"A tale as improbable as it is spellbinding, told with a deft touch and insightful clarity. Brian Kilmeade has done it again."
—GENERAL STANLEY McCHRYSTAL
(U.S. Army, Retired), author of *Team of Teams*

"The reader gets an inkling of the grit that made America great."
—ERIK PRINCE, author of *Civilian Warriors*

"A wild, page-turning history of one of America's most fascinating battles." —BRAD MELTZER, author of *The President's Shadow*

"A riveting introduction to one of the seminal battles in U.S. history. The War of 1812 folk legend of Old Hickory rides high on his horse again in this engrossing overview for readers of all ages. Highly recommended!" —DOUGLAS BRINKLEY, professor of history, Rice University, and author of *Rightful Heritage*

"The scholarship is impeccable, the topic immensely important, the story masterfully crafted. This little gem of a book belongs on the bookshelf of every history buff. What a triumph!" —JAY WINIK, author of *April 1865* and *1944*

"Kilmeade shows how the patriotism of Jackson and his generation made America great in the first place. A terrific read."
—JANE HAMPTON COOK, presidential historian and author of *The Burning of the White House*

ANDREW JACKSON

***** AND THE *****

MIRACLE OF NEW ORLEANS

BRIAN KILMEADE

AND **DON YAEGER**

ANDREW
JACKSON

★ ★ ★ ★ ★ AND THE ★ ★ ★ ★ ★

MIRACLE of NEW ORLEANS

THE BATTLE THAT SHAPED
AMERICA'S DESTINY

SENTINEL

An imprint of Penguin Random House LLC
375 Hudson Street
New York, New York 10014

Most Sentinel books are available at a discount when purchased in quantity for sales promotions or corporate use. Special editions, which include personalized covers, excerpts, and corporate imprints, can be created when purchased in large quantities. For more information, please call (212) 572-2232 or e-mail specialmarkets@penguinrandomhouse.com. Your local bookstore can also assist with discounted bulk purchases using the Penguin Random House corporate Business-to-Business program. For assistance in locating a participating retailer, e-mail B2B@penguinrandomhouse.com.

THE LIBRARY OF CONGRESS HAS CATALOGUED THE HARDCOVER EDITION AS FOLLOWS:
Names: Kilmeade, Brian, author. | Yaeger, Don, author.
Title: Andrew Jackson and the miracle of New Orleans : the battle that shaped
   America's destiny / Brian Kilmeade and Don Yaeger.
Description: New York, New York : Sentinel, an imprint of Penguin Random House, 2017.
   | Includes bibliographical references and index.
Identifiers: LCCN 2017027754 | ISBN 9780735213234 (hardcover) |
   ISBN 9780735213258 (epub)
Subjects: LCSH: New Orleans, Battle of, New Orleans, La., 1815. | Jackson, Andrew,
   1767–1845—Military leadership. | Generals—United States—Biography. |
   United States—History—War of 1812—Campaigns.
Classification: LCC E356.N5 K55 2017 | DDC 973.5/239—dc23 LC record available
   at https://lccn.loc.gov/2017027754

First Sentinel hardcover edition: October 2017
First Sentinel trade paperback edition: October 2018
Sentinel trade paperback ISBN: 9780735213241

Printed in the United States of America

Book design by George Towne
Map illustrations by Daniel Lagin

To the unsung men and women whose faithful military service has kept us free and made generals like Jackson famous. Your names and faces may not be known by the world, but you'll never be forgotten by me.

—BK

Our situation seemed desperate. In case of an attack, we could hope to be saved only by a miracle, or by the wisdom and genius of a commander-in-chief. Accordingly, on his arrival, [Jackson] was immediately invested with the confidence of the public, and all hope centered in him. We shall, hereafter, see how amply he merited the confidence which he inspired.

—**Major Arsène Lacarrière Latour**

Historical Memoir of the War in West Florida and Louisiana in 1814–15: With an Atlas (1816)

CONTENTS

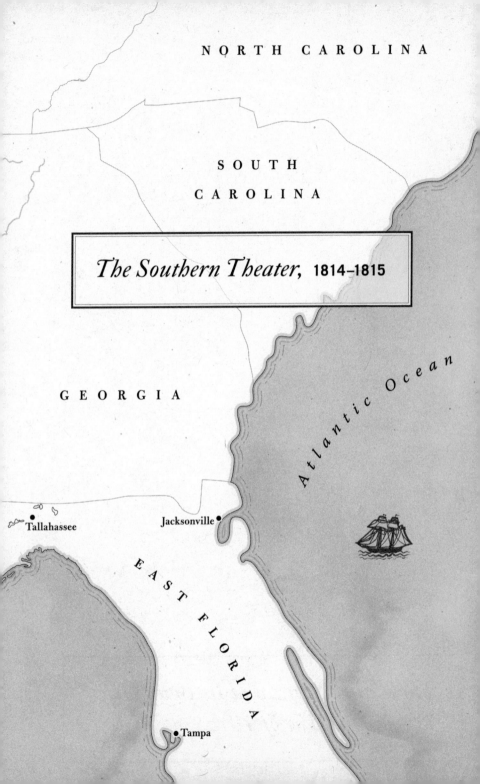

NORTH CAROLINA

SOUTH CAROLINA

The Southern Theater, 1814–1815

GEORGIA

Atlantic Ocean

Tallahassee

Jacksonville

EAST FLORIDA

Tampa

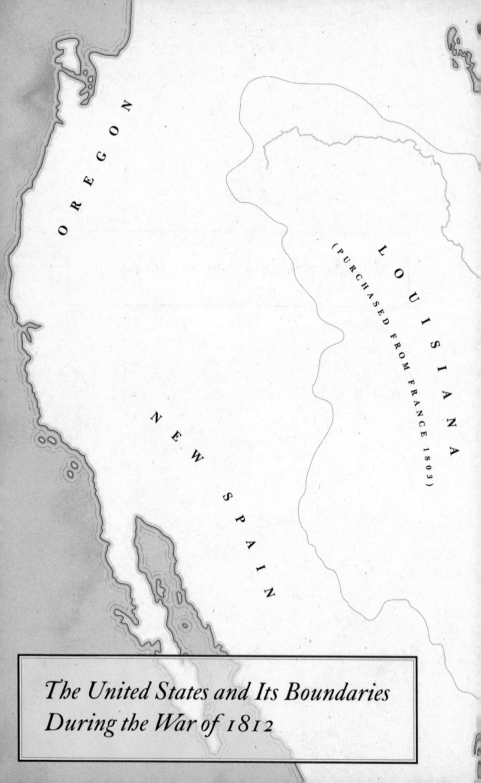

OREGON

LOUISIANA
(PURCHASED FROM FRANCE 1803)

NEW SPAIN

*The United States and Its Boundaries
During the War of 1812*

ANDREW JACKSON

AND THE

MIRACLE OF NEW ORLEANS

PROLOGUE

In the spring of 1781, the redcoats arrived in upland Carolina, and they brought terror with them. As they searched the countryside for the rebels, they turned the region the Jackson family called home into an armed camp. Elizabeth Jackson's youngest son, Andrew, though barely fourteen years of age, hated their presence—and quickly learned just how costly the fight for liberty could be.

On April 9, Andy and his brother, Robert, two years older, earned the wrath of the invading force by joining a battle to defend the local meetinghouse against a band of Tories reinforced by British dragoons. The fight went badly for the Americans, but the brothers, unlike a cousin who was severely wounded and captured, were lucky. They escaped and, after spending a night hiding in the brush, the two Jackson boys managed to reach their cousin's home to deliver the news of his fate. Once there, however, their luck ran out: a Tory spy spotted their horses and informed the British of their whereabouts.

A lesson in the cruelties of war was soon delivered. As the Jackson brothers stood helplessly at the point of British swords, the enemy set about destroying their aunt and uncle's home. Determined to make an example of these rebels, the redcoats shattered dishes. They ripped clothing to rags. They smashed furniture. Then, with the house in ruins, the commanding officer decided upon one more humiliation. He chose Andy Jackson as his target.

He ordered tall and gangly Andy Jackson to kneel before him and clean the mud from his boots. The boy refused.

"Sir, I am a prisoner of war, and claim to be treated as such."[1]

Enraged by the young American's defiance, the British officer raised his sword and brought it down on Jackson's head. Had Andy not raised his arm to deflect the blow, his skull might have been split open. As it was, the blade gashed his forehead and sliced his hand to the bone. Not satisfied at drawing blood from Andy, the soldier turned and slashed at his brother, tearing into his scalp, leaving him dazed and bleeding.

No one dressed their wounds. Instead, the Jackson brothers were marched forty miles, with neither food nor water, to join more than two hundred other rebellious colonists in a prison camp in Camden. There they were fed stale bread and exposed to the smallpox that raged among the prisoners kept in tightly packed conditions.

Their mother, Elizabeth Jackson, had already lost too much. Her husband, Andrew Jackson Sr., had worked himself to death shortly before Andrew was born, leaving the pregnant Elizabeth with two, soon to be three, young sons in the rugged wilderness of upland South Carolina. She had raised the baby and his brothers as best she could and tried to protect them from the dangers of the war, but the boys had joined the fight despite her pleas. Hugh, the oldest, had died at age sixteen of heat exhaustion after a battle the year before. Elizabeth was not about to lose her remaining sons now.

Traveling the long distance to their prison, she managed to per-suade their jailers to include them in a prisoner exchange. But freedom

didn't mean safety. Robert had fallen dangerously ill, his wound in-
fected, and the family of three had many miles to travel—on just two
horses. Robert, delirious, rode one, and the exhausted Elizabeth
the other.

Andrew walked. He made the journey barefoot, since the British
had taken his shoes. Although all three made it home through driving
rains, Robert died two days later. Elizabeth had no time to nurse her
grief—or her remaining son. As Andrew recovered from a fever, she
set off for Charleston, where two of the nephews she helped raise were
prisoners. She would never return. After completing a 160-mile journey, much of it through enemy territory, she became ill with cholera
and died. Andrew would learn he was an orphan when a small bundle
of her clothes was returned to his home.

Andrew Jackson would never forget the pain and humiliation of
that summer. His father, mother, and brothers were dead. He himself
bore the memory of British brutality, his forehead and hand forever
marked by the British officer's sword, a reminder of the callous cruelty
that had destroyed his family.

His mother may have left him alone, but she had not left him
without words to live by. Years later, he would report that she had told
him, "Make friends by being honest and keep them by being steadfast.
Never tell a lie, nor take what is not your own, nor sue for slander—
settle them cases yourself!"[2]

Andy wouldn't forget her advice, and he would take care to settle
more than just slander. Great Britain had left him an orphan, and one
day he would settle that score.

CHAPTER 1

Freedoms at Risk

These are the times which distinguish the real friend of his country from the town-meeting brawler and the sunshine patriot.... The former steps forth, and proclaims his readiness to march.

—Major General Andrew Jackson

On June 1, 1812, America declared war. After a hot debate, James Madison's war resolution was passed by a vote of 19–13 in the Senate and 79–49 in the House of Representatives, and, once again, the new nation would be taking on the world's premier military and economic power: Great Britain.

Twenty-nine years had passed since the colonists' improbable victory in the Revolutionary War, and for twenty-nine years the British had failed to respect American sovereignty. Now, the nation James Madison led had reached the limit of its tolerance. Great Britain's kidnapping of American sailors and stirring up of Indian tribes to attack settlers on the western frontier had made life intolerably difficult for many of America's second generation, including those hardscrabble men and women pushing the boundaries westward.

Though reluctant to risk the new nation's liberty, Madison was now ready to send a message to England and the world that America would stand up to the bully that chose to do her harm. The unanswered question was: Could America win? Less than thirty years removed from the last war, and with virtually no national army, were Americans prepared to take on Britain and defend themselves, this time without the help of France? The world was about to find out.

In fact, so many Americans opposed the war that the declaration posed a real risk to the country's national unity. The Federalist Party, mainly representing northerners whose economy relied on British trade, had unanimously opposed the war declaration. Many New Englanders wanted peace with Britain, and it was likely that some would even be willing to leave the Union in order to avoid a fight.

Yet peaceful attempts at resolving the conflict with Britain had already been tried—and hadn't helped the economy much. Five years earlier, when a British ship attacked the U.S. Navy's *Chesapeake,* killing three sailors and taking four others from the ship to impress them into service to the Crown, then-president Thomas Jefferson had attempted to retaliate. To protest this blatant hostility, Congress passed the Embargo Act, prohibiting overseas trade with Great Britain. Unfortunately, the act hurt Americans more than the British. In just fifteen months, the embargo produced a depression that cruelly punished merchants and farmers while doing little to deter the Royal Navy's interference and hardening New England's resistance to conflict. Further attempts at legislative pressure in the early years of James Madison's presidency had little effect, and British impressment had continued. By the time of the war declaration in June 1812, the number of sailors seized off the decks of American ships had risen to more than five thousand men.

To many, including Andrew Jackson, then forty years old, the attack on the *Chesapeake* alone had been an insult to American pride that demanded a military response. As Jackson wrote to a Virginia friend after learning of the *Chesapeake*'s fate, "The degradation offered to our government . . . has roused every feeling of the American heart, and war with that nation is inevitable."[1]

Yet America had waited, and the losses at sea mounted. At the same time, attempts to pacify the British had only resulted in further losses in America's new territory, "the West," which ran south to north from the Gulf of Mexico to Canada, bounded on the west by the Mississippi. There British agents were said to be agitating the Indians. For many years, the Five Civilized Tribes in the region (Cherokee, Chickasaw, Choctaw, Creek, and Seminole) had maintained peaceful relations with the European arrivals. But as more and more white settlers moved into native territories, tensions had risen and open conflict had broken out. In some places, travelers could no longer be certain whether the Native Americans they encountered were friendly; for inhabitants of the frontier, that meant the events of daily life were accompanied by fear. Stories circulated of fathers who returned from a day of hunting to find their children butchered, and of wives who stumbled upon their husbands scalped in the fields.

A major Shawnee uprising in the Indiana Territory in 1811 escalated the fear. And as the bloodshed increased, there were reports that the British were providing the Indians with weapons and promising them land if they carried out violent raids against American settlers. For Andrew Jackson, the threat had become too close for comfort when, in the spring of 1812, just a hundred miles from his home, a marauding band of Creeks killed six settlers and took a woman hostage. Jackson was certain the British were behind the attack on the little settlement at the mouth of the Duck River.

Westerners like Jackson fumed at the government's inability to resolve the country's problems, but their clout in Washington was limited. The decision makers from Virginia and New England had little sympathy for their inland countrymen. Eastern newspapers poked fun at the hill folks' backward ways, and much of the territory west of the Appalachian Mountains remained mysterious and wild, with few good roads and even fewer maps. The dangers faced by westerners were not felt by easterners, and their anguished demands for retaliation were scorned and dismissed by those whose wallets would be hurt by the war.

But eventually, despite many politicians' disdain for their hick neighbors to the west, Washington politics had begun to shift along with the nation's growing population. The West had gained new influence in the elections of 1810 and 1811, when the region sent a spirited band of new representatives to the Capitol. These men saw British attitudes toward the United States as a threat to American liberty and independence; they also saw the need for westward expansion, a move that the British were trying to thwart. Led by a young Kentuckian named Henry Clay, they quickly gained the nickname War Hawks, because, despite the risks, they knew it was time to fight.

Clay became Speaker of the House and he, along with the War Hawks and like-minded Republicans from the coastal states, put pressure on the Madison administration. Now, after years of resistance, Madison listened, and with Congress's vote, the War of 1812 began. America decided to stand up for its sovereignty on the sea and its security in the West.

The War Hawks in Washington were ecstatic about the declaration of war, and so was Jackson in Tennessee. At last he would have the chance to defend the nation he loved, to protect his family and friends—and, personally, to take revenge on the nation that had left him alone and scarred so many years before.

The Boy Becomes a Man

A quarter century before, Jackson had swallowed his grudge. When the Treaty of Paris made U.S. independence official in 1783, the orphaned sixteen-year-old adopted America as his family.

Relatives had taken him in after his mother's death. He became a saddler's apprentice, then, his ambitions rising, he clerked for a North Carolina attorney. Andrew Jackson's cobbled-together upbringing would serve him well, though he also gained a reputation as a young man who loved drinking, playing cards, and horse racing.

Admitted to the bar to practice law at age twenty, a year later he accepted an appointment as a public prosecutor in North Carolina's western district. That took him beyond the boundaries of the state, to the other side of the Appalachians. Jackson arrived in a region that, a few years after his arrival, became the state of Tennessee.

The red-haired, blue-eyed, and rangy six-foot-one young man made an immediate impression in Nashville, a frontier outpost established just eight years earlier. As Jackson put down roots, he became one of its chief citizens as his and his city's reputations grew. His rise gained momentum after he met Rachel Donelson, the youngest daughter of one of Nashville's founding families. Dark-eyed Rachel was the prettiest of the Donelson sisters and full of life. It was said she was "the best story-teller, the best dancer, . . . [and] the most dashing horsewoman in the western country."[2] Jackson was smitten, and after she extricated herself from a marriage already gone bad, he took her as his wife.

As a lawyer, a trader, and a merchant, Jackson bought and sold land. By the time Tennessee joined the Union, in 1796, he had won the respect of his neighbors, who chose him as their delegate to the state's constitutional convention. Jackson then served as Tennessee's first congressman for one session before becoming a U.S. senator. But he found life in the political realm of the Federal City frustrating—too little got done for the decisive young Jackson—and he accepted an appointment to Tennessee's Supreme Court. In the early years of the nineteenth century, he divided his energies between administering the law and establishing himself at his growing plantation, the Hermitage, ten miles outside Nashville. "His house was the seat of hospitality," wrote a young officer friend, "the resort of friends and acquaintances, and of all strangers visiting the state."[3]

His next venture into public service would suit him better: thanks to his strong relationships and sound political instincts, he was elected major general of the Tennessee militia, in February 1802. Maintained by the state, not the federal government, the militia was provisioned by local men who supplied their own weapons and uniforms and served short contracts of a few months' duration. Leading the militia was a good fit for Jackson's style, because it gave him the chance to serve the people he loved with the freedom he needed and the challenge he craved.

General Jackson repeatedly won reelection as well as the deep loyalty of his men. They liked what he said. He was often outspoken, and many shared his uncompromising views on defending settlers' rights. With rumors of war, he was ready to defend his people and was just the man to rally westerners to the cause of American liberty.

"Citizens!" he wrote in a broadside. "Your government has at last yielded to the impulse of a nation. . . . Are we the titled slaves of George the Third? The military conscripts of Napoleon the great? Or the frozen peasants of the Russian czar? No—we are the free-born sons of America; the citizens of the only republic now existing in the world."[4]

Jackson understood the stakes of the war, and he recognized the strategy as only a westerner could. Of critical importance to victory in the West was a port city near the Gulf Coast. As Jackson would soon say to his troops, in the autumn of 1812, "Every man of the western country turns his eyes intuitively upon the mouth of the Mississippi." Together, he observed, "[we are] committed by nature herself [to] the defense of the lower Mississippi and the city of New Orleans."[5]

The City of New Orleans

New Orleans was important—so important, in fact, that upon becoming president a dozen years earlier, Thomas Jefferson had made acquiring it a key objective. Recognizing the city's singular strategic importance to his young nation, he wrote, "There is on the globe one single spot, the possessor of which is our natural and habitual enemy. It is New Orleans."[6]

Knowing that Napoleon's plan for extending his American empire had suffered a major setback in the Caribbean, where his expeditionary force had been decimated by yellow fever, Jefferson sensed an opportunity. He dispatched his friend James Monroe to Paris, instructing him to try to purchase New Orleans.

Monroe had succeeded in his assignment beyond Jefferson's wildest dreams. Recognizing his resources were already overextended in his quest to dominate Europe, Napoleon agreed to sell all of Louisiana. That conveyed an immense wilderness to the United States, effectively doubling the size of the new country. The Louisiana Purchase had been completed in 1803 and, at a purchase price of $15 million for more than eight hundred thousand square miles of territory, the land had been a staggering bargain (the cost to America's treasury worked out to less than three cents an acre).

The Louisiana city of New Orleans was the great gateway to and from the heart of the country. America's inland waterways—the Ohio,

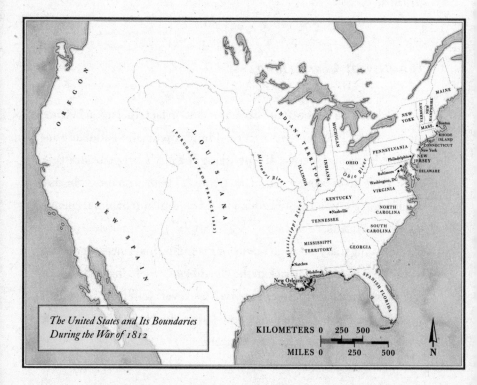

The United States and Its Boundaries During the War of 1812

KILOMETERS 0   250 500

MILES 0   250   500

N

the Missouri, and the numerous other rivers that emptied into the Mississippi—amounted to an economic lifeline for farmers, trappers, and lumbermen upstream. On these waters flatboats and keelboats were a common sight, carrying manufactured goods from Pennsylvania, as well as crops, pelts, and logs from the burgeoning farms and lush forests across the Ohio Valley, Cumberland Gap, and Great Smoky Mountains. On reaching the wharves, warehouses, and quays of New Orleans, the goods went aboard waiting ships to be transported all over the world.

Although Louisiana became a state in April 1812, the British still questioned the legitimacy of America's ownership of the Louisiana Territory—Napoleon had taken Louisiana from Spain and, to some Europeans, it remained rightfully a possession of the Spanish Crown. Jackson feared that sort of thinking could provide the British with just the pretext they needed to interfere with the American experiment—capturing New Orleans would be the perfect way to disrupt America's western expansion.

Now that America had finally gone to war, many nagging practical questions hung in the air in Washington. Who would determine America's military strategy? Who would lead the nation to war? The generals of the revolutionary generation were aging or dead. The passing of George Washington had sent the nation into mourning thirteen years before, and no military leader had the stature to take the general's place. Although the country had prevailed in the previous decade in a war on the Barbary Coast of North Africa, defeating pirate states that had attacked its shipping and held its men hostage, this was a bigger fight for even bigger stakes.

Although neither Mr. Madison nor the members of Congress could know it in June 1812, the burden of protecting the West would eventually settle onto the narrow but resilient shoulders of General Andrew Jackson, a man little known and less liked outside his region. But first Jackson had to convince the men in Washington that a general from the backwoods was the one to lead the fight. That would be anything but easy.

CHAPTER 2

How to Lose a War

Resolved, that we consider the war commenced against
Great Britain under existing circumstances unnecessary,
impolitic and ruinous.

—Citizens of Lincoln County, Maine, August 3, 1812

The *Boston Evening Post* soon dubbed the conflict "Mr. Madison's War." With no template to follow—he was the first American president ever to sign a formal declaration of war—James Madison was largely on his own.

There was nothing battle-hardened about Madison. Soft-spoken as well as short, he weighed perhaps 120 pounds. Genteel in manner, he was sickly and bookish, with a face that bore the age lines of a man of sixty-one years. He was a far cry from the strategist George Washington had been and had little choice when it came to military matters but to rely on the advice of his counselors. Many of them also lacked war experience.

Much of their guidance turned out to be less than sound. His advisers agreed that attacking Canada, which remained part of the British Empire, would be the perfect way to launch a war with Great

Britain and to gain a key bargaining chip in future treaty negotiations. Henry Clay, for one, believed a land war with the United States' neighbor to the north would end with "Canada at your feet."[1]

Madison's usually reliable friend Thomas Jefferson added his voice from Monticello. He thought the capture of Canada a sure thing. "The acquisition of Canada this year," he wrote, "will be a mere matter of marching."[2] All these words reflected the strong sense among American politicians that Canada, too, would like to be free of British rule and would welcome a liberating army from the United States. On the other hand, no one seemed to wonder what would happen if sending American troops north to invade Canada left the country's long coast unprotected, and few seemed to be considering the bigger danger to the South—if the British took New Orleans, they could hamstring its economy and prepare to squeeze the young nation.

If America was to fight in Canada, it might as well bring enough troops to win. Accordingly, several westerners, most notably Andrew Jackson, wrote to Madison to volunteer their military assistance. Jackson suggested moving 2,500 of his men to Canada within three months. But Washington never issued orders for Jackson's men to move, and Jackson became increasingly certain that the East Coast men Madison had running the war effort were incompetent.

Guiding the charge toward Canada was Madison's secretary of war, William Eustis, who had served as a regimental surgeon during the American Revolution. Neither a strategist nor a soldier, Eustis lacked battle experience, and it soon showed. Within six months, everyone in Washington knew that Dr. Eustis was no better prepared than Madison to direct the nation's military affairs.

Eustis's strategy had called for attacking Canada on three fronts. The first assault, which was to be launched from Fort Detroit, was directed by another veteran of the Revolution, General William Hull, who hadn't been in uniform for thirty years and looked like the grandfather he was with a shock of white hair. Though ordered to move on the British at a nearby Canadian fort, he folded when his men, along with a community of women and children, were bombarded by British guns. Hull surrendered Fort Detroit and the entire North-Western Army of the United States to a British and Indian force half its size.

The second assault, opened near Niagara in October 1812, also went badly wrong, this time because of division and lack of discipline within the American forces. When New York militiamen refused to cross the Niagara River into Canada to reinforce Ohio troops fighting the British, 950 Ohio militiamen were taken prisoner.

Desperate for a victory, Secretary of War Eustis placed all of his hope in the third assault. In a letter to Major General Henry Dearborn, another elderly warhorse who hadn't seen combat in three decades, Eustis warned him that he needed good news in time for Washington's January session: "Congress must not meet without a victory to announce to them."[3] Fighting in the vicinity of Lake Champlain, Dearborn and his men also failed. Some of the militia under his command refused to cross the border. Those who did march on Canada skirmished briefly with the enemy, only to find themselves, with the coming of darkness, shooting at one another. They retreated—from the British and their own friendly fire—ending the year's Canadian assault.

So much for what John Randolph of Virginia had told his fellow congressmen would be a "holiday campaign."[4] With the arrival of the year 1813, James Madison knew his war strategy needed to change.

The president felt embattled. Congress and the nation were deeply divided. During the congressional debates concerning the declaration of war, Madison's party had called the conflict a necessity, "a second war of independence." On the other side of the aisle, the Federalists regarded going to war as foolhardy and unnecessary, and they had unanimously voted against the president's war declaration. Though the War Hawks had prevailed, with bad news from the front, opposition voices had only grown louder.

There were too few troops to protect American cities, especially those on the coast, including Washington. The U.S. Navy had performed relatively well at sea, sinking a few British ships, but those victories meant little. The two dozen warships of the American fleet were outnumbered at least thirty to one by the Royal Navy, and already more enemy ships were arriving to blockade American ports.

Yet the divided Congress was often unwilling to provide funding for the military. The North, as demonstrated by the refusal of the New England militiamen to fight in Canada, was far from committed to the war. (From afar, Jackson offered a solution to the problem of soldiers refusing to fight: "I would hang them all."[5]) Even if Madison had the money and unity he needed, his military leaders were not what they should be: his generals were old, his secretary of war was incompetent, and his secretary of the navy was usually intoxicated. As the year 1812 ended, Madison faced a painful truth: those who wrote the military histories would surely wonder at the misguided way the United States had launched its Second War of Independence.

A Sense of Betrayal

Both Tennessee governor Willie Blount and his confidant General Andrew Jackson saw the immediate danger in the West of the British-supported Indians, and Jackson told Blount, on July 3, 1812, that he was ready and willing "to penetrate the Creek towns . . . [to] obtain a surrender of the captive and the captors."[6] But Jackson's offer to Washington, volunteering the services of his 2,500 Tennessee militiamen to serve the cause, produced no orders to march.

For months, Jackson awaited word from the War Department. He could do nothing but bide his time at the Hermitage and complain angrily about the "old grannies" in Washington.[7] Only in November did he get word from Governor Blount, writing on behalf of President Madison, ordering Jackson to protect the territory of the Mississippi Valley. Finally, the men in Washington were recognizing the needs of the West! Jackson was to assemble a force and proceed to New Orleans immediately to defend it from a likely British invasion.

Jackson issued a call to arms, and a flood of farmers, planters, and businessmen, many of them descendants of Revolutionary War veterans, poured into Nashville. These Volunteers, as their ranks would be called, were eager to fight for their country, to protect their homes, and to serve General Jackson.

Jackson had little time to organize and train his new recruits before they started for New Orleans in January 1813. Loaded into thirty boats, Jackson and more than two thousand men floated down the Cumberland River only to run into trouble. A cold snap blocked the river with ice, delaying the troops for four days. The unusually severe weather also brought frequent rain, hail, and snow, making the troops miserable. Jackson himself fell ill "with a severe pain in the neck and head," but he recovered.[8] When the ice melted, the boats continued on but not without accident. The difficult passage took five weeks and cost one boat and three lives.

On reaching Natchez, Mississippi, eight hundred miles downriver from Nashville, Jackson and his officers made camp, drilled their

Volunteers, and, with each passing day, grew more impatient. As instructed, they awaited orders regarding their final push toward New Orleans.

While encamped outside Natchez, Jackson took the opportunity to strengthen his relationships with his officer corps. Chief among them was John Coffee, Jackson's old friend and sometime business partner. Coffee was an imposing figure, with shoulders as broad as Jackson's were narrow, an ideal commander for Jackson's cavalry. There were other good men in Jackson's inner circle, including his chief aide-de-camp, Thomas Hart Benton, a young Nashville lawyer who had impressed Jackson with his diligence, and John Reid, Virginia-born and -educated, whose writing skills earned him the role of Jackson's secretary. Jackson also named William Carroll, a Nashville shop owner originally from Pennsylvania, to be brigade inspector.

The pause also allowed Jackson to begin the process of turning inexperienced volunteers into a fighting force. He and his officers watched as their troops cleaned and tested their weapons. The men practiced packing and unpacking their kits in order to be ready to march at a moment's notice. To a man, they were eager to take on the British forces said to be bearing down on New Orleans.

Finally, on March 15, 1813, a much-anticipated letter from the War Department arrived—only to humiliate and infuriate Jackson and his men, who had sacrificed their time, their money, and, in some cases, their lives to travel to defend New Orleans. As a result of America's many failures early in the war, General John Armstrong had replaced William Eustis as secretary of war in January, and Armstrong had decided to upend all of Eustis's strategy. "On receipt of this Letter," General Armstrong had written, "consider [your corps] as dismissed from public service."[9] Armstrong's focus would not be on the South but on the East Coast, where he thought the greatest jeopardy lay.

At first Jackson was confused about the missive's meaning. Could Armstrong really be telling him to disband his army and turn back? But the brief and pointed orders from the new secretary of war left no room for interpretation. The Volunteers were to abandon their plans to defend New Orleans and return home. Jackson's confusion gave way to shock and then anger. Eustis had been bad, but this move from Armstrong scarcely seemed an improvement.

Not that Jackson wouldn't be happy to go home. Deeply devoted to Rachel, his wife of almost twenty years, he carried a miniature portrait of her with him. They doted on four-year-old Andrew Jr., the boy the aging and childless couple had adopted as their own when one of Rachel's sisters-in-law birthed twins in 1808. The general would like nothing better than to be reunited with his family.

But what of New Orleans? As James Madison himself had put it years earlier, New Orleans held the key to "the country on the West side of the Mississippi."[10] Who would protect that essential port if Jackson turned back?

And what of the other military objectives on the Gulf Coast? For months, Jackson had argued that to defeat Great Britain, America needed to keep Florida's deep-water harbors out of British hands. Many of these small cities along the Gulf remained under Spanish rule, and the British were forming alliances with the Spanish in order to control the coast. Whoever held those forts was a threat to the likes of Mobile, as well as to the ultimate prize, New Orleans.

Yet in the face of what Jackson saw as the urgent need to protect the Gulf Coast and the mouth of the Mississippi, Secretary of War

Armstrong had not issued battle orders; he had told the general and his men to go home. Not only that, but Armstrong's letter specified that Jackson was to confiscate his men's weapons and to "take measures to have [them] delivered" to James Wilkinson, the overall commander of the American forces in the West.[11] Essentially, Armstrong was asking Jackson to disband his army, disarm his men, and leave them to find their way home as best they could. They would not be paid, nor would they be issued supplies.

Jackson faced a dilemma: he must follow orders—but to do so would put his men in grave danger.

Like Jackson, many of the men were sick; unlike Jackson, many of them were young and inexperienced. Together, when commanded by a seasoned leader, they could defend themselves from the British and Indians, but alone and scattered, they would be easy prey. *Abandon them?* Jackson was a tough man, but he wasn't cruel. Yes, he would obey the order to march home but he must do it his way.

He set about composing a reply.

"Must our band of citizen soldiers wander and fall a sacrifice to the tomahawk and scalping knife of the wilderness; our sick left naked in the open field and remain without supplies, without nourishment, or an earthly comfort?"[12] To do that, Jackson wrote, would be to choose their destruction.

That he simply would not do. If he had his choice, he would have led his men on defend New Orleans, since he was eager to "meet the invader and drive him back into the sea,"[13] as he had promised his recruits they would do together. But his more immediate concern was the well-being of the men in his charge.

As ridiculous as it seemed, he would have to turn his men around and lead them back to Nashville.

The Long Trek Home

The forty-mile march Jackson had made as a fourteen-year-old prisoner would not be the longest walk of his life. With no steamboat service to carry his army upstream against the current, Jackson and his Tennessee Volunteers faced a long march, one that would take them across five hundred miles of rugged ground, much of it in Indian country.

On March 25, 1813, they began the trek—but not before Jackson wrote to his congressman: "As long as I have funds or credit, I will stick by [my Volunteers]. I shall march them to Nashville or bury them with the honors of war—Should I die I know they will bury me."[14]

He wrote defiant letters to both Secretary of War Armstrong and General Wilkinson. He would not, could not, abandon his troops. "These brave men, at the call of their country, . . . followed me to the field—I shall carefully march them back to their homes."[15] He even wrote to the president: "I cannot believe [that] after inviting us to rally round the standard of country in its defense . . . you would dismiss us from service eight hundred miles from our homes, without money, without supplies." It has to be a "mistake," wrote Jackson.[16]

As the dispirited men, let down by their government but not by their general, marched north, illness spread through the ranks. Jackson soon had 150 men on the sick list, 56 of them so ill they could not sit unassisted. Jackson managed to commandeer wagons to carry some of them, but the eleven he found were not enough. He ordered his officers to surrender their horses to the sick. He asked no less of himself, turning over his three horses and walking so that ill Volunteers would travel easier.

"It is . . . my duty," he wrote to Rachel, "to act as a father to the sick and to the well and stay with them until I march them into Nash-ville."[17] He walked alongside his men; they covered an average of eigh-teen miles a day. He insisted upon order and discipline, but he led by example. He revealed no fatigue; he urged the troops homeward, and they understood his concern for their safety and comfort. As he moved along the column, this man, though well known for his violent and hasty temper, appeared to his men benevolent, humane, and fatherly. "There is not a man belonging to the detachment but what loves him," one reported.[18]

At forty-six, he was older than most of his troops—his face lined, his hair mostly gray—but Jackson made no complaint as he marched. Despite his slight build he was an imposing presence, with his erect posture. He did not need the gold epaulets and other adornments of a general's uniform to convey his authority. His intense blue eyes, people said, blazed when he was angry. But here Jackson was also the sympathetic man who urged his Volunteers toward home and safety. Admiration for him soared; among the ranks it was whispered that he was defying orders to shepherd them home, that he had reached into his own pockets to provide supplies. The men revered their general, who shared their hardships as they marched together toward Nashville.

Along the way, one soldier remarked upon Jackson's toughness. Then another observed that he was as "tough as hickory." Said aloud, the comparison rang true and, soon enough, his men took to calling their commander "Hickory" and eventually "Old Hickory."[19]

The nickname would last a lifetime, long enough for a truly great New Orleans adventure. Madison's administration had judged the fear for the city's safety to be a false alarm this time. But the threat would surface again in 1814, when this natural leader and his men would prove their military merit by fighting the hated British.

In the meantime, another danger to the people of the West was brewing. As Jackson had feared, the Indian trouble in the region was growing more serious by the day. A warring faction of Creeks called the Red Sticks (the tomahawk-like war clubs they carried were painted red) had allied themselves with the British. Soon enough, Andrew Jackson would have to face them down.

CHAPTER 3

The Making of a General

They must be punished—and our frontier protected . . . as I
have no doubt but they are urged on by British agents.

—**Andrew Jackson**

After marching his troops back to Nashville, Andrew Jackson
once again waited for Washington. His Volunteers' enlistments had yet to expire (most joined up for a year) but, with
no dispatch from the War Department ordering them into battle, the
general released his militiamen from duty in the spring of 1813, sending them home to tend to their families and their fields. Then he did
the same.

Life at the Hermitage had many obligations. A well-known horse
breeder, Jackson also raised cows and mules. He owned a sawmill and
a cotton gin; over the years, he had operated a store and a distillery,
and had even invested in a boatyard. Hundreds of his acres were
dedicated to growing the all-important cash crop, cotton.

As Jackson turned to his own interests during the spring of 1813,
Mr. Madison's War was concentrated more than a thousand miles north
of New Orleans. For once, good news arrived from Canada: the U.S.

Army had captured York, Ontario, in May, although drunken American soldiers had plundered the place, violating the rules of war by burning most of York's public buildings in celebration. But the rest of the news was bad for the Americans. The British continued to ravage the coast, burning the city of Havre de Grace, Maryland, in May. Reports circulated of women and children running for their lives as the attackers looted the town's church. A month later the ill-fated *Chesapeake* was captured once again by the Royal Navy. And then the president fell ill with "bilious fever." At Montpelier, their home in central Virginia, with Mr. Madison in a delirium, Mrs. Madison worried he might die.

In Tennessee, however, the summer passed peacefully until, with August giving way to September, life in Andrew Jackson's West took a sudden turn. In a matter of days, two events would alter the course of Jackson's life. One almost killed him, and the other accelerated his rise to the status of genuine American hero.

Caught in the Cross Fire

Years earlier, Jackson, known for his fiery temper, had fought several duels. As an angry twenty-two-year-old, he had issued a challenge over a minor courtroom disagreement, but both duelists had fired harmlessly in the air, realizing their argument was not worth dying for.[1] The more serious matter of a slander to Rachel Jackson's honor had led Jackson to an armed face-to-face with the sitting governor of Tennessee, John Sevier, in 1803. Once more, however, no blood was let, and the confrontation ended in a cascade of insults. In an 1806 duel, he killed a man who had called him a "worthless scoundrel" and a "coward."[2] Jackson had sustained a chest wound when a lead ball broke two ribs and lodged deep in his left lung (the injury would never entirely heal, causing periodic lung hemorrhages later in life). In 1813, however, Andrew Jackson most wanted to fight America's enemies, not argumentative opponents.

Then in June one of his officers, William Carroll, asked the general to be his second. Carroll was to duel Jesse Benton, the younger brother of another of Jackson's officers, Thomas Hart Benton; an exchange of insults between the two men had escalated until Benton, believing his honor as a gentleman had been questioned, demanded satisfaction. Jackson tried to talk his way out of participating, knowing he had nothing to prove and much to lose. "I am not the man for such an affair," he told Carroll. "I am too old."[3] But his attempt to negotiate a peaceful solution failed, and the duel was fought with the general standing by.

Unfortunately for Jackson, that was not the end of the matter.

In the June 14 duel, Jesse Benton sustained a wound to his buttocks, which some saw as a sign of cowardice, since it meant he had turned his back. Soon both Bentons were blaming Jackson, who had been charged with making sure the duel was fairly fought. The brothers publicly accused him of overseeing a duel "conducted . . . in a savage, unequal, unfair, and base manner."[4] The general, deeply offended, let it be known that he would horsewhip Lieutenant Colonel Thomas Hart Benton the next time they met.

On September 4, hearing the Bentons were in town, Jackson went to confront them, horsewhip in hand, at Nashville's City Hotel. The action quickly escalated. Gunshots were exchanged, and Jackson was left bleeding profusely after lead from Jesse Benton's pistol smashed the general's left shoulder and lodged in his upper arm. Jackson's blood soaked through not one mattress but two, and doctors saw no alternative to amputation. But Jackson refused.

"I'll keep my arm," he managed to say as he blacked out, and the respect and fear in which he was held meant no doctor would go against his order.[5]

Rachel arrived from the Hermitage to attend to her husband and, for many days, Old Hickory seemed suspended between life and death. But he refused to die. More than two weeks would pass before he could rise from his bed.

Then a courier brought news of an Indian massacre of settlers at Fort Mims, more than four hundred miles away. Red Stick Creeks were responsible, led by Chief Red Eagle, also known as William Weatherford, the son of a Native American mother and a Scots trader. Red Eagle and his band of Creeks had surprised the inhabitants of a small village inside a crude stockade near the Alabama River. The news was shocking: although protected by militiamen, on August 30, 1813, all but a handful of the roughly three hundred inhabitants— including many women and children—had been slaughtered. As a U.S. Army major reported from the scene some days later, the devastation was terrible, with the remains of "Indians, Negroes, white men, women and children . . . in one promiscuous ruin. . . . The main building was burned to ashes, which were filled with bones. The plains and the woods around were covered with dead bodies."[6]

Emerging from his fever-induced delirium, Jackson absorbed the news and saw the call to action: Fort Mims must be avenged and, soon enough, Governor Blount and President Madison so ordered. (It wasn't lost on Jackson that Fort Mims, located within range of the Gulf Coast, would bring him much closer to New Orleans, once again raising concern about a possible British invasion.) Though he still lay on what might have been his deathbed, Major General Andrew Jackson issued his own orders, on September 24, 1813, for his "brave Tennesseans" to assemble. The two thousand men of his division were to gather at Fayetteville, Tennessee, in two weeks' time.

Jackson's left arm and shoulder were unusable, thanks to his injuries, but he made his men a promise. "The health of your General is restored," he told them. "He will command in person."[7]

Not even a near-fatal gun brawl could keep Andrew Jackson from doing his duty.

Marching to Battle

A month to the day after the City Hotel gunfight, the first of the Tennessee Volunteers headed south. John Coffee, now a brigadier general, sat on his horse at the head of the army since Andrew Jackson, though gaining strength, was still recovering. But Old Hickory sent a message that was read to the men. "The blood of our women and children, recently spilled at Fort Mims, calls for our vengeance," he exhorted. "It must not call in vain."[8]

Jackson would not be far behind Coffee, mounting his horse three days later. Pale and drawn, he pushed himself hard, even though his left arm was in a sling, Jesse Benton's bullet still lodged in the bone. As November approached, he caught up with his Volunteers, and they made their way into Creek country. Supplies would be a continuing problem so far from civilization, but Jackson would not be deterred.

Impatient though he was, Jackson considered with care information on the enemy provided by friendly Creeks, Choctaws, and

Cherokees. Setting aside his deep distrust of Indians, he urged his commanders to make allies of Native Americans who had chosen not to join the Red Sticks' uprising. Out of instinct rather than military training—of which he had little—Jackson understood that intelligence concerning his enemies' forces would be invaluable.

When his spies reported a large enemy force a dozen miles south of his encampment on the Coosa River, Jackson ordered General John Coffee and his brigade of nine hundred horsemen to attack the Red Sticks at the island community known as Tallushatchee.

Jackson was not there, but a young enlistee named David Crockett witnessed the battle. "I saw some warriors run into a house," he remembered years later. "We pursued them until we got near the house, when we saw a squaw sitting in the door, and she placed her feet against the bow she had in her hand, and then took an arrow, and, raising her feet, she drew with all her might, and let fly at us, and she killed a man. . . . His death so enraged us all, that she was fired on, and had at least twenty balls blown through her. This was the first man I ever saw killed with a bow and arrow."[9]

The American force, outnumbering the Tallushatchee defenders five to one, decimated the Red Sticks, just as Jackson had ordered. After counting 186 dead warriors, Coffee reported, "Not one . . . escaped to carry the news."[10]

Jackson arrived to inspect the smoking ruins of Tallushatchee. No wholesale slaughter of families had occurred, and Coffee's forces held eighty-four prisoners, all women and children. Jackson's interpreter, an Indian trader fluent in Creek, brought a Native American infant to the general. The boy had been found in the embrace of his dead mother. When urged to give the child nourishment, the surviving Creek women had refused. "All his relations are dead," they reportedly said, "[so] kill him too."[11]

Having lost his own mother in wartime, Jackson was moved by the orphaned boy. Only hours after ordering the assault on the Indian camp, the general mixed a few grains of brown sugar with water and coaxed the tiny child to drink.

"Charity and Christianity says he ought to be taken care of," he wrote to Rachel.[12] The boy, named Lyncoya, would be adopted as a member of their family, to be raised and educated at the Hermitage as if he were the couple's blood child.

As he had been ordered to do, Jackson avenged the Fort Mims massacre. Yet, while the warrior Jackson could be ruthless, the aftermath at Tallushatchee revealed his strong instincts as a father not only to his men but to the meek and the vanquished.

Jackson Takes Talladega

Six days later, Jackson faced a test of his personal toughness.

Not all the Creeks had taken up arms against the Americans, and Jackson promised to protect the friendly Indians, who also included Cherokees and Choctaws. As he assured one Native American ally, "If one hair of your head is hurt, . . . I will sacrifice a hundred lives to pay for it."[13]

He got his chance with the arrival, at sunset, on November 7, 1813, of an express rider. Having grunted and rooted his way through Red Stick lines, disguised beneath the skin of a hog with head and hooves still attached, the messenger brought word that an estimated one thousand warriors had besieged the settlement of friendly Creeks at Talladega. William Weatherford—Red Eagle—and his Red Sticks stood poised to do to their brothers, who were allied with the enemy, what they had done to the settlers at Fort Mims.

Andrew Jackson was in no condition to field this call to action. As if the wounds to his useless left arm were not enough—he needed help mounting his horse, and simply unfolding a map posed a challenge—a case of dysentery racked him. For years, he had suffered almost constantly from intestinal problems, ranging from bouts of diarrhea to constipation, but now the discomfort was so intense that he had trouble sitting up straight. Still, pain could not be allowed to stand in the way, and slouched against a tree, he rapidly conceived a plan. Jackson and his men were on the march by midnight.

As he rode to the endangered Indian settlement at Talladega, he leaned forward in the saddle, almost hugging the neck of his horse, attempting to ease his abdominal pain. The ride was more than twenty-five miles long, but by sunset the following day, Jackson's army, consisting of twelve hundred foot soldiers and eight hundred men on horseback, made camp within range of their destination. Again Jackson did not sleep, but questioned his scouts about the terrain as he formulated a battle plan. At 4:00 a.m., he ordered his sleeping men awakened. His battle orders, as Jackson himself described them in a letter to Governor Blount, called for the advance of the infantry "in three lines—the militia on the left, and the volunteers on the right. The cavalry formed the two extreme wings, and were ordered to advance in a curve."[14]

With the bulk of his forces fixed in position, he ordered three mounted companies of men armed with rifles and muskets to advance. Jackson expected the hostile Indians to attack this American vanguard, which could then fall back as if in retreat. The Indians in pursuit would come into the range of his larger force, where his cavalry could trap them in a deadly crossfire.

The fight began with a roar of Indian guns as Weatherford's Red Sticks, naked but for their red war paint, burst from a dense thicket. They were "like a cloud of Egyptian locusts," Davy Crockett wrote, "screaming like all the young devils had been turned loose, with the old devil of all at their head."[15]

The plan unfolded as designed, and the Red Sticks ran directly into Jackson's trap. A hail of American bullets began to take a terrible toll, though the Indians, some with guns, many armed only with bows and arrows, fought back. There should have been no escape—but Weatherford and a large contingent of Creeks swarmed through a gap in the line. Though some of Jackson's men pursued them, seven hundred warriors escaped into the hills.

When the dead were counted, Weatherford had lost 299, Jackson 15. And Jackson gained a new nickname: to the Red Sticks, he became Sharp Knife.

The inexperienced general, despite a useless left arm, his body more than a little wasted by dysentery, had masterminded his first big battle and led his men to victory. Although Jackson, as ever, was ready to carry on the honorable fight, the result at Talladega would be the last good news for many weeks to come.

CHAPTER 4

A River Dyed Red

The power of the Creeks is I think forever broken.

—Andrew Jackson

Andrew Jackson faced new challenges as the winter of 1813–14 approached. In the back of his mind was the worry about a British advance on New Orleans (in fact, a British admiral had quietly proposed such a move a full year earlier[1]), but much more immediate concerns occupied Jackson's attention.

His Volunteers had little food and no feed for their horses. With expected supply shipments delayed, Jackson saw that his starving troops were growing more restless by the day. He realized that, despite the victory at Talladega less than a month before, his army was about to come apart at the seams—and if his Volunteers deserted, he would be able to fight neither Indians nor the British. After weeks of cajoling, Jackson finally had to threaten his men to restore order.

When one brigade of frustrated Volunteers prepared to head for home in early December, Jackson showed his resolve. Facing the desertion of troops, he planted his mount in their path. Because his left arm was still in a sling, he rested his musket on the horse's neck.

Looking down the barrel at the mutinous men, he warned, "You say you will march. I say by the Eternal God you shall not march while a cartridge can sound fire!"[2]

General Coffee and Major John Reid took up positions on either side of Jackson. No one moved for long minutes—until several loyal companies broke ranks and assembled behind the trio. Out of fear and respect for General Jackson, a few of the rebels moved in the direction of the camp. Others followed, and no one headed back to Tennessee that day.

Jackson also faced a deadline. The first Volunteers had enlisted for one year and expected to be discharged from service on December 10. Many lacked the clothing necessary for a winter campaign, and their farms and families awaited their return. "If they do not get home soon," one officer told Jackson, "there are many of them who will be literally ruined."[3]

Their commander sympathized with their plight, but he saw the enlistment period differently. Because they had been dismissed for the summer, these soldiers, Jackson reasoned, had yet to serve twelve months. And their task remained unfinished, with the dangerous Red Stick Creeks still at large.

Jackson was again forced to face down his own men. He told them they could depart only "by passing over [my] body."[4] He tried to shame them into remaining, saying they were about to become "the tarnishers of their own fame" as they went into "inglorious retirement."[5] He said he expected reinforcements would soon arrive—and some did. But several of those regiments were also nearing the end of their enlistments, on January 1 and January 14, 1814. Finally, realizing there was little he could do to salvage the campaign, Jackson released the majority of his men without extending their obligations.

Meanwhile, Jackson's health deteriorated. Year's end found him still unable to maneuver his left arm into the sleeve of his coat unassisted. His army was dwindling by the day. About all he could do was write home to Tennessee.

At "1/2 past 11 o'clock at night," on December 29, 1813, he opened his heart to his wife, Rachel. He bemoaned "the shameful desertion from their posts of the Volunteer infantry . . . and the apathy displayed in the interior of the state by the fireside patriots." But his letter offered his wife assurances. "Be not uneasy . . . if I have trials, and perils, [God] has fortified me with fortitude to do my duty under every circumstance."[6] In the next hour, he wrote harder words to his old friend Governor Willie Blount, reminding him that the fight had to be carried on to protect the people from the Creeks. The Indians needed to be "exterminated or conquered," said Jackson, and he challenged the governor to act. "Are you, my dear friend, sitting with your arms folded?"

Jackson's letter was an insistent demand for help. "Arouse from your lethargy," he wrote. "Give me a force for 6 months in whose term of service there is no doubt . . . and all may be safe. Withhold it, and all is lost."[7]

Before Blount could react, still more enlistments ended and the army encamped with Jackson amounted to just 130 able-bodied soldiers. And the dangers had grown: Jackson's spies brought word that British troops had landed at Pensacola. This could mean only one thing: as long expected, the enemy had to be preparing to assault the Gulf Coast—and, in particular, its most important city, New Orleans. Jackson knew he must, somehow, keep his army together. He must prevail against this first foe—and be ready for the next.

Meanwhile, Red Eagle's fame continued to grow. On December 23, with Jackson struggling to keep his army together, Weatherford confronted a force of Mississippi militiamen. Again outnumbered, the Red Sticks fled and Red Eagle, riding his prized gray, Arrow, took the only avenue of escape he saw. Racing along a high bluff overlooking the Alabama River, he pointed the horse toward the precipice and drove his spurs into Arrow's flanks.

From a height of roughly fifteen feet, both rider and horse took flight. They seemed to float in midair before plunging into the water. The astonished Mississippi militiamen watched: neither man nor animal was visible, entirely submerged. Then Weatherford surfaced, still astride his mount. With one hand, he grasped the horse's mane; with the other, he held his gun aloft.

The troops unleashed musket volleys as Arrow swam for the opposite bank but, despite the hail of lead, man and beast reached the shore. Safely out of range, Red Eagle dismounted and inspected his steed for wounds. Finding none, he rode off.[8]

The Creek chief survived to fight another day. As for Andrew Jackson, he could only hope that when that day came, the two of them would finally look each other in the eye across the line of battle.

Battle Preparations

Early in the new year, fresh recruits finally arrived from Nashville. Although the 850 men had little or no military experience, Jackson wasted no time. He ordered a march deep into enemy territory.

The new force met the enemy, fighting skirmishes with Red Eagle's braves at two Red Stick villages late in January 1814. Though he and his men managed to prevail, the battles were hard fought, and Jackson himself was nearly killed when he rode directly into the fighting. "In the midst of showers of balls, of which he seemed unmindful," one officer recalled, "he . . . [rallied] the alarmed, halting them in their flight, forming his columns, and inspiriting them by his example."[9]

After that near-debacle, Jackson pulled back to drill his inexperienced men. His army continued to grow, and not just with fresh recruits from Tennessee. Jackson's reputation was beginning to travel farther afield, and, for the first time, U.S. Army regulars were put under his command in addition to the Volunteers, raising the total troops in Jackson's army to more than 3,500 men.

The Battle of Horseshoe Bend

Before long, spies reported that William Weatherford and a thousand warriors waited almost a hundred miles away in a village overlooking the Tallapoosa River. Jackson was determined to make this the Creeks' last stand. This enemy posed a dual danger: they were a threat to frontier life, and they had chosen to ally themselves with the nation's larger enemy, Great Britain. The British were known to be providing the Creeks with supplies—a few months before, American militiamen had intercepted the Creeks with wagonloads of supplies offloaded from the British at Pensacola.

Jackson's scouts—among them, Davy Crockett—informed him that the Indians were camped at a place called Horseshoe Bend. The enemy used a great U-shaped curve in the river as a moat to protect them on three sides. The Creek warriors, together with several hundred women and children, inhabited a cluster of huts at the southern end of the hundred-acre peninsula. A narrow neck to the north

provided the only land entry, across which the Red Sticks had constructed a breastwork. Built of large timbers and earth, this fortress
wall was 8 feet tall and 350 yards wide. It was lined with portholes
through which the Indians could shoot at attackers.

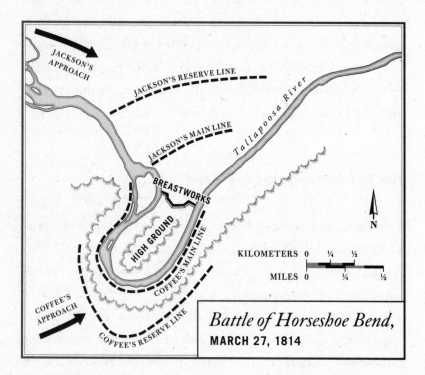

General Jackson was impressed. "Nature furnishes few situations
as eligible for defense," he reported to Governor Blount, "and barbar-
ians have never rendered one more secure by art."[10] Even though his
men outnumbered the Creeks, conquering this fort would be no
easy task.

Despite Jackson's inexperience with military strategy, he was undaunted. After all, he had attributes that couldn't be taught: unrivaled courage, natural leadership, and—he would soon discover—uncanny battlefield instincts. Working with his advisers, he devised a plan.

At first light on March 27, 1814, General John Coffee's cavalry headed out with a band of Cherokees and friendly Creeks. Per Jackson's orders, they were to take positions south of the enemy village along the bend of the Tallapoosa on the opposite bank. From there they could shoot any Red Sticks attempting to escape Jackson and his men.

Meanwhile Jackson marched the rest of his army directly toward the breastwork. They halted, remaining at the ready while artillery- men set their two cannons. At 10:30 a.m., with word that Coffee and his men were in place, the cannoneers fired.

The cannonballs did little damage, bouncing away or thudding harmlessly into the sturdy breastwork. Any Red Stick who showed himself was quickly the target of heavy musket fire from Jackson's line, but, remaining behind their earthworks, the Creeks mocked their attackers with war whoops.

At the other end of the peninsula, a different attack had begun. When Jackson's gunners started firing on the fort, some of the Indians in Coffee's command charged the river. Under fire, they plunged into the water, swam across the river, and seized their enemies' canoes on the opposite bank.[11] After paddling back in stolen vessels, they ferried two hundred Indians and thirty Tennessee militiamen to the Creek side and began to fight their way toward the Red Stick village, about half a mile away from where Jackson's men were fighting. They soon set the huts aflame and marched on to join Jackson in attacking the Indian fort.

When Jackson saw the billowing smoke rising from the village, he ordered his men to charge. He'd prepared his troops for this moment: "In the hour of battle," Jackson's general orders from three days earlier read, "you must be cool and collected. When your officer orders you to fire, you must execute the command with deliberateness and aim. *Let every shot tell.*"[12]

His men did as ordered and, despite a storm of enemy bullets and arrows, the first attackers soon reached the ramparts. There they fought muzzle to muzzle, the Tennesseans and Indians shooting point-blank at one another through the portholes.

The first man to scale the wall and go over the top, Major Lemuel Montgomery, collapsed onto the breastwork, lifeless, shot through the head. A platoon leader named Sam Houston next led the charge, brandishing his sword. A Red Stick arrow penetrated his upper thigh, but Houston didn't fall. He leapt to the ground inside the fort, his uniformed men close behind.

Overwhelmed by this breach of their trusted wall, Red Stick defenders retreated into nearby brush and woods. They fired on the invaders, but the attackers had every advantage—more men, more guns, the momentum of the battle. Even so, the Indians continued to fight.

So did Sam Houston. At his order, another officer withdrew the barbed arrow from Houston's left thigh, opening a gaping wound. When Jackson called to men to attack the Creeks holding a nearby redoubt, Houston picked up a musket and led the charge. This time he took two musket balls, one entering his right arm, the other his right shoulder.

The battle raged on, with Jackson's men clearly winning the day. Even so, the outnumbered Indians refused his offer of surrender in the early afternoon, firing upon Jackson's messenger and his interpreter, wounding one of them. The Creeks preferred a fight to surrender, and the battle went on. "The *carnage* was *dreadful*," Jackson would write to his wife.[13]

A few Red Sticks would escape in the night, but the morning body count totaled 557 Indian corpses. Many more Creeks had died trying to escape; the Tallapoosa River, dyed red with human blood, had carried away an estimated 300 braves. On Jackson's side, just 43 soldiers lost their lives, while his Indian allies lost 23.

Red Eagle no longer commanded a viable fighting force and, by mid-April, most of the other Creek chiefs had presented themselves at Jackson's camp under flags of truce. They accepted that they were not in a position to dictate peace terms. But General Jackson was, and, before negotiations could begin, he made one simple demand: He wanted the man behind the Fort Mims massacre. Only when William Weatherford was in his hands could the Creek War be ended.

A few days later, a lone Indian arrived in Jackson's camp. The stranger had a freshly shot deer tied across the rump of his horse; he was directed to the general's tent and rode up just as Jackson was emerging.

"General Jackson?"

Jackson looked up in surprise at the man riding the handsome gray horse. Bare to the waist, the light-skinned Indian wore buckskin breeches and moccasins.

His next statement was still more surprising. "I am Bill Weatherford."

More than anything else, his desire to avenge Fort Mims had driven Jackson over the preceding months. Now the man responsible for the massacre stood unarmed before him.

His first response was anger at Weatherford's nerve. "How dare you show yourself at my tent after having murdered the women and children at Fort Mims!" he exclaimed.

His second response was puzzlement. Had Jackson's men captured the Indian leader, the general would no doubt have ordered his speedy execution. It had never occurred to him that Weatherford might surrender. Now Jackson had to decide what to do with him.

"I had directed that you should be brought to me confined; had you appeared in this way, I should have known how to treat you," he told Weatherford.

"I am in your power," the man replied. "Do with me as you please. I am a soldier. I have done to the white people all the harm I could; I have fought them, and fought them bravely: if I had an army, I would yet fight, and contend to the last: but I have none; my people are all gone. I can now do no more than weep over the misfortune of my nation."[14]

To the surprise of his men, Old Hickory did not order Weatherford's imprisonment or execution. Instead, Jackson offered Red Eagle a deal: He would grant him his life and liberty if he would serve as a peacemaker to the Creeks who were still fighting. If he chose to fight again, "his life should pay the forfeit of his crimes." If he chose peace? "[You will] be protected."[15]

Weatherford took the deal, telling Jackson that "those who would still hold out can be influenced only by a mean spirit of revenge; and to this they must not, and shall not sacrifice the last remnant of their country. You have told us where we might go, and be safe. This is a good talk, and my nation ought to listen to it."[16]

The man's manner and words left a deep impression on Major Reid. Weatherford, he wrote, "possessed all the manliness of sentiment—all the heroism of soul, all the comprehension of intellect calculated to make an able commander. . . . His looks and gestures—the modesty and yet the firmness that were in them."[17]

Unlikely as it might seem, Andrew Jackson recognized a kindred spirit "as high-toned and fearless as any man he had met with."[18] Here was a man who understood the rules of war, a man who knew the time had passed for bloodshed between the Creeks and the settlers. And he could help assure the peace.

With the U.S. victory at Horseshoe Bend, the Creek War was effectively over. The Creeks recognized that their only choice was to bargain, and, with the help of Red Eagle, Jackson negotiated the Treaty of Fort Jackson. On August 9, 1814, the Creek chiefs signed it, agreeing to give the United States—and the man they called Sharp Knife—more than twenty-two million acres of land. American settlers were now safe and had room to expand.

Red Eagle had helped make the case for peace, having retired from making war. As for Jackson, even with an Indian treaty in hand, he had no such luxury. He was already hearing the sound of British footsteps moving toward New Orleans.

Major General Jackson

Word of Jackson's battlefield success reached the War Department.

This man Jackson, whom they had mistrusted as a stubborn and crude westerner, was outperforming Washington's military strategists and its aging generals.

His troops both loved and feared him. To everyone's surprise, he had made an effective fighting force out of volunteer militiamen. He knew when to be tough, and he knew when to temper that toughness with kindness. He was fearless in battle, but not reckless. In fact, he balanced his courage with great caution and surprising patience for gathering intelligence and listening to the advice of others. He knew when to stand firm on his convictions but wasn't blind to the possibility of compromise. Finally, and most important, he possessed a natural instinct for military strategy that made up for his lack of formal training.

Even Secretary of War John Armstrong, whose orders Jackson had quarreled with in Natchez, recognized Jackson's potential. "Something ought to be done for General Jackson," he wrote to President Madison after news of the triumph at Horseshoe Bend elated the nation's capital, where politicians were weary of a war that was draining the treasury, brought too few victories to cheer, and had gone on far longer than expected.[19] Something would be done for Jackson and, on June 18, 1814, militia general Jackson was promoted to the rank of major general of the regular U.S. Army, a larger and more powerful command.

Jackson's rise to national prominence could not have come at a better time. After two decades spent fighting France, the British had forced Napoleon to abdicate in April. That meant the Royal Navy and the immense army of the victorious Duke of Wellington could be sent to engage in the fight in North America. An invading force was already cruising the Mid-Atlantic coast, worrying President Madison and his cabinet. What would unfold elsewhere wasn't clear—but, with Jackson in command of the Seventh Military District, which encompassed Louisiana, Tennessee, and all of the Mississippi Territory, it became Jackson's job to ponder what might happen in his region.

This was also a responsibility he had long wished for. As he wrote

Rachel from his quarters in Creek country, near the Coosa River, "I owe Britain a debt of . . . vengeance."[20]

In Jackson's view, the enemy's ultimate objective was clear enough: the British wanted New Orleans. Anyone who could read a map knew that by capturing the city, His Majesty's forces would consolidate control of the North American continent from the Gulf Coast to Canada—and that could end the United States' westward expansion. For Jackson, that prospect was unacceptable.

In August 1814, his army was small. His Tennessee Volunteers had returned to their farms and shops after defeating the Indians, and he had just 531 enlisted soldiers. But Jackson's knowledge of what the British might do was even smaller. He knew neither when the British warships might land nor how many troops they carried. What he was certain of was that he and his army had to move south immediately. With the Creeks disposed of, he could focus on protecting the coast from his European enemy.

Two days after the Creek treaty was signed, Jackson and his little army set off toward the Gulf of Mexico, marching as quickly as they could. The new reality of a British threat fed an existing fear: those who read the papers already knew the British could be ruthless. The previous summer the Crown's men, rampaging through the Virginia countryside, committed terrible atrocities. One woman seeking to escape was said to have been "pursued up to her waist in the water, and dragged on shore by ten or twelve of these ruffians, who satiated their desires upon her, after pulling off her clothes, stockings, shoes, etc."[21] Another report claimed a sick man was murdered in his bed. According to one congressman, "The town of Hampton, and the surrounding country were given up to the indiscriminate plunder of a licentious soldiery."[22] Such stories, linked with rumors of the impending British approach, prompted General Jackson, sitting in his saddle for four hundred miles, to think very hard about possible strategies for preventing the same from happening to the people of the Gulf Coast.

Yet even for the most powerful military in the world, an attack on New Orleans would be no simple matter. The Royal Navy might lead the siege, but to get to New Orleans its ships would have to sail a hundred miles up the Mississippi. Along the way, they would face American guns, changing tides, and several sharp turns in the river, making for a slow and dangerous approach to their objective. Though he had no naval experience, Jackson understood these obstacles and guessed that the British would avoid a river assault.

Assuming the British would launch an overland attack against the city, Jackson considered his possibilities. The Mississippi delta south of New Orleans, a swampy morass of bayous, would be practically impossible to march across. And the British had no easy land access from the north. Thus, Jackson and his advisers concluded that their enemy would come from the east.

If the British were to send a land force from the east, where would they land? Jackson believed that the most likely site was Mobile, a city 150 miles to the east, with its own protected bay. When, on August 22, he rode into Mobile with his army, he was already thinking one move ahead. Although he had never visited New Orleans, he would, somehow, find a way to protect this city unlike any other.

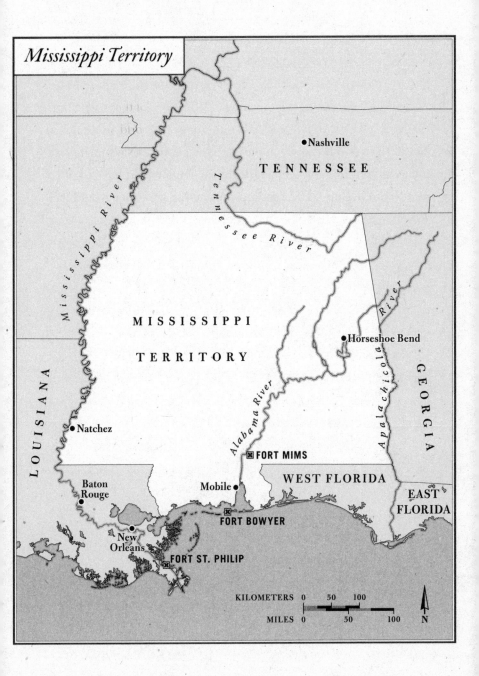

Mississippi Territory

TENNESSEE

●Nashville

Mississippi River

Tennessee River

MISSISSIPPI

TERRITORY

Horseshoe Bend●

Alabama River

Apalachicola River

LOUISIANA

GEORGIA

●Natchez

☒ FORT MIMS

Baton
Rouge●

Mobile ●

WEST FLORIDA

EAST
FLORIDA

New
Orleans●

☒
FORT BOWYER

☒ FORT ST. PHILIP

KILOMETERS 0   50   100

MILES 0   50   100

N

CHAPTER 5

The British on Offense

I have it much at heart to give [the Americans] a complete drubbing before peace is made, when I trust their . . . command of the Mississippi [will be] wrested from them.

—Admiral Alexander Cochrane to Earl Bathurst, July 14, 1814

Would New Orleans welcome America's protection? The answer to that question was far from certain. The most important city in Jefferson's Louisiana Purchase was in transition. An American possession since 1803, Louisiana had been a state for only two years, and its loyalty to the Union was not yet proven.

The young and precariously American city was also a place of contradictions. Though isolated amid low-lying mudflats, in a climate where withering tropical heat and violent hurricanes were normal, New Orleans had nevertheless become a center of European refinement and culture. An outpost of law and order in the wilderness, it was still home to more than a few outlaws. The most important city in the newest American state, it was French in spirit, but had

also been a possession of both the British and the Spanish; many
of its inhabitants didn't even speak the language of their new government. In the event of invasion, Jackson would have to shape an
unprecedented unity among a motley population of French colonials,
Native Americans, freed slaves, American woodsmen, and even
pirates.

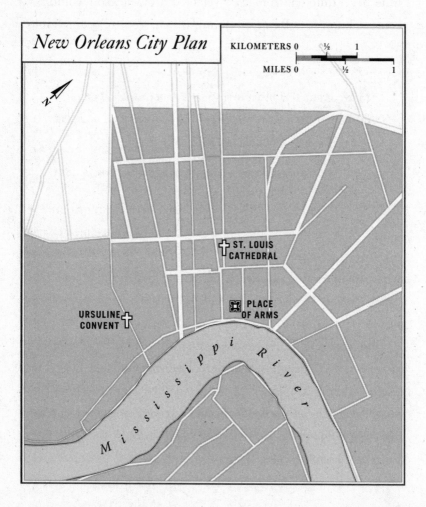

New Orleans City Plan

KILOMETERS 0 ½ 1
MILES 0 ½ 1

ST. LOUIS
CATHEDRAL

URSULINE
CONVENT

PLACE
OF ARMS

Mississippi River

New Orleans had been a place of constant change simply because of its geography. A natural bank, or levee, had risen along a crescent-shaped turn in the meandering Mississippi and, over the centuries, Native Americans had found the spot, located about a hundred miles upstream from the Gulf of Mexico, a convenient place to travel farther inland. Their overland route took them to a slow-moving stream at a water level different from the river's (Andrew Jackson would soon come to know it as Bayou St. John), which, in turn, drained into a shallow body of water called Lake Pontchartrain. That enormous lake emptied into Lake Borgne and, eventually, the Gulf, north and east of what had become New Orleans.

In 1718, an early European arrival in the region, Jean-Baptiste Le Moyne, sieur de Bienville, founded a community at the watery crossroads and called it La Nouvelle-Orléans, in honor of France's ruler, Philippe II, duc d'Orléans. The settlement began as little more than an array of shacks, and most of those were obliterated by a massive flood in 1719. Bienville supervised a rebuilding, with taller and sturdier levees constructed to protect his settlement, which, behind the wall of earth, sat several feet below the Mississippi at high tide. The growing town became the capital of French Louisiana in 1722, but later that same year a hurricane destroyed most of New Orleans's buildings.

Slaves brought from Senegal dug drainage canals and built higher levees, and as they pushed the water back, Bienville's village grew into a good-size town. As settlers poured in, New Orleans gained its first cathedral and a convent for Ursuline nuns. The Ursuline sisters established a school for girls and a hospital where soldiers and slaves alike were treated for ailments common to the region, like malaria and yellow fever. When the Seven Years' War in Europe shifted the political landscape (the 1756–63 conflict was known to Americans as the French and Indian War), Louisiana was ceded to Spain. But the Spaniards' luck during their decades in charge proved no better than that of the French. Three major hurricanes hurtled through; a great flood swamped most of lower Louisiana in 1782; and two great fires nearly flattened the city of New Orleans in 1788 and 1794.

Nevertheless, by the time of Mr. Jefferson's Louisiana Purchase, New Orleans had become a European-style city with an aura such that a contemporary visitor described the place as a "French Ville de Province."[1] The oldest quarter was a central checkerboard of streets, the Vieux Carré, which retained a grid planned long before by French royal engineers. In the next decade, the population more than doubled to eighteen thousand inhabitants.

In the heat and humidity of its bayou country, lower Louisiana proved a perfect melting pot for blending cultures. There were slaves and free persons of color and many Native Americans (the area had once been Choctaw territory). During and after the French and Indian War, French-speaking Acadians from Canada's maritime provinces had been expelled by the British, and thousands of them took refuge in Louisiana. These "Cajuns" established their own unique culture in nearby bayous. A German community had been established upstream. On New Orleans's streets and wharves, Spanish, Dutch, Swedish, and French were spoken. River trade had lured many frontiersmen from Kentucky, Tennessee, and Ohio, adding English speakers to a city where once they had been few.

When war was declared in 1812, Louisiana had no long-term allegiance to the United States, but the British increasingly interfered with trade, and goods quickly accumulated at the city's docks, generating profits for no one. Louisiana's governor, William Charles Cole Claiborne, had been dispatched from Washington—first appointed to the post by President Jefferson and then elected after statehood—but the city's powerful Creoles, as white New Orleanians of Spanish or French heritage were called, had little respect for him. In truth, no one in New Orleans controlled the levers of power, and the city's competing interests coexisted but didn't necessarily cooperate.

This was amply demonstrated by the fact that a brash band of privateers—some called them pirates—sold their contraband openly in New Orleans, flouting the law. They paid no customs duties on the coffee, linens, silks, iron, mahogany, spices, and wine they smuggled into the city using hollowed-out cypress canoes and other flat-bottomed boats adapted to the marshy waterscape of the delta. Although they operated outside the law, these men were essential to the local economy and publicly advertised their wares. Few among New Orleans high society showed a willingness to crack down on the purveyors of much-desired bootlegged goods.

Persuading the city's population of sturdily independent peoples to support one another and fight together would be Jackson's first challenge: corralling a throng of rich and poor, blacks and whites, speakers of many tongues, Americans and men of mixed allegiance wouldn't be easy.

Yet there was still a chance that cooler heads would prevail, and a diplomatic end to the war might be reached before any confrontation with the British took place at or near New Orleans. On the other side of the Atlantic, in fact, there were a number of Americans vitally concerned with avoiding what loomed as a potential military disaster in Louisiana.

The Negotiations: Ghent, Belgium

Many months before, President Madison had sent his diplomats to discuss an end to the conflict with representatives of the British Crown. After many delays, the ministers from both countries finally sat down together in August 1814 to talk treaty. If the Americans had hoped the end of the French wars would lead the British to tender peace offerings, they were very much mistaken. Even on day one of the talks, the U.S. envoys understood—perhaps more than anyone in Washington—the very real British threat to the Gulf of Mexico.

One of them, Albert Gallatin, had kept his ears and eyes open on his way to Ghent, in Flanders, the site of the peace talks. He was an old friend of President Madison's, having previously served as secretary of the treasury. During a stopover in London in the spring, Gallatin had heard things.

Some of what he picked up was common street knowledge. The London *Times* stated in its pages the position that many Britons held: "Mr. Madison's dirty swindling maneuvers in respect to Louisiana and the Floridas remain to be punished."[2] A few members of Parliament even called for New Orleans to be handed over to Great Britain. The dutiful Gallatin took notes of the chatter and wrote home, relaying it to Secretary of State James Monroe.

"To use their own language," he warned, "[the British] mean to inflict on America a chastisement that will teach her that war is not to be declared against Great Britain with impunity."[3] Gallatin added ominously that he had heard whispers that a force of between fifteen and twenty thousand men was on its way across the Atlantic Ocean.

THE BRITISH ON OFFENSE 59

Their aim was clearly to deliver punishment, not peace, to the colonies they'd lost thirty-one years before.

After writing from London, Gallatin had made his way across the English Channel where he joined forces with the rest of the American negotiating team, including the sharp-spoken Kentucky politician Henry Clay and John Quincy Adams, son of founding father John Adams, the most experienced of the American envoys.

As Speaker of the House of Representatives, Henry Clay had helped persuade his colleagues in Congress to declare war, asserting that capturing Canada would be a simple matter. Two years later, humbled by American military failures in Canada and elsewhere, Clay resigned as Speaker to accept the posting to Europe. There he hoped his considerable negotiating abilities would help salvage an honorable peace.

But Clay, like Gallatin, was deeply worried as the August meetings with the British representatives got under way. Although Madison had agreed to the proposal for peace talks back in January, Lord Castlereagh, the British foreign secretary, and the men around him had dragged their feet ever since. Clay had to ask himself: *Why are there so many delays in sending a team to talk peace?*

Tall and congenial, Henry Clay was a hail-fellow-well-met sort of man who liked his liquor. He could walk into a roomful of strangers and depart with new friends, even if, as a demon cardplayer, he had managed to take some of their money. Now, in Ghent, those same gambling instincts put Minister Clay on edge. He could smell risk when he encountered it, and he had come to think the British were slow to open the treaty talks for a reason: *With a large force from Great Britain attacking the United States, mustn't the odds favor the superior British troops?* he thought. Clay believed the Crown's representatives were awaiting news of battlefield successes in North America. In the meantime, the king's statesmen had little incentive to negotiate.

This all made painful sense to Clay. He was a man who understood better than most the advantage of having bargaining chips on one's own side of the table. And British victories on the battlefield could provide just that to his enemy.

When, at last, the Britons did sit down to present their terms of peace on the afternoon of August 8, 1814, at one o'clock, the aura of doom darkened for Madison's diplomats. The demands made on behalf of Foreign Secretary Lord Castlereagh were harsh, involving unacceptable limitations on fishing rights in the Atlantic as well as a large buffer zone for the Indians in the center of the North American continent.

The American envoys recognized that the British demands were those of a conqueror—and that the United States had by no means been conquered. At least not yet.

In the days that followed, the British and American negotiators continued to meet and exchange notes about possible treaty terms. But they made little progress. As Clay wrote home to Secretary of State Monroe ten days into the talks, "I am inclined to think . . . that their policy is to consume as much time as possible . . . [in] the hope that they will strike some signal blow, during the present campaign."[4]

Both sides in the Ghent negotiations awaited news from the front.

"Bloody Noses"

As the peace negotiators talked across the Atlantic, an express messenger arrived in Mobile, bringing Jackson bad news. His hunch had been correct: the British were indeed planning to land along the Gulf

Coast east of New Orleans. The dispatch Jackson received at five o'clock on the evening of August 27, 1814, reported that three warships, the HMS *Hermes, Carron,* and *Sophie* from the Royal Navy station at Bermuda, had already landed a small force of men and armaments at Pensacola in Spanish Florida.

With British boots on the ground just fifty miles east of his station, Jackson wondered what might happen next. A large invasion seemed likely; another source, this one writing from Havana, reported that a loose-lipped British officer had bragged about a plan to capture Pensacola, to move on to Mobile, then to march overland to New Orleans.[5] London had already sent thirteen additional warships with ten thousand troops aboard, the officer claimed, with still more soon to follow.[6]

When Jackson looked at his own forces, they seemed laughably small. He had arrived with his five-hundred-man Third Infantry force and found that Mobile was manned by just the Thirty-Ninth Tennessee Regiment. Scattered over his large southwestern command—from Tennessee to the Gulf Coast—were fewer than two thousand more troops. Only the Third and the Thirty-Ninth had ever seen combat.

That night Jackson put pen to paper, writing home to Tennessee, asking to be reinforced with the entire state militia. In particular, he wanted General Coffee and his cavalry. He wanted Cherokees and artillerymen, and he needed transport and supplies.

Action was required; the threat was real. "Before one month," he warned, "the British . . . expect to be in possession of Mobile and all the surrounding country." If he did not get the support he needed, he was not sure he could stop the British from taking this key port and then moving on to New Orleans.

But Jackson couldn't afford to sit around waiting for reinforcements: his first task would be to get Fort Bowyer into fighting shape.

Because of its location thirty miles south, at the opening of Mobile Bay, Fort Bowyer would be the first line of defense if British ships moved on Mobile. Enemy vessels would have to pass within range of the fort's guns as they sailed through the narrow channel at the entrance to the bay. But from Jackson's position, that was both good and bad: its location was certainly a strategic advantage, but, having been abandoned due to a lack of men a few months earlier, Fort Bowyer was far from ready to repel a sustained attack.

Jackson needed a man he could trust to get the fort back in line. He chose Lieutenant Colonel William Lawrence for the task. A career U.S. Army officer from Maryland, Lawrence set out immediately from Mobile for the seaside battery. A tall, stern man with a full head of curly brown hair, he loaded his 160 infantrymen into boats along with supplies and all the munitions he could muster.

On reaching Fort Bowyer, Lawrence saw the challenge before him. The semicircular battery was really just a wall of sand and earth. With its low walls lined on the inside with resinous pine boards, the fort could be set afire by one well-placed shell. No hardened shelter protected the fort's ammunition and, worst of all, more than half of its twenty guns were mounted on outmoded Spanish carriages, making them difficult to aim and operate.

Lawrence and his men threw themselves into the task and, with the British expected to arrive at any moment from their new base at Pensacola, worked night and day, reinforcing the little bastion on the spit of sand with wood, stone, sand, and whatever else came to hand. Even after sunset, the Americans remained ready for action, always expecting to see British sails on the horizon. They didn't know how many days they had to prepare.

Back in Mobile, Jackson continued his writing campaign. One of his correspondents was Governor William Claiborne. Jackson was looking beyond Fort Bowyer and Pensacola, worrying about New Orleans.

Though born and educated in Virginia, the ambitious young Claiborne had, by the age of twenty-five, already earned a law degree, moved west, and served as a congressman (he won Andrew Jackson's vacated seat in 1797). After a decade as governor of New Orleans, he carried himself with what some saw as a haughty confidence; he relished his power and influence in Louisiana. The governor was respected for his administrative abilities but not loved by those he governed, with whom he, as a Virginian, had little in common.

Jackson's letter to him was a warning: "The present intention of Britain," he told his former Washington colleague "is to make an attack on [Mobile], and New Orleans. Part of the British force for this purpose, has landed at Pensacola, and the balance, hourly expected."

The letter was also an urgent call to arms: "You must summon up all your energy, your quota of militia must be in the field without delay. . . . The country must and shall be defended."[7] From Mobile, the best Jackson could do was to urge Claiborne to raise the alarm. Somehow, Jackson hoped, the governor would begin pulling Creoles and Anglos, Indians and freemen, and the rest to fight together.

The British clearly expected to win Mobile and to move on to New Orleans. The odds that Jackson's small army could repel them seemed slim. But the pugnacious General Jackson, channeling his long-simmering anger, was as always ready to fight. Writing home to Tennessee, he reported on the prospect of the British taking Mobile, resolving solemnly, "Th[ere] will be bloody noses before this happens."[8]

The Burning of Washington

When Jackson wrote to the secretary of war in Washington, he did not know that, days earlier, partly due to John Armstrong's incompetence, the nation's capital had sustained a terrible attack.

Back on August 16, a British fleet of some fifty warships had been sighted in Chesapeake Bay. Though its presence was clearly a sign of nothing good, the Americans were unsure what to expect. In an eerie parallel to Jackson's situation near New Orleans, Madison and his men in Washington received only fractured reports concerning the enemy force; British strategy and even their ultimate objective were uncertain. One option was to attack Annapolis, Maryland's capital. General Armstrong didn't think that likely; he was certain the enemy would attack Baltimore, a busy commercial city. Armstrong assured Madison that Washington was safe—he thought it had little strategic value—but others worried that if the armada veered into the nearby Patuxent River, the British could land troops and move on the capital.

On August 20, Secretary of State James Monroe took it upon himself to find out and rode to a nearby hilltop from which he could see the enemy fleet. And there, before him on the shore of Benedict, Maryland, he saw the British had established a base camp and soldiers were coming ashore. Their exact target still wasn't certain, but there was no doubt an invasion had begun.

On August 24, the British played their hand: At the little town of Bladensburg, eight miles from Washington, the British attacked. The town's American defenders—a mix of militiamen from Washington, Baltimore, and Annapolis, almost none of whom were in uniform—were no match for the men in bright red coats. Dragoons on horseback led

the charge across the bridge that defined the sleepy village on the East
Branch of the Potomac River. A flood of British infantryman followed,
bearing polished bayonets that glinted in the sun. To the intimidating
sound of exploding rockets overhead, the king's veteran troops drove
into the American line. General Armstrong had expected his troops to
hold off the outnumbered British—there were some four thousand British troops facing perhaps seven thousand American defenders—but he
was wrong. Led by the British general Robert Ross and Sir George
Cockburn, a hot-tempered admiral in the Royal Navy, the enemy sliced
through the line of intimidated militiamen, captured Bladensburg, and
headed straight for Washington.

Madison and the other government officials had been watching
the battle from an overlook and had to rush back to Washington, making it there just in time to join a larger retreat. Before fleeing, the First
Lady and others had sought to save a few precious relics—a portrait
of Washington, a copy of the Declaration of Independence in the Library of Congress—but a few hours later, after stopping for an afternoon dinner, the British marched into a nearly empty Washington.
Then shots rang out, as hidden snipers fired into the ranks of the
150-man British force. The angry British commander regarded the
snipers' behavior as "dastardly and provoking." He promptly ordered
the house from which the muskets fired set afire.

That would be the first of a series of conflagrations. Next it was
off to the president's house. When the British arrived there, they found
Mr. and Mrs. Madison's dinner table still set, the aroma of cooking
food still wafting up from the recently abandoned kitchen. They drank
the president's wine and ate a generous meal before building bonfires
in the rooms and retreating to the street to watch the mansion burn.
By nine o'clock, great billows of flame reached into the sky; the

Capitol had also become an inferno and by morning it was a roofless, smoking ruin, and the light gray stone of the president's house had been burned black.

The British made a point of sacking the offices of the Washington newspaper the *National Intelligencer*, building a bonfire to burn its type and presses. The *Intelligencer* was known for printing stories critical of Cockburn, and he was determined to teach its editor and readers a lesson. "Be sure all the c's are destroyed," he is said to have told his men, "so that they can't abuse my name anymore."

In the end, it wasn't the brave efforts of the American people that put out the fires or stopped the destruction. Only the arrival, with miraculous timing, of a powerful storm prevented more of the city from being damaged by the flames. Rain poured down and strong winds blew, lifting British cannons off the ground, according to some reports. Others claimed that the storm formed a tornado, a rare phenomenon in Washington. Whatever the case, the British were discouraged and the fires quenched thanks not to the work of men, but to an act of God.

Although the British returned to their ships several days later, President James Madison and the U.S. Congress were left homeless. The attack tore the fabric of the nation, too, with hopes of a peace deal growing dim. Many of the northern states had refused to go to war; the Eastern Seaboard was ill equipped to fight off its attackers, and when it came to protecting the new nation's capital, no one had fought. Perhaps more than ever before America needed something—or someone—to knit the country back together.

The events of August 24 also meant that when Jackson's dispatch arrived in Washington, it didn't land on John Armstrong's desk. That desk was gone—the building the War and Treasury Departments shared had also been torched—and John Armstrong had been dismissed. At Madison's request, James Monroe took on a second job in the cabinet, becoming secretary of war as well as secretary of state. Yet even Monroe, despite his good intentions, would not be able to provide much help to his Tennessee general, given that the national government was struggling to survive and reestablish itself.

Meanwhile, one of the first British ships to arrive in the Gulf of Mexico was about to make its presence felt. But the British success did something they never expected. It galvanized more ambivalent Americans, who now found themselves motivated to support the war as they realized that America was facing not only the possibility of defeat, but of complete destruction.

A Message from the British

On the morning of September 2, 1814, the British *Sophie* sailed into view, sailing directly for the shallow channel that led to Barataria Bay, south of the city of New Orleans. The two-masted warship, armed with eighteen guns, dropped anchor several miles from shore. British gunners fired a cannon, but the men on shore recognized that it was a greeting, not an act of war.

Since 1805, the island of Grand Terre had been home to the men who thought of themselves as coastal privateers. They had fled the Caribbean island of Santo Domingo following the slave rebellion that led to the founding of the independent nation of Haiti. Their adopted home in Barataria Bay offered access to New Orleans via the muddy waters of shallow streams, bayous, and channels camouflaged by reeds and grasses. In turn, the city provided a ready market for captured goods. Led by a pair of brothers, Jean and Pierre Lafitte, the pirates had constructed dozens of warehouses deep in the bayous on Grand Terre Island, all the while maintaining businesses in the city, including a store on Royal Street (where Jean could often be found) and a blacksmith shop, operated by Pierre, on St. Philip Street. The store offered a wide range of hard-to-find goods to the well-to-do of New Orleans, and the shop doubled as an in-town warehouse.

The British had arrived in Barataria Bay to seek a parley. Like Jackson, the British understood that they would need local knowledge of the New Orleans landscape in order to take the city. They expected to conquer Mobile first but were confident enough of their success that they were looking ahead, and the HMS *Sophie* approached Grand Terre hoping to find the guidance they needed.

Who better to provide it? With their fleet of perhaps thirty vessels, the pirates routinely attacked shipping in the Gulf, taking as prizes passing merchant ships flying the British and especially the Spanish flag. After capturing their prey—their artillery was considerable, their daring greater—the pirates would disappear into the sanctuary of the bayous, beneath the canopy of live oaks laden with Spanish moss. These backwater buccaneers knew the terrain around New Orleans as no one else did.

From the deck of the *Sophie,* British sailors lowered a longboat, flying a flag of truce, into the waters. Two uniformed officers were aboard—one was the *Sophie*'s commander, Captain Nicholas Lockyer—along with a handful of sailors who rowed for shore.

Soon a second boat launched from the beach, rowing toward the small British vessel. One Baratarian stood in its bow, and four pirates manned the oars.

When the two bobbing vessels were within hailing distance, a British voice called out, in French, "We are looking for Jean Lafitte."[9]

"Follow me," called the tall, thin man with the long mustache standing in the bow.

With the two boats now headed for the beach, more and more Baratarians assembled on the shore to greet them. Some in boots, some barefoot, the pirates in their brightly colored pantaloons and blouses stood in contrast to the uniformed men of the Royal Navy. Knives, cutlasses, and pistols hung from their belts, and bandannas covered their heads. These men deserved the name that Andrew Jackson soon coined for them: they were "piratical banditti."

When the boats were drawn onto the sand, the pirates crowded toward the handful of British visitors. With no more than a movement of his head, the tall man stepping from the pirate boat made it plain that the men on the shore should keep their distance. He then turned to the leader of the English, Captain Lockyer.

To the visitor's surprise, the elegant man identified himself, speaking in his native French.

"Monsieur," he said, "I am Lafitte."

He beckoned them to follow.

The British Proposition

Jean Lafitte's comfortable house had a broad covered gallery, a deep porch in the Caribbean style, which looked out on the Gulf. There Lafitte served his British guests fish and game, Spanish wine, and the fruits of the Indies. He offered Cuban cigars.[10] Only then did he examine a packet of letters handed him by the visitors. They contained the terms of a British proposal.

"I call on you, with your brave followers, to enter into the service of Great Britain, in which you shall have the rank of a captain," Lafitte read. "Your ships and vessels [will] be placed under the orders of the commanding officer on this station."[11] Lafitte and his men were being invited—or were they being forced?—into British service.

Lafitte looked upon his guests and they, in turn, studied this unusual man. At thirty-four, he was something of a mystery. Some said he was born in Bordeaux. Or was his birthplace Haiti? He was dark-haired and sunburned. Rumor had it he had served in both the British and the French navies and had been incarcerated for a time in a Spanish prison, but no one seemed certain. Clearly he was not a man to be easily intimidated, and he had a shrewd and adventuresome look. Renowned for his skills both as a fencer in battle and as a dancer in society, he carried himself with a gentleman's grace.

Through his translator, Lockyer assured Lafitte the offer was a generous one. For his cooperation in fighting the United States, Lafitte would be paid $30,000 in cash. There would be grants of land for him and his men, pardons for former British subjects, and other guarantees.

Next Lafitte gained confirmation of the rumor he had already heard: yes, New Orleans was to be attacked by the British.

But along with the carrot came the stick: Should Lafitte and the Baratarians choose not to side with the British, a great armada of ships would make Grand Terre their target. The refusal of the offer to join forces would result in the obliteration of the village at Barataria, along with every pirate sailing vessel.

The message was clear: *Join us or we will destroy you.*

When Lafitte spoke, his words to the British officers were measured and diplomatic.

He needed to consider the proposal before him, he said. His habit of closing one eye when he spoke suited his words; he could not, he explained, give an immediate answer. They were his guests, but as they had seen on the beach, he reminded them, they were among violent men, many of whom were hostile to the British. He needed to discuss any proposed alliance with his fellow privateers. But he promised his English visitors safe passage back to their ship in the morning. With their little boat now under pirate guard, the men of the Royal Navy had no choice but to agree.

Good to his word, Jean Lafitte saw his visitors off the following morning and, after their departure, he drafted a formal response.

He opened his letter with an apology for being unable to give an immediate answer, but the pirate leader stood firm: He needed time to decide. After taking two weeks to put his affairs in order, he would meet the British again with an answer. When he finished writing, he ordered his letter be delivered to the HMS *Sophie* and, later in the day, he watched the warship as her unfurled sails caught the breeze. The *Sophie* headed out to sea, making for the deep Gulf waters and a return to Pensacola.

The Baratarians and the British would indeed meet again—but on terms yet to be determined.

Lafitte wrote a second letter, this one addressed to a trusted friend in New Orleans. Writing as a "true American," Lafitte confided that he wished to be of service to his adopted country. "I make you the depository of the secret on which perhaps depends the tranquillity of our country,"[12] he wrote, before recounting the story of the arrival of the British ship at Grand Terre.

Lafitte had decided to play the double agent, offering the Americans fair warning of the British plan.

His third letter of the morning was addressed to Governor William Claiborne. "I tender my services to defend [Louisiana]," he told Claiborne. "I am the stray sheep, wishing to return to the sheepfold."[13]

Whether General Jackson wanted the help of the piratical banditti or not, Lafitte had just declared himself at his service in the fight to save New Orleans.

CHAPTER 6

Jackson Unleashed

I was born for a storm, and a calm does not suit me.

—Andrew Jackson

More than a week would pass before Andrew Jackson learned of the British visit to Barataria. He was 150 miles away in Mobile—and worrying about the security of that port. For him the stakes were clear: if he didn't hold Mobile, the British would have a clear road to New Orleans.

Knowing Fort Bowyer was Mobile's first line of defense, Jackson wanted to be sure he could keep the town safe and secured. On the evening of September 13, 1814, the general, together with a small guard of infantrymen, climbed aboard a schooner. Sailing south that evening toward Fort Bowyer, the little craft was well short of its destination when, at about eleven o'clock, another schooner hailed Jackson's vessel. She brought bad news: It was too late for Jackson to inspect Mobile's defenses. "A number of British armed ships . . . lay off the bar, and from their maneuvering and sounding, etc., showed a design of attacking that fort, or passing it for Mobile."[1]

Jackson, with no wish to be captured by a vastly superior force,

ordered the crew to reverse course and return to Mobile. There was
no way for him to consult with Colonel Lawrence. At this point, all
he could do was pray that the little fort withstood the attack and prepare Mobile to face the British if it didn't.

Unknown to Jackson, a small force of 72 Royal Marines and 130
Indian recruits had landed nine miles east of Fort Bowyer three days
earlier. Armed with a cannon and a howitzer, they planned to attack
the fort from behind, while four warships, mounted with seventy-eight
guns, would attack from the sea. Even now, the *Hermes*, the *Carron*,
and the sloops *Sophie* and *Anaconda* were sailing around Mobile Point,
getting into position.

By the afternoon of September 15, all was ready. The British announced their presence with the roar of cannons, firing their guns in
unison at four o'clock in the afternoon. Fortunately for the Americans,

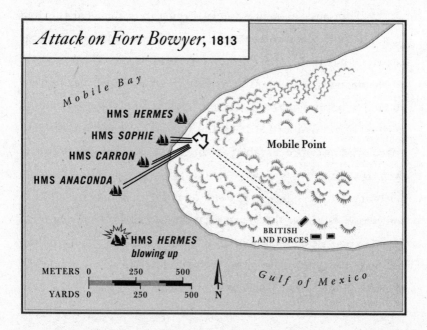

Attack on Fort Bowyer, 1813

Mobile Bay

HMS *HERMES*

HMS *SOPHIE*

Mobile Point

HMS *CARRON*

HMS *ANACONDA*

HMS *HERMES*
blowing up

BRITISH
LAND FORCES

METERS 0   250   500

YARDS 0   250   500   N

Gulf of Mexico

the wind wasn't cooperating, which meant just two of the British warships, the HMS *Sophie* and the flotilla's flagship, the HMS *Hermes*, had managed to maneuver into firing range.

With enemy shots and shells bombarding their fortification, Colonel Lawrence and his men returned fire. They had little time to answer that attack from the sea before the attack from the land began.

At the center of the approaching British land force were Creeks and Choctaws the British had recruited as their allies. Wearing British red coats over their bare legs, the Indians were flanked by confident—and more completely clad—Royal Marines. The British veterans expected Fort Bowyer to fall as easily as Washington had three weeks earlier. But as the combined force marched boldly toward Fort Bowyer, Lawrence's men dampened their hopes. A barrage of cannon shot pinned the British down, halting their advance. As the ground force took cover and attempted to regroup, Lawrence concentrated on the seaside battle.

Along the seawall, the American gunners had found the range and were making the cannonballs count, shooting away the bowsprit of the *Hermes*. Yet as great clouds of gun smoke enveloped both the fort and the ships, neither side seemed to be gaining the upper hand. The Americans were holding their own, but there was no reason to believe that the British, attacking from both sides, would not be able to wear them down and prevail once the Americans ran out of ammunition.

Then, with a lucky shot, an American cannonball tore through the anchor cable that was holding the *Hermes* in firing position. Suddenly cut loose, the ship drifted helplessly toward the fort, carried by the incoming current. While sailors frantically tried to get the sails to catch the falling wind and carry the *Hermes* out of range of American guns, shots thudded into her hull and shredded the ship's sails and rigging.

Just as the crew managed to turn the ship, her keel scraped the sandy bottom. The *Hermes* had run aground. Trapped just six hundred yards from Fort Bowyer's guns, the ship was now an easy—and stationary—target.

With American artillery fire raining down, the British commander had no choice but to abandon ship. By seven o'clock that evening, the departing sailors set fire to the crippled vessel before fleeing to the British ships waiting safely out of range. As night fell, the great flames aboard the *Hermes* rose into the sky. For three hours, the ship burned slowly but steadily, a brilliant light show against the dark sea. Then the flames reached the gunpowder in the ship's hold. In a moment, the *Hermes* exploded, blasted into fragments that rained down on the sea and shore.

Waiting and Wondering

Thirty miles away, the earth trembled. Feeling the ground shake in Mobile, Andrew Jackson looked south toward Fort Bowyer and there, at the horizon line, he saw the *Hermes* light the sky.

From his faraway vantage he couldn't be sure what had happened at Mobile Point. What he did know was that the reinforcements he had sent the day before had been turned back, their ship prevented from reaching the fort by the much larger HMS *Hermes*. If Lawrence and his men were to hold Fort Bowyer against the British, they would do so on their own. There was nothing else he could do.

As he watched the sun rise the following morning, General Jackson still didn't know whether Fort Bowyer was safe. More anxious hours would pass before a dispatch from Colonel Lawrence finally arrived, reporting the destruction of the *Hermes* and the flight of the three other British ships. The British had sustained significant casualties (thirty-two killed, thirty-seven wounded). The fort's defenders reported just four dead and five wounded.

Although the men defending Fort Bowyer had been outnumbered by roughly ten to one, Jackson's strategy and Lawrence's hard labors produced a victory. Lawrence's band of 158 soldiers had prevented the British from winning a beachhead and, more important, gaining access to a harbor from which they might march overland to invade New Orleans. Washington may have fallen, but little Fort Bowyer still stood. The Americans had finally held.

"Success has crowned the gallant efforts of our brave soldiers," Jackson wrote, passing the good news to Secretary of War James Monroe in Washington.[2] He intended to keep that success going.

"Defence of Fort McHenry"

Far away, a full one thousand miles to the north and east, another fort had just been bombarded by the British, and a major American victory had been won. The fight for the nation's third-largest city would help launch a turnaround of U.S. military fortunes—and national morale would rise as Francis Scott Key's poem about the events in Baltimore Harbor reverberated around the country.

Before dawn, on September 12, 1814, British troops had gone

ashore east of Baltimore for a land assault on the city. The British ground forces had been stunned when, only minutes into the first skirmish, an officer on horseback returned at speed from the vanguard, calling for a surgeon. The infantrymen recognized the riderless horse that followed: it belonged to the commanding general, Robert Ross, the man responsible for the burning of Washington. He had fallen from his steed, mortally wounded with a musket ball to his chest. The old gentlemen's agreement not to target officers had been breached during the Revolution—to the outrage of the British—and targeting officers had since become an accepted strategy.

Despite Ross's loss, the British were undeterred. At first light the next day, the people of Baltimore were awakened by the sound of mortars exploding overhead. A convoy of British frigates and a half-dozen bomb vessels were firing on Fort McHenry, which guarded the entrance to Baltimore's harbor. The Americans had sunk ships in the channel to prevent the British from sailing in, hoping to keep them out of range of the town. A relentless barrage of mortar shells continued all day and into the night; the hollow projectiles, some of which weighed up to two hundred pounds, flew in a high arc, remaining in flight up to thirty seconds. Many exploded in midair, scattering deadly shrapnel in all directions, accompanied by exploding rockets that brightened the sky like fireworks. The artillery attack ceased briefly at one o'clock on the morning of September 14 when an attempt by British barges to land troops west of Fort McHenry was rebuffed, but the pounding soon resumed. Finally, shortly before dawn, the gunners ceased their fire.

Five miles downstream from the port of Baltimore and in British custody, Francis Scott Key had watched the great fight unfold. Commissioned by President Madison to negotiate the freedom of a Maryland doctor detained by the British after the burning of Washington,

Key was aboard a British ship awaiting the outcome of the battle. From the ship's deck he watched the fireworks of the bombardment, then waited in the darkness, watching and wondering. He did not know what the silence meant, but he worried: *Had Baltimore fallen?* He paced the deck of the ship, periodically peering through a spyglass at Fort McHenry, fearing he would see, instead of the Stars and Stripes, the Union Jack or a white flag of surrender.

A feeling of pride swelled his breast as the morning mist cleared, revealing an American flag still flying over the fort. The British attack had failed.

Finding an envelope in his pocket, Key began to compose a poem on the back of a letter, seeking to express the relief he felt. He had a tune in his head—once before, he'd written a celebratory

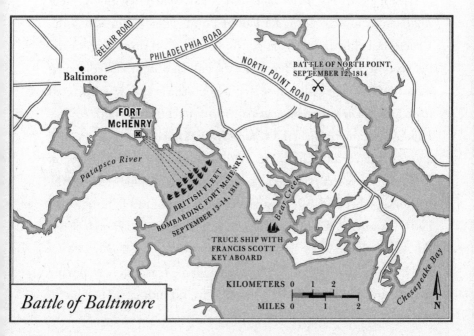

Battle of Baltimore

poem to fit the melody—and he jotted down his thoughts and sentiments, as well as a couplet that would ring familiar in the ears of his countrymen for generations to come. "'Tis the star spangled banner, O! long may it wave / O'er the land of the free and the home of the brave."[3]

That morning the Royal Navy withdrew, retreating to the Chesapeake. No longer held captive, Key landed in Baltimore and completed his ballad. A friend arranged for freshly printed broadside copies of the poem bearing the title "The Defence of Fort McHenry" to be distributed on the streets of the city, on September 17. Three days later, when the *Baltimore Patriot and Evening Advertiser* resumed publication, the newspaper published the poem in its pages.

Earlier in the war, Francis Scott Key, a Federalist by affiliation, had opposed the decision to go to war. But recent events—the burning of Washington, the fight for Baltimore—had allied him with President Madison, who was calling for national unity after Washington's destruction, exhorting "all the good people . . . in providing for the defense" of the nation.[4] Though Key's anthem was published anonymously, it would help the cause. In the coming weeks, it was reprinted in no fewer than seventeen newspapers, in states from Georgia to New Hampshire, among them the *Federal Republican* of Georgetown, long an outspoken critic of both Mr. Madison and his war.[5] Francis Scott Key's four verses had sparked a patriotic fire that would help draw the nation together and, after years of defeats, America's fighting spirit had been stirred. Washington may have fallen, but the Union Jack did not fly over Baltimore.

Even so the British would strike again, reasonably believing that the greatest naval power on earth would ultimately be able to conquer New Orleans. The only thing standing in their way was Andrew Jackson.

On to Pensacola

After the Fort Bowyer victory, Jackson's sense of elation was short-lived. He knew it was only a matter of time before the next attack. Without sufficient land forces to defend the entire coast, his job, above all, was to outguess his enemy. For the moment, Jackson himself would remain at Mobile. He would work his network of spies, monitoring British military moves from Florida to Louisiana and in the Caribbean.

Where would the British strike next? His first guess had been a good one: the British attack on Fort Bowyer confirmed that the enemy had hoped to use Mobile as a base for their move on Louisiana. But even after Lawrence and his guns had repelled them, who was to say the enemy wouldn't return another day to the mouth of Mobile Bay with a much larger flotilla of ships, perhaps accompanied by Royal Marines and infantry?

Jackson would take no chances. "We will be better prepared to receive them on the next visit," he wrote to an old Tennessee friend serving in Congress.[6] As he waited for reinforcements, he set about further improving the defenses at Fort Bowyer. He ordered Colonel Lawrence to salvage the cannons from the blasted wreck of the *Hermes*. If the British returned, they would find the fort even harder to take than before.

Meanwhile, Jackson also plotted his next move: once Fort Bowyer was reinforced with the new guns, the best course, Jackson decided, would be to eject the British force from Pensacola, the next large port town some fifty miles east of Mobile.[7] That seemed the obvious next step. As his aide-de-camp John Reid observed, unless Pensacola could be taken from British hands, "it was vain to think of defending the country."[8]

Pensacola was in Spanish territory, and the Spaniards were not proving friendly to the Americans. The Spanish governor, Don Mateo González Manrique, had granted the British Royal Navy safe harbor in Pensacola two months earlier, which meant that the British were free to land troops there for an overland assault on New Orleans—and the young country would be in danger as long as the British held the harbor. Taking it might not be easy, though; the British ships could repel a water attack, and any force attempting a land attack would meet up with un-friendly Red Sticks living in the swamps surrounding Pensacola.

Knowing these dangers, Jackson decided he would attack nonetheless—only he would need reinforcements. As October tilted toward November, the task of refortification at Fort Bowyer neared completion and, leaving the place in Colonel Lawrence's good hands, General Jackson led a column of five hundred army regulars headed for Pensacola. He and his troops took a circular route, looping north in order to meet up with General Coffee and, on October 25, the old friends joined forces. Coffee brought eighteen hundred men, each on horseback, all with their own rifles.

The generals and their combined force crossed the Alabama River at the Fort Mims ferry. In the coming days, more Tennessee troops joined them—rangers from West Tennessee, militiamen from East Tennessee—and the ranks of the army swelled with 750 Choctaws and Chickasaws.

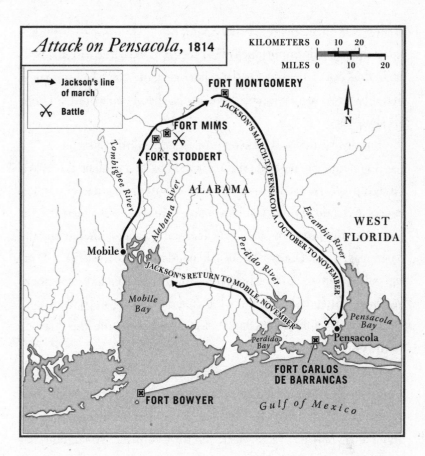

Although his army now numbered more than four thousand troops, Jackson was politically very much on his own. In official correspondence, Secretary of State James Monroe warned Jackson away from Pensacola. President James Madison's government was afraid that the United States, already at war with one powerful European foe, risked a war with Spain, too, if they threatened Pensacola. Yet Monroe had also made it known to Jackson in "*strong* terms" via back channels that the general "would receive all the support in the power

of the government, relating to the Spaniards."⁹ Monroe clearly understood the strategic importance of Pensacola in the battle with the British in the Gulf of Mexico. On the other hand, the savvy Jackson knew
that if his move on Pensacola went badly, the blame would fall onto
his shoulders.

But duty called and Jackson proceeded toward Pensacola.

The target lay nestled on the north bank of a protected bay. Although the town itself consisted of little more than a trio of parallel
streets and a downtown public square, Pensacola possessed several
protective ramparts. In particular, Jackson was concerned with Fort
Barrancas, which Don Manrique had handed over to the British. Stra-
tegically essential, Barrancas sat nine miles to the southwest overlooking the opening to the harbor, which meant arriving ships were in its
line of fire. To control Fort Barrancas was to control the finest harbor
on the Gulf Coast.

On November 6, Jackson's army halted two miles west of Pensacola.

First, the general tried approaching in peace.

He sent Major Henry B. Piere of the Forty-Fourth Infantry forward
under a flag of truce. Piere was to tell the Spanish commandant that
he did not come with demands of war but with suggestions for preserving neutrality. Then he would present Jackson's written demands: the
United States wanted control of the fortifications around Pensacola,
in particular Fort Barrancas, with its strategic overlook at the entrance
to Pensacola Bay.

But before he could arrive in the town to present the American
case, Piere and a small escort took artillery fire from one of the city's
fortifications. They retreated to consult with Jackson.

Jackson was a man with a hair-trigger disposition, but he could
also be a man of calm in chaos when necessary. In this case, he held

his temper and tried a second peaceable approach, this time sending as his emissary a Spanish prisoner captured the previous day. Through the messenger, Jackson demanded an explanation for the firing on his men. Governor Manrique hedged, blaming the British. They had fired on Piere without the governor's authorization, he claimed, and he assured Jackson that he would, of course, talk with Jackson's representative.

That evening, Major Piere, now welcomed by the governor, went to Pensacola to deliver Jackson's demands. The governor read Jackson's note: "I come not as the enemy of Spain; not to make war but to ask for peace." But though Jackson used words of peace, his demands hinted at the consequence of war should his request be ignored. The governor should give him Barrancas, he insisted—and he gave the Spaniard one hour to respond. Governor Manrique deemed the terms unacceptable, insisting that his duty did not permit him to do as Jackson asked. Piere brought the news back to the American camp.[10]

Done negotiating, Jackson grimly laid out his plan for storming the town. Manrique left him no alternative: they would have to do this the hard way.

Meanwhile, in Ghent . . .

The American diplomats in Europe didn't have it much easier, as the peace negotiations proceeded at a snail's pace. The British commissioners had to write home to London whenever the Americans made a proposal, forcing the U.S. delegation to spend weeks waiting in the three-story house they shared on the Rue des Champs.

The American team had little in common. John Quincy Adams,

Henry Clay, and Albert Gallatin disagreed over the style and tone of their responses to the British demands and differed in style of life, too. As the days and weeks passed, Adams couldn't help but notice when, rising to read his Bible before dawn, he heard Henry Clay retiring to his room after a long night of cigars, port, and cards. About the only thing the envoys agreed upon was what they told their betters in Washington: "We need hardly say . . . that there is not at present, any hope of peace."[11]

When the news had arrived, on October 1, of the August burning of Washington, John Quincy Adams spent a sleepless night worrying about the fortunes of his country. A habitual diarist, he found, on the morning after hearing of his capital's capture, that his sense of shock remained so great that "it was almost impossible to write."[12]

The American team had little choice but to continue talking until a subtle British move shocked them anew. The British asked that the treaty include two Latin words: *uti possidetis*. Meaning "as you possess," the term specified that the land held by each side at ratification of the treaty would remain with its possessor.

The precise purpose of the simple little phrase wasn't clear, but Gallatin thought he knew. He had suspected for some time that the British were attempting to capture the mouth of the Mississippi, writing to Monroe six weeks earlier, "It appears to me most likely that their true and immediate object is New Orleans."[13] Now that they had introduced this term into the treaty, he was even more certain. If the British were able to conquer New Orleans before the treaty was signed, America's westward expansion would be cut off, and the future shape of the United States would be determined by the British.

From a distance of five thousand miles from New Orleans, the diplomats could do little. They could issue warnings that Jackson and his men were in grave danger; they could wring their hands at the worrisome prospect that their independent nation was in danger. (As Gallatin wrote to the U.S. ambassador to France, "A belief is said to be entertained that a continuance of the war would produce a separation of the Union, and perhaps a return of the New England states to the mother country.")[14]

Gallatin was right to be worried. Late in 1814, delegates of the New England states met secretly in what became known as the Hartford Convention to discuss their complaints about Madison and his war. Several delegates pushed for secession even as the British moved toward New Orleans.

For now, the thought of secession was only one of the looming difficulties. The diplomats considered all the obstacles and could offer no optimism at the likelihood their negotiations would succeed. As Clay bluntly put it to Monroe, "The safest opinion to adopt is . . . that our mission will terminate unsuccessfully."[15]

Jackson and his American soldiers would get no help from Ghent—and, in the coming weeks, the predictions of Ministers Gallatin and Clay would prove all too correct.

Back to New Orleans

Unaware of the dark turn in British negotiations, General Jackson nonetheless continued to move to the defense of New Orleans. He waited for no man—in Europe or in Washington—and under the cover of night, on November 7, 1814, he marched all but five hundred of his men into the woods on the outskirts of Pensacola. The town's Spanish defenders, believing the Americans were still in their original camp, kept their guns pointed toward the nearly empty tents, while their British allies repositioned their warships to bear on the westward approach to Pensacola.

At daylight, the token force Jackson left behind made a feint toward Pensacola from the west, while the much larger army, which Jackson had led around the town in darkness, attacked along the narrow beach from the northeast.

Taking both the Spanish and the British by surprise, the combined force of Choctaws, Jackson's infantrymen, and General Coffee's brigade quickly overwhelmed the first band of startled defenders. As the Americans entered the town, Spanish musket fire raked the attackers from gardens and houses along the center street, but the Royal Navy was no help. Unprepared, their supporting fire came too late.

The fight lasted only minutes, as the Spanish corps, numbering fewer than five hundred men, was no match for the attacking Americans. A U.S. Army lieutenant lowered the Spanish flag and Governor Manrique, looking old and ill, brandishing a white flag, appeared in the street looking for an American officer. General Jackson was summoned and rode into town with an escort of dragoons for the formal surrender.

The Spanish agreed to relinquish control of Fort Barrancas, and Jackson sent men off to take charge of it, but before they could get there, the retreating British lit a fuse that ignited three hundred barrels of powder stored in its magazine. The explosion left the fort unusable, and the enemy fleet was seen heading out to sea.

The British had relinquished the fort and, though Jackson had not won quite the victory he expected—he had come to capture Fort Barrancas, only to see it destroyed—Pensacola had been rendered defenseless. The British would not be able to use it as a base of attack, and Jackson needed to waste no men garrisoning the town or the blasted hulk that had been Fort Barrancas.

General Jackson had repulsed the British at Pensacola. His men had sent one British warship to the bottom of the sea at Fort Bowyer, and twice the Royal Navy flotilla had been forced to abandon good harbors on the Gulf Coast. The British had hoped to enlist the rebellious Creeks into their ranks, but Jackson had vanquished his Indian foes, too.

The preceding months had seen Andrew Jackson emerge as the best general in service to the American cause. President Madison knew it. So did James Monroe, who scurried around the ruins of Washington to find money for Jackson to pay his army's bills. Despite the nation's empty coffers, Monroe somehow came up with $100,000. And the secretary of war promised more troops would be sent to his winning general.

But Jackson could feel the pressure rising. His health was far from perfect, with his left shoulder still nearly useless and his gut a constant discomfort. He saw the line he had to walk, taking care not to overcommit his inexperienced force while aggressively challenging the British. He would have to balance rage and reason as he took on his new task: by disrupting the larger British strategy—enemy ground troops wouldn't be landing any time soon at either Pensacola or Mobile—he had put New Orleans directly into the line of fire.

Suspecting the increased danger to New Orleans, Jackson pushed his men hard, hurrying back whence they had come. A mere three and a half days later, on November 11, 1814, they were back in Mobile.

The general found a stack of letters waiting for him. Some had been mailed from Washington, where James Monroe sounded almost panicked. Word from his ministers in Ghent persuaded the secretary of state of the certainty of an imminent assault on New Orleans. The worried Monroe wrote to his Tennessee general he had "strong reason" to think that the British would soon attempt "to take possession of that city [on which] the whole of the states westward of the Allegany mountains so essentially depend."[16] Other letters had come from New Orleans, where Governor Claiborne feared an attack was imminent.

For more than three months, Jackson's secret informants—a merchant in Havana, a spy in Pensacola, well-connected Indian chiefs, and others—warned of British invasion plans. Now, however, the arrival of the flood of ever-more-anxious letters from Washington and New Orleans meant that reports of a British attack no longer seemed exaggerated.

On Tuesday, November 22, 1814, Andrew Jackson and his army began a new trek, this time to Louisiana to defend America's heartland from a looming enemy.

CHAPTER 7

Target: New Orleans

I expect at this moment that most of the large seaport towns of America are . . . laid to ashes; that we are in possession of New Orleans, and have command of all the rivers of the Mississippi valley and the lakes, and that the Americans are now little better than prisoners in their own country.

—Lord Castlereagh, British foreign secretary

The armada in Jamaica's Negril Bay was stunning to see. Along a four-mile stretch of pristine white beach, a forest of tall masts swayed in the gentle tropical breezes. No one on the west coast of Jamaica or anywhere else in the Caribbean had seen anything like it before. The fifty large vessels, each flying the Union Jack, amounted to the largest naval force ever assembled in the hemisphere.

On November 26, 1814, the hardened old Scotsman in command surveyed his flotilla, proud of its power. He watched with care as his captains carried out his orders to set sail. After months of planning, this was an exhilarating moment.

High on the poop deck of the eighty-gun HMS *Tonnant,*

fifty-six-year-old Vice Admiral Sir Alexander Forrester Inglis Cochrane, his hair turned white, looked older than his years. His courtly
manner revealed his pedigree: he was a younger son of an earl. Though
softened by age—round through his middle, jowls overhanging his
high collar—Cochrane revealed a steelier side. As one of the admirals
in his command remarked, Cochrane was "a rough, brutal, and over-
bearing officer."[1]

From his flagship, he looked upon five other ships of the line, each
armed with seventy-four guns; his enemy, the U.S. Navy, had no ships
that were their equal. There were eight three-masted frigates with
thirty-eight or more cannons, along with smaller two-masted brigs
and schooners with a single mast. Lower in the water sat the sloops of
war and barges, along with uncounted transports and other smaller
craft. As one observer remarked, the vessels were "so closely wedged
together that to walk across the decks from one to the other seemed,
when at a little distance, to be far from impracticable."[2]

Cochrane had risen in the ranks during the war with Napoleon.
After commanding the HMS *Ajax* in Egypt, he served in Martinique,
Santo Domingo, and then in Guadeloupe, where he won a knighthood
and earned the assignment to take on the United States. Sir Alexander
had bided his time since the Americans had declared war on Great
Britain two years before, but his charge now was to bring home victory, a task he accepted with grim determination.

He had sworn to "give to Great Britain the command of . . . New
Orleans." He had promised to hand the Americans "a complete drubbing before peace is made." He would deliver to the king complete
"command of the Mississippi."[3] And now he had the force to do it: the
more than ten thousand Royal Navy sailors and officers that manned
the formidable show of sail around him constituted just half of the

British force Cochrane would soon send into battle. Belowdecks, an army of foot soldiers waited as British tars hoisted the sails of the fleet.

Since his arrival in Jamaica nine days earlier, Cochrane had watched a parade of vessels sail in from Ireland and France and, like the *Tonnant*, from the Chesapeake Bay. After dropping anchor in Negril Bay, the warships disgorged thousands of troops dressed in red and green and even tartan uniforms. There were detachments of engineers, artillerymen, and rocketeers. The ground troops under the command of Major General John Keane included two black regiments from the West Indies.

Only a few men among this amphibious force had been certain of their destination. But this day the word got around and reached the ear of Lieutenant George Gleig, of the Eighty-Fifth Light Infantry. Gleig, who would help write the story of Cochrane and the invading force, noted in his journal, "It was soon known throughout the fleet that the conquest of New Orleans was the object in view."[4]

So far in 1814, the Americans had done little to persuade Cochrane they were worthy opponents. He and his ships had delivered the army to Maryland that had so effortlessly overrun Washington. True, the siege at Baltimore in September had failed after a sharp-eyed sniper killed Robert Ross, Cochrane's commanding general, and Fort McHenry at the mouth of Baltimore Harbor proved more resilient than expected. But that only upped Cochrane's desire to vanquish the Americans once and for all.

Cochrane's interest in beating the Americans was personal. Many years before, he had fought in the American Revolution, but it had been an older brother, Charles, who died at the hands of the rebellious colonists. At the deciding battle of that war, in Yorktown, Virginia, in 1781, a cannonball parted Charles Cochrane's head from his body.

That painful loss, it was said, led to Sir Alexander's hatred of Americans. He had nothing but contempt for the "American character." He dismissed the former colonists as no better than dogs: "Like spaniels," he said, "they must be treated with great severity."[5]

Cochrane had another motive, too. Back in Scotland, Sir Alexander would inherit neither property nor title. That meant New Orleans, an immensely valuable prize, represented exactly the change in fortune he needed (among the crew, there was talk of the "beauty and booty" to be had in the Louisiana city). For hundreds of years, the law of the seas had permitted officers and crew to share in the spoils of war and, with exports at a standstill because of the war, New Orleans's warehouses were packed with sugar, tobacco, hemp, and, in particular, bales of cotton. The goods were worth a great deal of money, perhaps £4 million. As the commander, Cochrane's portion of the plunder would be the largest of all.

British confidence ran high. Among the many ships departing Negril Bay were cargo vessels for carrying off the spoils, together with civilian administrators and barristers, an admiralty judge, customs officials, and tax collectors. It was a battalion of bureaucrats, complete with wives and daughters, a British team ready to take control of the city they planned to capture. And Cochrane had promised his naval superiors at the Admiralty in London he would deliver a resounding triumph. It was inconceivable that these American upstarts could hold out against the most powerful military force in the world.

Though not all Cochrane's forces had arrived, the fleet would delay no longer. More British soldiers were expected any day, along with General Sir Edward Pakenham, who was to take command of the invading army. But the British force was about to be on its way to New Orleans without him.

There, Cochrane vowed to his men, he would have his Christmas dinner.

Arriving in New Orleans

What Admiral Cochrane could not know was that, a thousand miles north on the Gulf Coast, another man with a personal stake in the war was headed to New Orleans to stop him. Andrew Jackson, born in a log cabin, was very different indeed from the high and mighty Cochrane, whose family roots lay in a great castle in Scotland. Jackson wasn't looking to win fame or enhance his wealth but, like Cochrane, he had a personal grudge against the country that had killed his brother. And both men knew the stakes.

Jackson didn't know for sure that Cochrane's force was on its way from Jamaica, but he suspected the British navy would be coming—and soon. Accordingly, he had chosen an overland route from Mobile. He wished to gather intelligence on the way; as he wrote to Monroe, he wanted "to have a view of the points at which the enemy might effect a landing."[6]

Before leaving Pensacola, Jackson had written to Rachel, confiding how ill he felt. "There [were] eight days," he wrote to his wife of the preceding month, "that I never broke bread." He had consulted an army doctor, who administered an herbal concoction containing mercury. Jackson reported the purgative cleansed his system but—no surprise, given how thin he already was—it left him "very weak."[7]

Though Jackson was a man whose sense of duty seemed to empower him to press on no matter his physical condition, he could lower his guard with Rachel. When they first met a quarter century before, he had arrived seeking only a bed at the boardinghouse that Rachel's widowed mother ran. Instead, the long-orphaned Jackson found a family to replace the one he had lost. In particular, the strapping young man had been drawn to the handsome young woman who had recently escaped a violent first marriage. In each other the two found solace.

In two decades of marriage, he and Rachel had shared public embarrassment when the shadowy status of her divorce from her first husband became public. She had matured into a short and plump woman, he ever more gangly, wasted by his battle with dysentery and other intestinal problems. But Andrew and Rachel developed an intimate bond. Despite a shared dislike of being separated, over the preceding thirteen months they had spent no more than thirty days together. As the British approached, he realized he needed to be with her.

In a perfect world, he wrote to Rachel, he might travel home to the Hermitage and "return to your arms on the wings of love and affection, to spend with you the rest of my days in peaceful domestic retirement."[8] But knowing that he had to travel to New Orleans for the biggest battle of his life, he instead asked for her to travel to him. "It is my wish," he had written from Mobile, "that you join me at . . . New Orleans." He would arrange for her to travel by riverboat in early December. In the meantime, he traveled toward the city on horseback.

Jackson's plan had allowed twelve days for the trek. Against the odds, his army reached its destination in ten, covering some three hundred miles, slogging through forests and fields. Where they could, Jackson's army followed the Federal Road but often had to blaze its own trail. His soldiers cut down many trees to support the horses and wagons as they crossed flooded streambeds.

On nearing New Orleans Jackson and his officers had been ferried across Lake Pontchartrain, landing after dark on the last day of November. When the morning haze burned off the large lake, they headed south for the last half-dozen miles, paralleling the meandering waters of Bayou St. John.

According to witnesses who saw them, Jackson stood out as the oldest of the riders, "a tall, gaunt man, of very erect carriage, with a countenance full of stern decision and fearless energy, but furrowed with care and anxiety." His iron gray hair peeked out from beneath the leather cap he wore to keep off the morning chill. Tall dragoon boots, much in need of polish, protected his legs, but even the loose blue cloak that hung from his shoulders couldn't hide how emaciated the man was. His complexion looked "sallow and unhealthy," but "the fierce glare of his bright and hawk-like gray eye betrayed a soul and spirit which triumphed over all the infirmities of the body."[9]

One lady of the neighborhood who saw Jackson on the morning of December 1, 1814, as he rode along the Bayou St. John road, said he looked like "an ugly, old Kaintuck-flat-boatman."[10] She was a native of New Orleans, a Creole. She would not be the last Creole to look askance, at least at first, at the general charged with saving their city.

Meeting the General

As Jackson neared the city limits, carriages were sent to greet him, and the general and his aides gratefully accepted the offered ride. Seated in unaccustomed luxury, they looked with curiosity at the city they were to defend.

The cobbled streets of New Orleans were abuzz with expectation at meeting the man some already called the "Savior of New Orleans."

As Jackson's carriage arrived at 106 Rue Royale, the handsome house chosen for his headquarters, he was greeted by the men of the town decked out in ties, gloves, and hats for the occasion. Everyone expected the British, but first they would welcome this tall Tennessean.

Climbing down from his carriage, Jackson was greeted by Governor Claiborne and the city's mayor, an affable Creole named Nicholas Giroud. As gray skies gave way to rain, the assembled crowd listened to Claiborne and Giroud give speeches in preparation to handing off responsibility for the city's defense to General Jackson. But mostly those in attendance wanted to hear from this gaunt American. What would the rough soldier from upriver have to say to a city of French and English speakers, merchants and pirates, freemen and slaves, woodsmen and Indians, a city that wasn't even sure it wanted to be American?

Unfortunately for Jackson, he spoke no French at all, but he was saved by his old congressional colleague Edward Livingston, who spoke it fluently. From the second-floor gallery, Jackson spoke to the crowd and Livingston translated for his friends and neighbors. Jackson assured them of his determination, promising to "drive their enemies into the sea, or perish in the effort."[11]

Jackson's words were met with cheers, but Livingston knew New Orleans high society well enough to understand that his neighbors were still unsure what to make of this weathered general. A transplant from New York, Livingston understood what it took to win the approval of the Creole upper class. He had worked hard to be accepted, but it was only when he married Louise Davezac, a well-born young widow from French Santo Domingo, that he had felt secure. With Louise on his arm, his entrée to the French culture of New Orleans was assured and, from their home on Royal Street, the Livingstons had become central figures in the city's society.[12]

Livingston decided to invite New Orleans's finest and Jackson to dinner to help the general secure the confidence of the city's elite. His wife's reaction to the idea demonstrated just how badly the introduction was needed. When Livingston told Louise that he had invited the Tennessean to take a seat at her table of fashionable friends, she expressed some annoyance. The man's fame had preceded him, of course, but wasn't he supposed to be a "wild man of the woods—an Indian almost"?

Jackson may have been a man of the woods, but he could hold his own with the haughty. When he entered the Livingston drawing room that afternoon, the other guests saw a man "erect, composed, perfectly self-possessed, with martial bearing." In place of his worn and dirty traveling clothes he wore a full dress uniform, and "the soldier who stood before them [was] one whom nature had stamped a gentleman." When dinner was announced, he exhibited perfect manners, offering his hostess his arm and, during dinner, he proved agreeable company. Mr. Livingston—soon to be Jackson's aide-de-camp—and the general departed early. But one guest who remained, both surprised and favorably impressed, remarked, "Is this your backwoodsman? He is a prince!"[13]

In a matter of hours, Jackson had left a strong impression on the inhabitants. In the same span, Edward Livingston had demonstrated he could be invaluable to the general. Livingston possessed skills as an orator and a translator, as well as a deep knowledge of Creole society. He was also an attorney, and his opinions on martial law might soon be put to use. In recognition of the man's usefulness, Jackson made him a colonel. In the coming weeks, Livingston would function as Jackson's military secretary and confidant. His inside knowledge of the peculiar circumstances of New Orleans society would prove invaluable.

Surveying the Surroundings

A wise general imprints on his mind the local topography as he prepares to do battle. So Andrew Jackson began with the maps, even as he wondered whether the fight would commence in two days or twenty-two.

New Orleans was the nation's seventh-largest city. The dense streetscapes at its center were packed together in the Vieux Carré and a few surrounding suburbs that stretched along the Mississippi riverbank and atop curving ridges just inland.

The swampy land surrounding New Orleans looked nothing like the rugged rolling hills that encircled Jackson's Nashville. The city resembled an island amid a marsh, with little dry land in any direction. Jackson was in the midst of a vast wetland, with millions of acres of waterlogged swamps dominated by towering cypress trees. A breeding ground for mosquitoes, the swamplands provided a better habitat for water snakes and alligators than for man.

Thanks to trade from upriver, New Orleans had become a place where people got rich. To his surprise, however, Jackson found that the city's people knew little of their larger surroundings. "The numerous bayous and canals," he noted, "appear to be almost as little understood by the inhabitants as by the citizens of Tennessee."[14]

Clearly, this was a precarious place, one subject to fires and hurricanes and floods. But Jackson's job was to cut through all the paradoxes and mysteries to figure out how to keep it out of British hands. As one of the engineers on Jackson's staff, Major Howell Tatum, noted in his log, "The first days of the General's arrival at New Orleans [were] devoted to the acquisition of such information, upon various points, as were deemed necessary, in order to enable him to adopt the most efficacious plan for the defense of Louisiana."[15]

First, that meant identifying—and then obstructing—any and all routes the British might take to attack the city. To help with that process, Edward Livingston brought the architect Arsène Lacarrière Latour to Jackson's headquarters on Royal Street. Jackson was impressed, both with the man and with the maps of New Orleans and its vicinity. Because Latour displayed the kind of knowledge the general needed, Jackson promptly named him principal engineer of the U.S. Army's Seventh Military District.

From afar, Jackson's pet theory had been that the British would put their troops ashore well east of the city—namely, landing at Mobile—then march in a great arc north of their objective. When they reached the Mississippi River upstream from New Orleans, Jackson reasoned, they could commandeer boats and barges; then, carried by the current, they would attack from the river. That thinking had led Jackson to secure both Mobile and Pensacola.

Even now, after moving his army to New Orleans, Jackson understood the British might still return to Mobile Bay and overpower Fort Bowyer, making an overland attack route possible. In order to prevent that, Jackson had dispatched General Coffee; he and his Volunteer cavalry had parted with Jackson on the march from Mobile, going on to Baton Rouge. Coffee's job would be to halt any such assault from upstream or, on Jackson's orders, to come at double time to New

Orleans, when and if intelligence reports determined the British were approaching via another route.

That left half a dozen other distinct paths for a possible British invasion. Jackson had no way of knowing which the enemy would choose but, again, he would have to take steps to obstruct their progress, whatever the angle of approach.

Three of the possibilities involved rivers, the most obvious being

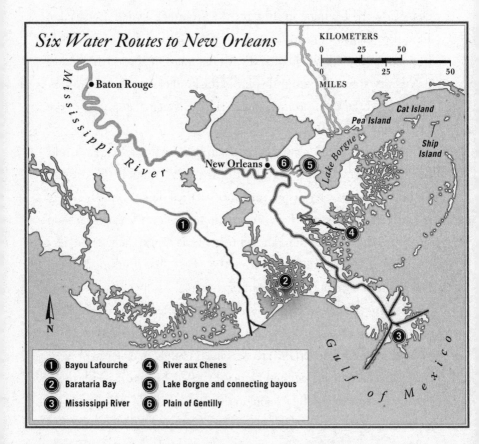

the Mississippi itself. That approach was guarded by fortifications well downstream; but those he needed to inspect personally. In a day or two, he'd go there.

Bayou Lafourche, which lay to the west, was another option for the British. A narrow but deep stream that veered south off the Mississippi between Baton Rouge and New Orleans, it emptied into the Gulf. If the British could sail up Bayou Lafourche and reach the parent river, they could then attack New Orleans from upstream. However, the breadth of the river and its ever-changing currents would make attacking from the opposite bank difficult. This seemed to Jackson and his advisers an unlikely—though still possible—British strategy.

To the east of the city was the River aux Chenes, which connected to Bayou Terre aux Boeufs. Both of these watercourses were sluggish but navigable for small boats. Again, Jackson was doubtful that the British attack would approach via these waters.

The other three angles of attack were via larger bodies of water.

Barataria Bay, south of the city, was linked to a maze of smaller waterways. Even though the pirates routinely used this network of streams to bring their goods to New Orleans, landing an army was another matter, especially without skilled pilots—and, it seemed, the Lafittes and the corsairs of Barataria had rejected the British offer. Again, the likelihood was low.

East of the city, Lake Borgne offered two plausible lines of attack: If the British could take possession of this large inlet, they might move on New Orleans via Bayou Chef Menteur, which led to a mile-wide strip of dry land called the Plain of Gentilly. Or they could carry the boats some five miles from the lake toward the Mississippi. On reaching the far side, however, the army could then march along the dry land that bordered the river through a series of plantations directly to the city. These two attack routes seemed to pose the greatest risk.

After absorbing the larger picture using the maps provided to him by Latour, Jackson and Governor Claiborne issued orders on December 2. Jackson sent guards to the least likely lines of attack, where they would watch and report if he had gambled wrong and the British were coming that way. Commanded by General Jacques Villere, detachments of the Louisiana militia marched out to the bayous and toward Barataria Bay armed not only with guns but also with axes. Their job was to clog the waterways with enough logs and other debris to slow the progress of boats carrying an oncoming army. Guards were then to be posted to speed the word if the enemy did approach. Jackson wasn't going to commit many soldiers to these low-probability lines of attack, but the sentries would become part of the intelligence network he needed to monitor enemy movements.

Because there was one route that might allow Royal Navy warships to get within firing range of the city, Jackson himself headed downriver the next day. As the engineer Latour reported, Jackson, "adhering to his constant practice of seeing everything himself," and his command, with Latour as their guide, went to inspect the fortifications on the banks of the Mississippi.[16]

Fort St. Philip was about sixty-five miles downstream; it was manned by regular troops and armed with two dozen cannons. This was enough to make it a formidable obstacle to a British onslaught, but Jackson knew that an attacking armada would have vastly greater firepower that would probably overcome the American defenders. He ordered the construction of new batteries before moving on to the next fort.

Closer to the city, he visited Fort St. Leon, which overlooked one of the Mississippi's many great bends. The abrupt curve was known as English Turn, having gained its name in 1699, when the future founder of New Orleans, the sieur de Bienville, persuaded a band of English explorers to turn back because, he said, France had already claimed the territory. Jackson hoped to convince the British to turn back there, too, and planned to take advantage of the difficulties the British navy would have navigating the arching bend. Sailing ships needed a change of wind in order to make the curve, which meant a naval force coming up the river might have to linger for hours exposed to Fort St. Leon's guns. To increase chances of holding the British there, Jackson again ordered the construction of added artillery batteries.

The scouting trip down the Mississippi left Jackson and his officers feeling confident. "It is almost impossible for an invading enemy to gain possession of New Orleans," noted his aide, the engineer Tatum, "by ascending the Mississippi. . . . At the *English Turn* . . . heavy cannon . . . would destroy every armed vessel that dared to attempt the ascent."[17]

After his six-day tour of the Mississippi, Jackson returned to New Orleans on December 9 and informed Claiborne that, given the added batteries, the river could be well defended.

But Jackson still needed to evaluate the last and perhaps the most likely approach for the British, via Lake Borgne. Repelling an attack there would be a challenge, but the general was ready and willing. He had already, almost single-handedly, lifted the morale of New Orleanians. As the engineer Latour reported, "The citizens were preparing for battle as cheerfully as if it had been a party of pleasure, each in his vernacular tongue singing songs of victory. The streets resounded with 'Yankee Doodle,' the 'Marseilles Hymn,' the 'Chat du Depart,' and other martial airs."[18] In a matter of less than a fortnight, Jackson had brought a new sense of unity to the city's factions, turning them into a patriotic force eager to fight off the British no matter which approach Cochrane and his invading army chose.

CHAPTER 8

Losing Lake Borgne

The courage and skill which was displayed in the defense of
the gun vessels . . . against such an overwhelming force as they
had to contend with, reflects additional splendor on our naval glory.

—Master Commander Daniel T. Patterson to the secretary of the navy

The weather was fair—the thermometer read a tropical eighty-
four degrees—when Admiral Cochrane and his fleet left
Jamaica. But, as Andrew Jackson took his tour of the Mississippi's fortifications, the British encountered a severe storm in the
Gulf of Mexico. During the last few days of the passage swells rocked
the warships violently enough that the soldiers on board stayed below.
"So great was the motion," Lieutenant George Gleig noted, "that all
walking was prevented."[1]

After the storm exhausted itself, on December 9, 1814, blue skies
appeared and, with sight distances increased, the sailors spied the
Chandeleurs, a string of barrier islands with few signs of habitation.
Just thirty miles beyond lay the mouth of Lake Borgne. There, the

British intended to land the ground troops who would march through to New Orleans.

There was a distinct chill in the air as the fleet's flagship, the HMS *Tonnant*, along with the other tall ships, dropped anchor in the deep water off the Chandeleurs. Smaller warships sailed deeper into the sound, reefing their sails as they found anchorage between Cat and Ship Islands.

When one of the smaller ships, the HMS *Sophie*, approached the

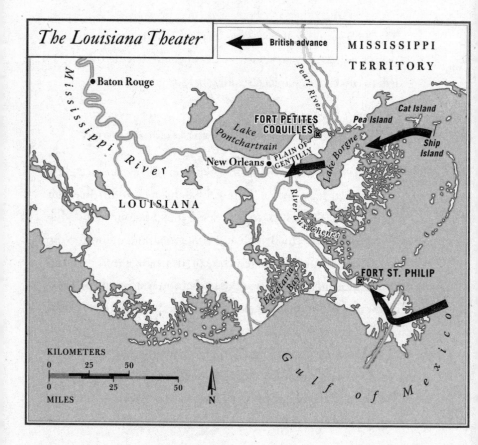

nearby coast, it came upon two small American gunboats, which sailed quickly away, presumably to warn their army of the coming attack. The captain of the *Sophie,* Nicholas Lockyer, may have wished to follow, but the coastal waters were tricky. A sandbar lay dead ahead, guarding the mouth of Lake Borgne, and the lake's shoals were known to pose a danger to all boats with more than the shallowest draft. The Americans, knowing the waters, escaped unscathed as the British watched, unable to stop them from ruining Cochrane's surprise. Within a day or two, Andrew Jackson would know that his fears were confirmed and that a huge British invasion force was heading toward Lake Borgne.

Patterson and Jones, USN

Lacking experience with warships, Andrew Jackson had no choice but to rely on the men of the U.S. Navy. But he didn't know quite what to think of Daniel Todd Patterson.

Although Patterson was just twenty-eight, his career in the navy had already spanned more than fifteen years. He had served two years in the West Indies before shipping out as a midshipman aboard the USS *Philadelphia* during the war with the Barbary pirates. In the Mediterranean, after the big frigate's grounding in the harbor at Tripoli, he had been a prisoner for eighteen months. Yet even that experience had added to his store of naval knowledge, because the *Philadelphia*'s captain had used the time wisely, running an informal academy to tutor his young officers while in captivity.

Patterson had served on the Mississippi River, rising to the rank of lieutenant while commanding a dozen gunboats operating at

Natchez in the Mississippi Territory. Having been elevated to the rank of master commander in 1813, he now ran the New Orleans station. Married to a daughter of New Orleans and with a growing family, Patterson called the city home.

A stout, compact man, Patterson carried himself with confidence, but that very boldness gave Andrew Jackson pause. Writing from Mobile on his arrival there in August, the general had summoned Patterson to help defend Mobile Point—only to have Patterson flat out refuse to come. In the most respectful terms (he wrote that it was his "most ardent wish" to cooperate with the U.S. Army), Patterson had told Jackson that he thought coming to Mobile was a fool's errand. In his judgment, if he went to Jackson's aid, the more powerful Royal Navy would inevitably blockade his vessels in Mobile Bay, rendering his gunboats useless for the more important job of protecting New Orleans.

Whatever the merits of Patterson's argument, this smacked of insubordination even if, strictly speaking, the chain of command called for Patterson to report to the secretary of the navy rather than to Jackson.

On the general's arrival in New Orleans, the two men had been thrown into a collaboration. Patterson, as the city's naval commander, had joined Jackson and his engineers on their reconnaissance trip down the Mississippi. He proved useful, his counsel valuable in improving the fortifications along the river. Jackson began to appreciate that, after almost five years in New Orleans, Patterson knew the city and, in particular, the big river, the many lakes, and the seascapes that surrounded it.

Furthermore, Jackson had to admit, Patterson was no yes-man; he was willing to stand up to his superiors. Having himself seen the need from time to time to disobey orders, Jackson had a grudging respect for the fact that Master Commander Patterson was clearly his own man.

Patterson had also thought long and hard about protecting New Orleans. Some of his thinking appeared suddenly prescient, because he had been pleading with the secretary of the navy for twelve months to send him more men, matériel, and warships. New Orleans was in danger: "The great depot of the western country," he warned, was "left open to the enemy."[2] Jackson recognized that he and Patterson had shared the same fears for many months.

Back at headquarters on 106 Royal Street, the two men considered how to protect the city from a northeastern attack via the lakes. Having never seen a gunboat, Jackson looked to Patterson; as a former gunboat commander, Patterson knew the vessels intimately. They were small by the standards of naval ships, typically fifty to sixty feet in length and eighteen feet wide, with a shallow draft and rigged with mast and sails. Armed with a large-bore cannon each and several smaller guns, the little vessels were notoriously top-heavy, making them unstable in heavy seas. Still, Patterson advised, they were well adapted to the shallow waters of the Gulf Coast.

Five U.S. Navy gunboats already actively patrolled the waters near the mouth of Lake Borgne. The gunboats were served by a schooner, the *Sea Horse,* to carry dispatches, and the *Alligator,* a converted fishing boat used for transporting men and supplies from shore to ship. Armed with a total of twenty-three guns, the little flotilla was manned by 182 officers and seamen.

Its commander was Lieutenant Thomas ap Catesby Jones. He and his sailors were to be General Jackson's eyes and ears, watching and reporting to Patterson frequently concerning the enemy's movements. If challenged by the British, Jones was under instructions to retire to the Rigolets, the narrow strait that was the passage from Lake Borgne to Lake Pontchartrain. There he was to "wait for the enemy, and sink him or be sunk."[3]

Jackson agreed that Patterson's plan seemed sound. The mouth of the big lake offered defensive advantages, and the two men believed that Jones and his well-armed boats could hold off any small craft Admiral Cochrane might send his way. Patterson also assured Jackson that no deep-draft warship could possibly sail into Lake Borgne.

Jackson wrote to James Monroe. "The gun boats on the lakes," he told the secretary of war confidently, on December 10, "will prevent the British from approaching in that quarter."[4]

Neither man knew that Lieutenant Jones and his men, on that very morning, awakened to the sight of a flotilla of enemy vessels at anchor and, with the chiming of every hour, even more ships were sailing into view. All Jones could do was watch and wait from a safe distance.

Gunning for the Gunboats

As the fog lifted on the morning of December 10, British sailors and officers alike looked curiously at the tall grasses that lined an unfamiliar shoreline. As one artilleryman noted, the landscape resembled "trembling prairies," with no beaches in sight, and only matted reeds and soggy ground where the water and land merged.[5] One thing was obvious: moving troops and hauling big guns on this terrain would not be easy.

But Admiral Cochrane had a strategy.

Though the new army commander, General Pakenham, would arrive any day from England—replacing the previous expedition leader, Robert Ross, who had been killed in September in the Battle of Baltimore—Cochrane couldn't wait for Pakenham to arrive to begin getting the troops off the ships and into fighting position. He favored ferrying the troops across Lake Borgne to a landing site. On the advice of two former Spanish residents of New Orleans, Cochrane thought the beachhead on the far side might be Bayou Bienvenue, a waterway said to be navigable by good-size barges.[6] From there a short march of a few miles would take the invading army to the outskirts of New Orleans.

Before any of this could happen, however, Lake Borgne would have to be cleared of enemy ships. Though there were only five small American gunboats in the lake, their cannons were a grave danger to the open boats the British would use to ferry soldiers ashore. Cochrane would not expose his men to that kind of danger and gave an order: "[No] movement of the troops could take place till this formidable flotilla was either captured or destroyed."[7]

From his anchorage outside the waters of Lake Borgne, Cochrane gave the reliable Nicholas Lockyer, captain of the *Sophie,* command of the venture to exterminate the gunboats. Having visited the pirate Lafitte in Barataria Bay, patrolled the Gulf, and commanded the attack on Lake Bowyer, he was the Briton most experienced in the ways and waters of the Gulf Coast.

On the night of Monday, December 12, a mix of seamen in blue coats and marines in red jackets boarded forty-two barges. Three unarmed ship's boats accompanied the barges and, taken together, the vessels carried 1,200 men.

Lockyer's assignment: *Dispose of the gunboats.* Capture them, if possible, Cochrane ordered; the shallow-draft boats might well be useful in the operation to come. But, most of all, the admiral wanted them out of the path of his amphibious assault.

On Guard

Aboard one of the American gunboats in Lake Borgne, Lieutenant Thomas ap Catesby Jones watched and waited for the British attack. For the past three days, the twenty-four-year-old commander had played a cautious game of cat and mouse with the enemy. He had ventured near to the channel near Ship Island where many of the Royal Navy ships rocked with the tides, close enough to confirm how many ships were there, and had then retreated, dispatching one of his boats with a report to Patterson. As the number of British ships increased, Jones had decided it was "no longer safe or prudent for me to continue on that part of the lakes."[8] He retreated to the mouth of Lake Borgne just north of Malheureux Island.

From there, on December 13, he spotted the British barges at 10:00 a.m. As he watched the flotilla proceed westward, he knew that the assault on New Orleans had begun. Cochrane would be taking the route Jackson had thought most likely, crossing the lakes to land his men and march on the city.

Seeing how much larger the British force was than his own, Jones quickly took action. Reasoning that the British were likely to reach vital supplies waiting on the nearby shore, he dispatched the schooner *Sea Horse* to blow up the goods, wanting to prevent them from falling into enemy hands. There was little else he could do; though he might be able to inflict some damage on the barges, his little fleet of gunboats was much too small to stop the enemy completely.

Lieutenant Jones watched as the British convoy made steady though laborious progress across the lake. The front of the imposing flotilla was half a mile wide and moved relentlessly westward despite strong headwinds. As noon came and went, Jones waited for the enemy force to make a move south toward shore—and to New Orleans—to unload the troops. But the flotilla did not change course.

At last, as the hour struck two, a terrible intuition struck Lieutenant Jones: *The British intended to attack his gunboats.* They weren't yet looking to land an army. He and his men were their objective. Jones's reaction was immediate. If the British wanted to destroy his little fleet—and they clearly had the manpower to do it—the time had come to retreat deeper into Lake Borgne. Per Patterson's orders, Jones prepared to sail his badly outnumbered force to the narrow strait, the Rigolets, where he might make a stand. If that failed, he could retreat into Lake Pontchartrain.

Ordered to weigh anchor and set sail, his men soon discovered that days of sustained winds and low tide had made the marshy waters off Malheureux Island uncommonly shallow: three of the gunboats ran aground on the sandy bottom. In a frantic effort to lighten the craft, Jones's men threw all dispensable heavy items overboard, but the boats still refused to budge. They sat helplessly, watching the British approach, until 3:30 when, finally, the rising tide floated the boats free.

Just a few minutes later, Jones noticed that, while most of the British boats were still heading for him and his recently freed flotilla, three of the British barges were veering northward toward shore. Their unmistakable target was the schooner *Sea Horse,* still visible on its mission to keep the supplies on land from falling into British hands. With darkness falling, the *Sea Horse* attempted to fight off its attackers, firing a deadly discharge of grapeshot at the British boats. The rain of iron balls brought the British attack to a temporary halt and gave the *Sea Horse* time to make for the shore, but the reprieve was short-lived. As Jones watched, four more launches broke from the flotilla's ranks to join the attack on the *Sea Horse*.

By the time the combined British force of seven boats closed in on the schooner, the *Sea Horse* was moored at the shoreline, and some of its crewmen were on dry land, readying their cannons, two six-pounders, to fire on their attackers. The sun was setting, and from a distance Jones could only watch and wonder in the growing darkness as gunfire echoed across the lake. Would the outnumbered Americans be able to hold out?

Jones didn't have long to wonder. Within half an hour, the British discovered that the single American ship put up a better fight than they'd expected. Despite their advantage in numbers, the British lost one boat and sustained many casualties before pulling back.

But the British retreat was no victory for Jones's men. Although the Americans on the *Sea Horse* had fought off this first attack, they remained trapped—and they understood they would not be able to hold off a second assault. Unwilling to let the ship fall into enemy hands, they made a painful decision. At 7:30 p.m., a tremendous explosion rent the air, sending flames high into the sky. The Americans had blown up the *Sea Horse* and the supplies. Neither would be of any use to the British.

As the *Sea Horse* burned, Jones and the men aboard the five gunboats continued north, attempting to avoid a fight with the many barges. For a few hours, they made progress but, as midnight approached, the wind failed them. They were well short of the shallow passage north of Malheureux Island that would lead them to safety when it became clear their sails would carry them no farther. But the British boats, powered by oarsmen, would be unaffected by the stillness. Though the enemy had stopped for the night nearly ten miles back, they would easily catch Jones and his men when they resumed their pursuit at daybreak. At one o'clock in the morning, Jones decided he and his becalmed force had only one option: they must turn and fight.

Summoning the commanders of the five gunboats, he laid out the plan. They would form a line across the mile-wide strip of shallow water where they were becalmed, anchoring the boats at the stern. The tide retreating from Lake Borgne would keep their bows—and thus their cannons—pointing at the oncoming British. His intent, Jones explained, was to put them "in the most advantageous position, to give the enemy as warm a reception as possible."[9]

Laboriously moving their craft into place, the gunboat commanders did as ordered before dropping anchor and attempting to get some much-needed rest. In the morning, they would face the fight of their lives.

Morning, December 14

The day started early. British sailors had begun rowing at 4:00 a.m. With the first light of day, Captain Nicholas Lockyer spied the American flotilla. Less than ten miles ahead, the gunboats, five abreast, were obviously looking to hold the line against the British onslaught.

Lockyer's orders were to capture or destroy any American ship he saw, whatever the cost. The previous evening the *Sea Horse*, trapped and alone, had been the first victim. Now Lockyer spotted a second quarry. The *Alligator*, sailing back toward the gunboats after delivering Jones's letters for Commodore Patterson, attempted to make a run past the British barges despite the light winds. Lockyer ordered the small boat's capture, and his barges moved on the *Alligator* too quickly for her to escape. Though the Americans attempted to ward off the British with their cannons, the shot splashed harmlessly into the lake. Recognizing they would soon be overpowered by a force that numbered in the hundreds, the eight-man crew of the American vessel surrendered. Lockyer could now note in his log that the *Alligator* no longer flew the Stars and Stripes but henceforth would sail with Cochrane's convoy.

With the *Alligator* captured, Lockyer's barges resumed their progress toward Jones's gunboats, now anchored in place. The outgoing tide meant that Lockyer's tired oarsmen worked against the current. But the veteran captain knew the ripples coming his way meant something

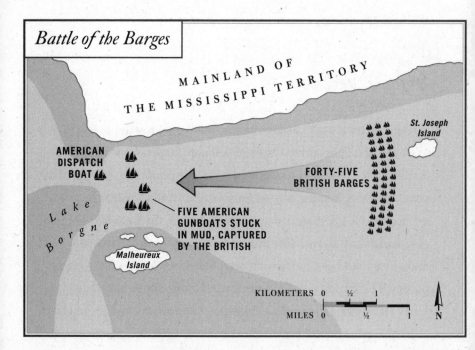

Battle of the Barges

MAINLAND OF THE MISSISSIPPI TERRITORY

St. Joseph Island

AMERICAN DISPATCH BOAT

FORTY-FIVE BRITISH BARGES

Lake Borgne

FIVE AMERICAN GUNBOATS STUCK IN MUD, CAPTURED BY THE BRITISH

Malheureux Island

KILOMETERS 0   ½   1
MILES 0   ½   1

N

else, too. His opponent would not be retreating this morning. With the push of the tide and no wind to fill his sails, Jones had no choice but to wait and fight.

The more than forty British boats continued to close in on the Americans. As they neared the five gunboats, they saw unmistakable signs of the American determination to fight: Jones's men had hung their boarding nets on the sides of the vessels. These webs of thick rope, like coarse spiderwebs, would hamper British marines seeking to board once the close fighting began.

Now nearly within striking distance, Lockyer ordered a pause just outside the range of American guns. It was 10:00 a.m., and his men had been rowing for six hours. As the Americans watched and waited anxiously, the British commander gave his men thirty minutes to breakfast and rest. Confident of victory, the British were in no rush, and they would defeat their unhappy prey much more easily if they were refreshed.

The Fight

The American boats waited in an uneven row, despite the best efforts of Jones's men. In the night strong currents from Lake Borgne had carried two gunboats a hundred yards forward of the planned line of defense. One of them, at the center, was Jones's, and his position meant he would be the first target of the cannons in the prows of the British barges.

When the British had finished their meal and began their progress toward Jones's men, the U.S. Navy guns sounded first. The Americans' long-barreled cannons possessed greater range than the shorter

British guns, but at a distance of more than a mile, the barges made small targets. Undamaged and undeterred, the British flotilla drew closer with every stroke of the oars.

Soon, with the American boats within the range of his guns, Lockyer issued the order for his gunners to fire. With an ear-shattering roar, the British carronades boomed as one. Jones's men returned fire and, as the British boats grew nearer and nearer, the British marines aimed their muskets at the little flotilla.

The maneuverable British boats held an advantage over Jones's gunboats, which remained fixed at anchor. Three British barges led by Lockyer's closed rapidly on Jones's boat, their first target. This would be a battle of commanders.

Jones's gunners landed shot in two of the attacking barges, and with water rising through holes in their hulls, the British boats began to sink. But the undamaged third barge soon pulled alongside Jones's boat, and Royal Marines attempted to board the American ship. Fighting with pistols and swords, the U.S. Navy crew of forty-one men repulsed the attack, wounding or killing most of the British officers. Lockyer himself sustained a wound, but he continued to rally his men as four more barges from his column joined the fight.

The Americans fought valiantly, but just as it appeared they might again repulse a wave of attackers, a musket ball smashed into Lieutenant Jones's left shoulder, and he fell to the deck. As his men carried their commander below, he ordered, "Keep up the fight! Keep up the fight!"[10] His second in command took charge of the defense, but the attackers had shot away the gunboat's defensive netting and British marines soon managed to clamber over the gunwales of the American ship. After a few minutes of bloody hand-to-hand action, the British gained possession of the gunboat's deck.

Lockyer himself sustained another wound in the fight, but, lying on the deck, he ordered the cannons aboard Jones's gunboat turned on the other American craft. Because Jones's boat had drifted well in front of the others, they were easily within its line of fire. Jones's vessel sent shot cascading at the other U.S. Navy ships even before its flag came down.

The end of the battle neared. According to Jones's report, "The action continued with unabating severity until 40 minutes past 12 o'clock, when it terminated."[11] By then, all the gunboats belonged to the British.

In a fight that lasted just less than two hours, the British prevailed. But the Americans had fought hard, despite being outnumbered almost seven to one. The British casualties numbered at least 17 killed, 77 wounded. On the American side, 10 men died and 35 were reported wounded.

British surgeons set about treating the injured, including Captain Lockyer and the American commander, Lieutenant Jones, now held captive by the British. Neither officer would see further action in the battle for New Orleans. But Captain Lockyer had handed his admiral the signal advantage of clear sailing on the lakes.

Despite his losses—his men, his gunboats, he himself a prisoner— the American lieutenant had, in turn, done Andrew Jackson a significant service: the brave action of Jones and his men bought the general vital time. The first British warship had been sighted off the Gulf Coast almost a week earlier; at the moment of their victory at Lake Borgne, not so much as a platoon of the British army had stepped ashore. True, the handful of American gunboats had been captured (Jones's was promptly renamed the HMS *Destruction*). But Jones and many of his men, despite being held prisoner, continued to serve their country, telling their interrogators tall tales about the size of Jackson's army. Now Admiral Cochrane might have unfettered access to land his army for the march to New Orleans, but he did not know with any accuracy what the troops aboard his ships were about to march into.

CHAPTER 9

The Armies Assemble

Our lakes are open to the approach of the enemy, and I am
with my feeble force prepared to meet him and die in the last
ditch before he shall reach the city.

—Andrew Jackson, December 16, 1814

When, hours later, the news of Lieutenant Jones's defeat
reached New Orleans, its citizens were terrified. But
General Jackson was not in the city to hear the news.
A full day would pass before Jackson learned that the American defense on the lakes had been shredded like the sails on the U.S. Navy
gunboats.

While Jones was being taken captive, Jackson had been north of
town, scouting the terrain, believing the lake waters were well protected. If the British did attack from the north—and even without
knowing about Jones's loss, the location of Cochrane's armada in Mississippi Sound suggested to Jackson that they would come from that
quarter—then the general must have a clear picture in his mind of the
lay of the land.

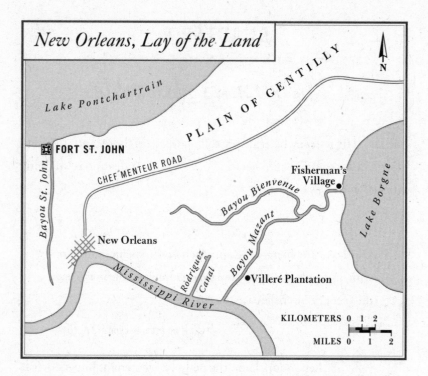

Despite a recurrence of his dysentery, which made riding a horse intensely painful, Jackson ventured to the head of Lake Borgne. There he inspected the end of the large lake opposite from where Jones confronted Lockyer. Next Jackson went west to look at the expanse of Lake Pontchartrain, then traveled along the Chef Menteur Road, which seemed to him the best and most likely route for a British attack on the city. He issued many orders. Streams he saw were to be blocked, defenses enhanced, guards stationed, and a chain of sentinels organized to bring him word of any British appearance.

Then, on December 15, he received the bad news of Jones's defeat. Having assured now secretary of war James Monroe just days before that the lakes were still secure, he learned that, quite to the contrary, they were not. Jones's flotilla now belonged to the British and the American lieutenant was their prisoner.

Jackson galloped back to his headquarters in New Orleans, knowing that, almost overnight, he had to pull together his army to protect the city. His journey had taken a toll on his worn body and, too ill to stand, he lay upon a sofa, dictating orders to his aides and reinforcing himself with sips of brandy.

With barely a thousand regular troops in his command, he wrote to General Coffee, the man he called his "right arm."[1] His order sounded like a plea: "You must not sleep until you reach me, or arrive within striking distance."[2] He sent a letter to Natchez, where he hoped it would reach William Carroll, another Tennessee militia general. Carroll was on his way downriver with some 1,400 men with arms and ammunition.

Jackson also anticipated the arrival of General John Thomas's Kentucky militia, an estimated 2,500 troops. And he worried about a shipment of guns and munitions, en route from Pittsburgh since November 3.[3] Would it arrive on time?

Even as General Jackson fretted, he received some spiritual assurance. From their convent overlooking Ursuline and Chartres Streets, four nuns wrote him a letter. They wanted to do their bit, volunteering to take in wounded men. Since word of the British arrival in the region had reached them, they had already taken the precaution of sending the boarding students and orphans in their care out of New Orleans and had plenty of space.[4] But most of all, they offered their prayer for Jackson and his men and for the safety of the city they had come to love.

The people of New Orleans needed prayers desperately—and not just prayers for ammunition and troops to stand up to the fighting force that had defeated Napoleon. Most immediately, it looked like it might take a miracle to pull the city's factions together. The townsfolk had been comforted by Jackson's return, but one of his attempts to unite the city's population against the British almost destroyed the fragile unity he had achieved in his weeks in New Orleans. Against the advice of some Louisianans, Jackson accepted into his army two battalions of freemen of color. Though he required that officers of the two corps be white men, he also ordered that black soldiers be treated the same way as white volunteers, a shocking attitude in a society that doubted the humanity and trustworthiness of nonwhites. When one paymaster objected, Jackson made his position clear. He needed every man he could get and was determined not to worry about the prejudices of the white men: "Be pleased to keep to yourself your opinions . . . without inquiring whether the troops are white, black or tea."[5]

The people of New Orleans, no matter their skin color, whether French or American, male or female, young or old, devout or not, would have to rally behind General Andrew Jackson if the city was to fight off its attackers. Outnumbered and outgunned, they were unlikely to defeat the British even if they did unite. Divided, they had no chance.

The Grand Parade

Jackson turned his attention to calming a panicked populace and persuading everyone to pull together.

New Orleans was a city that loved a parade, and Jackson decided there was no better way to cheer and inspire the anxious townspeople. He announced there would be a procession into the city's central downtown square, the Place d'Armes, on Sunday, December 18.

On the day of the parade, the people of New Orleans crowded together in the doors and windows lining the square. Even more townspeople lined the balconies and roofs, and the surrounding streets were packed with sailors and laborers and freemen.

With the towering old Spanish Cathedral of St. Louis as the backdrop, and accompanied by the roll of drums and the cheers of the crowd, two regiments of Louisiana state militia marched in, most dressed in civilian clothes. Not all carried guns, and those who did brought what they had, shouldering a mix of rifles, muskets, and fowling pieces. The militia was followed by uniformed companies resplendent in full parade dress. Major Jean Baptiste Plauché, a cotton broker who had volunteered when he felt the call of duty, led one battalion of 287 men, which consisted of two generations of local businessmen, planters, and lawyers. Stirred to patriotic fervor, women of the town waved scarves and handkerchiefs as their husbands and sons marched by.

But would they cheer for the next wave of marchers? As martial music was played, the troops of Frenchmen were followed by a well-drilled battalion of 210 freemen, most of them Haitians, commanded by a bakery owner, Major Jean Daquin. Choctaws marched, too, commanded by Pierre Jugeat, a trader who had married into the tribe. Here was a test of the unity that Jackson hoped the parade would create. The townspeople had celebrated their own; now would they celebrate these protectors who didn't look like them and whom they sometimes regarded with suspicion?

It's possible there was a break in the cheering, but if there was, it was not long enough to record. Whatever the motive—fear of the

British, a change of heart, or the frenzy of the moment—the people of New Orleans together honored even these troops that they had so recently questioned.

Proudly following the Haitians and Choctaws were representatives of the city's high society. Thomas Beale, a gentleman from Virginia, had just days before persuaded several dozen of his friends—a range of merchants and New Orleans professionals—to don blue hunting shirts and wide-brimmed black hats and to shoulder their long Kentucky rifles.[6] These sharpshooters called themselves Beale's Rifles and many of them wore miniature bouquets of flowers pinned to their shoulders, good luck tokens from wives and mothers.

The force that filled the square, some 1,500 men, seemed suddenly formidable and impressive. Together with the militiamen en route, the number of troops defending New Orleans had doubled in the sixteen days since Jackson arrived. This army had come together in a matter of weeks. Even more remarkably, the patchwork force of the high- and low-born seemed prepared to work together to save their city, perhaps in answer to the nuns' prayers, perhaps because of Jackson's leadership genius.

Although the total number of soldiers was not large, Jackson made a point of giving each group representation on his staff. In addition to Livingston and Claiborne, a mix of merchants, French nationals, and other locals held freshly issued officer ranks. Now, because of Jackson's careful delegation and savvy reading of the city's mood, a once-divided New Orleans was caught up in the fervor of the moment, and morale soared as they saw the clear proof that they would not go unprotected. The parade had been a stroke of genius, galvanizing the fighting force of freed slaves, Indians, pirates, woodsmen, militiamen, and French colonials.

But the general wasn't there only to display the growing power of his army. He wished to deliver a message himself. Riding his favorite horse, Duke, Jackson cut an imposing figure as he rode to the center of the square. Again, he entrusted Edward Livingston to deliver his message in French and, as the cheers quieted, Livingston began his translation.

First, he complimented the people of New Orleans on their bravery even as he exhorted them to further heroism: "The American nation shall applaud your valour, as your general now praises your ardour." Jackson's promise, he told them, was of victory: "Continue with the energy you have began, and he promises you not only safety, but victory."[7] Then he addressed the various factions, with specific words for the militia, for the Creoles, and for the blacks.

But Jackson's action to unify the city went one step further. He left his appreciative audience reassured and inspired—but he had also, just the day before, issued a declaration of martial law. Henceforth, anyone entering the city would have to report to the office of the general; those wishing to leave needed written permission from Jackson or a member of his staff. The streets would go dark at 9:00 p.m. Every able-bodied man was expected to fight, while the old or infirm would police the streets. The legality of the declaration wasn't clear, but Jackson would stop at nothing to beat back the British.

The declaration of martial law also meant that men, whatever their color or nationality, could be conscripted forthwith to become sailors—and Commodore Patterson chose to put this new authority to immediate use. With the loss of the flotilla on Lake Borgne, Patterson's force had shrunk to one warship on the Mississippi, the schooner USS *Carolina*, and a converted merchantman, the USS *Louisiana*. Reportedly a speedy ship before she was armed with sixteen guns, the

Louisiana had no crew, but now, under Jackson's authority, Patterson and his officers could draft the sturdiest sailors they could find to man the ninety-nine-foot sloop. In a matter of hours, the new tars of the *Louisiana* were drilling on its decks.

Jackson's words in the Place d'Armes calmed the city; panic had ebbed as the citizens witnessed his preparations and leadership, and little grumbling was heard. Applause had rippled across the crowd as Livingston brought the speech to a close, and when the troops in the Place d'Armes were dismissed, they melted into the crowd of well-wishers. Everyone knew this might be his last chance to visit with family before the call to fight.

The urgency of their need to defend family and friends was one of the few advantages the Americans had. Jackson and his men might be less experienced than the British, but they had the added motivation of fighting for their homes and their loved ones. If they lost, they had nowhere to go, unlike Gleig and his men, who could return to their families in England.

The stakes of the battle weighing on him, Jackson, ailing and anxious, returned to his quarters more determined than ever to hold off the British. Little did he know that the invaders were already well on their way.

Men on the Move

On the morning before Jackson's parade, the British had begun their advance. Because deep-draft warships could not penetrate Lake Borgne, the British embarked once again in barges. Stroke by wearying stroke, oarsmen propelled the first loads of British soldiers westward from the navy's anchorage in Mississippi Sound into the lake.

The danger of the American gunboats had been eliminated, but the trip across the lake was still not an easy one for the British. The men sat so tightly packed that shifting position was almost impossible, and storms that blew across the lake soon made the ten-hour, thirty-mile journey truly miserable. As the infantry officer Lieutenant Gleig noted, he and his men were pummeled by "heavy rains, such as an inhabitant of England cannot dream of, and against which no cloak will furnish protection."[8] The open boats posed a particular hardship to African-Caribbeans, dressed in light clothing and unused to chilly temperatures, and many of them died later after becoming ill in the cold.[9]

Many hours into the journey across the lake, the invaders' first destination came into view. Known to the Creoles as Isle aux Pois, but called Pea Island by the British, this swampy mound of land, little more than a sandbar, would serve as a staging point in the attack. The soldiers disembarked and then the empty boats reversed course back to the fleet. At least three round-trips would be needed to move the full invading force to Pea Island, meaning the sailors would have to row the thirty-mile distance five times before returning to the ships once again for stores and artillery.

Even then, however, the job of ferrying Cochrane's force was only half complete: Pea Island with its wild ducks and alligators sat at the northern end of Lake Borgne, halfway to the beachhead from which the troops could march on the city. Another hard row of some thirty miles was necessary before the march to New Orleans could commence.

Pea Island offered neither buildings nor trees for shelter. The soldiers, stiff and wet from the crossing, carried no tents and suffered as bad weather continued. After the rain slowed to a stop, the conditions improved little. The temperature dropped rapidly at night and, with a sharp wind off the water, the soldiers' uniforms stiffened with frost. The dinner fare wasn't very appetizing, consisting of "salt meat and ship biscuit . . . moistened by a small allowance of rum . . . not such as to reconcile us to the cold and wet under which we suffered," as one officer noted.[10] Even Admiral Cochrane and the commanding army general, John Keane, far from the comforts aboard the HMS *Tonnant,* had to adapt, their island quarters makeshift shelters of thatched grasses.

Five full days were required to move the first several thousand troops to Pea Island but morale remained high. "From the General, down to the youngest drum-boy, a confident anticipation of success seemed to pervade all ranks; and in the hope of an ample reward in store for them, the toils and grievances of the moment were forgotten."[11] As the troops assembled, there was heady talk of a "speedy and bloodless conquest," as well as of rich booty, because even the lowliest of cabin boys could expect a share of the spoils when the wealth of New Orleans was divided up.

On its way into battle, despite the hardships of the trip, the finest army in the world had little doubt that New Orleans would soon be theirs.

The British Make Landfall

While the British shuttled their troops to shore, Jackson waited blindly. He knew the enemy now controlled Lake Borgne, but what route would they take from the lake?

One clue arrived compliments of a schooner captain named Brown. Sailing on Lake Borgne, together with his pilot, a black man named Michaud, he had seen a daunting sight, "count[ing] three hundred and forty-eight barges, carrying each forty or fifty men, infantry, cavalry, and two regiments of Negroes." Brown was brought to Jackson.

Where, the general asked, did they observe this flotilla?

"They disembarked at Ile-aux-Poix," Brown replied.[12] Jackson wished to know more, but the schooner captain could offer no further details.

Jackson was left to ponder—as he advised the secretary of war— where the enemy would "choose his point of attack."[13] He knew from his own reconnoitering that the best approach from Pea Island could be along the Plain of Gentilly, so Jackson dispatched defenders, in- cluding a regiment of Louisiana militia and a battalion of free blacks. Because it was also possible that His Majesty's soldiers would take a route south of the plain, Jackson ordered another Louisiana regiment downriver to be posted at Jumonville. At the Villeré plantation just downstream, a picket was posted to watch for danger from that ap- proach, while another division of the militia marched toward English Turn, in case the British came that way. Every fort in the vicinity was manned and everyone was on watch and alert.

The most direct routes were now covered, but Jackson still had two problems. First, he did not have enough ammunition for his men. Second, he had insufficient knowledge of the bayous to truly plan to repel every possible attack. He had examined the local topography to the best of his ability, but it wasn't enough. To ensure the safety of the city, he would need to add one more group to his motley coalition of troops.

Partnering with the Pirates

For months, Jackson resisted making a deal with the devil. When Governor Claiborne had forwarded Jean Lafitte's warning back in September concerning the British attempt to recruit the pirates of Barataria Bay, Jackson had written back, angrily dismissing the Lafitte brothers and their fellow privateers as "hellish banditti." Claiborne concurred: Louisiana's governor was a sworn enemy of the privateers and, in September, had even ordered a raid of Barataria Bay, driving the outlaws into hiding elsewhere in the marshes south of the city.

Yet the Lafittes still had powerful friends in New Orleans and, with the danger of invasion on everyone's mind, attitudes softened toward Jean who, at great risk to himself, had relayed word of the British approach. The motives of the pirates were hard to decipher— were they really pro-American or was Lafitte just looking for pardons for past offenses?—but many in the Creole community wanted to enlist their help under these desperate circumstances. Indeed, on December 14, the Louisiana legislature passed a resolution promising amnesty for their piratical transgressions if the Lafittes and their men helped fight the British.

With the British now so near at hand, Jackson consulted Edward Livingston. For three years, Livingston had been Jean Lafitte's legal adviser. Until now, Jackson had followed William Claiborne's lead and regarded the Baratarians as infamous bandits. But Jackson's army was low on matériel—and he had gotten wind of Lafitte's boast that he could outfit an army of thirty thousand.

The time had come for Monsieur Lafitte and General Jackson to meet.

After obtaining a pass into the city from a federal judge—there remained a warrant out for his arrest—Jean Lafitte arrived at the three-story brick house on Royal Street. Major Latour, now a trusted member of Jackson's brain trust, offered to bring his friend Lafitte in. He did the introductions and helped bridge the language gap.

Jackson listened to Monsieur Lafitte's proposal, as he "solicited for himself and for all the Baratarians, the honor of serving under our banners . . . to defend the country and combat its enemies."[14] Jackson had his doubts—more than once he had dismissed Lafitte and his men as "pirates and robbers." Still, this proposal was beginning to make sense.

Lafitte explained he could offer more than his allegiance. He claimed to have one thousand men, all willing to fight. Just as important to Jackson, however, was the cache of powder, shot, and essential flints—some seven thousand of them, he said—which were needed to provide the spark used to fire muzzle-loaded flintlock muskets and pistols.

The general and the pirate regarded each other. The two shared little in life experience, yet both had a native gift for leadership; they were men around whom other men rallied. They had differing moral codes but shared a respect for what they regarded as fairness and natural law. Just as Jackson had recognized the Red Stick chief Weatherford as a man who, at great risk to himself, had confronted Jackson seeking common cause, he began to see Lafitte in the same light. The pirate just might prove to be a key ally.

Lafitte knew the backwaters of this region intimately.

The man who stood before Jackson promised him men and munitions.

The artillerists in his band were famously skilled.

His stores of gunpowder would be invaluable.

A deal was struck, and Jackson dictated a note saying, "Jean Lafitte has offered me his services to go down and give every information in his power. You will therefore please to afford him the necessary protection from insult and injury and when you have derived the information you wish, furnish him with a passport for his return, dismissing him as soon as possible as I shall want him here."[15]

Lafitte's intelligence would be critical, and some of his privateers would be assigned to help protect Bayou St. John north of the city and to reinforce Fort St. Philip downstream on the Mississippi. Others would be organized into two artillery companies. The stores of munitions the pirates had accumulated would be removed to Jackson's magazine. Lafitte himself would then join Jackson's officer corps.

Together, they would seek to save New Orleans.

Across the Sea, in Ghent

Across the Atlantic, a quieter confrontation brewed. The American and British negotiators in Ghent grew closer to a meeting of the minds and, as November became December, the Americans had begun to think a treaty was within reach. The differences between the parties seemed to have been whittled down to talk of fishing rights off the New England coast and navigation of the Mississippi.

These discussions had revealed a regional rift between the American negotiators. John Quincy Adams saw no great harm in trading away access to the Mississippi and, to him, the right to fish off his native coast was an essential and absolute right. He felt bound to protect it, partly because his father had negotiated similar terms in the

Treaty of Paris when the American Revolution ended. For the Kentuckian Henry Clay, however, the importance of the fisheries was dwarfed by the matter of navigating the great river that defined the westernmost boundary of his state. For him, the Mississippi was central to the development of his nation's middle, and he could never agree to compromise those American rights.

In the midst of these distractions, the American ministers briefly furrowed their brows at a new wrinkle the British introduced to the discussion.

In early December, the English diplomats returned once more to the language concerning territory captured by either party in the war. At first, the renewed discussion seemed a simple continuation of the earlier negotiations concerning the Latin phrase *uti possidetis* ("as you possess") and the restoration of territory with a peace. But the wrangling over language puzzled the ever-thoughtful John Quincy Adams. He pondered the British insistence on splitting linguistic hairs concerning who owned what and when—and what it might mean in practical terms.

In Louisiana, he knew, a battle for New Orleans might just be unfolding. If so, the city would be successfully defended or it would fall. Neither he nor anyone else—in Europe or in North America—knew what the outcome would be.

Yet a great deal might hinge on that result: half hidden in the diplomatic and legal language of the document lay a grave danger—one that, despite Adams's suspicions, remained undetected by Adams and the American negotiators.

What would happen if the British captured New Orleans?

In the new draft of the document, all "territories, places, and possessions" captured by one side were to be returned. Regardless of the outcome when Admiral Cochrane's forces met up with General Jackson's, the Treaty of Ghent would assure that Louisiana remained the property of the United States of America. Right?

However, to a legalistic eye, wasn't that subject to interpretation? What if there was a deeper subtext to the British insistence upon the insertion of the word *possessions*? Given that the British had never accepted Louisiana as a legitimate American *possession*—the Crown regarded the territory as the rightful property of the king of Spain, taken wrongly by Napoleon and therefore illegally transferred to the United States of America—might this open-ended treaty invite dispute?

And in the event the British captured New Orleans, did they intend to keep it?

What none of the Americans knew was that Edward Pakenham, the new general sent to defeat the Americans in the great battle for New Orleans, had very specific instructions. The British secretary of state for war, Earl Bathurst, had instructed Pakenham precisely. Even if he heard a treaty had been signed, Earl Bathurst ordered, "hostilities should not be suspended *until you shall have official information*" that the treaty had been ratified. The British commander was, quite specifically, to fight on to gain "Possession of the Country."[16]

If Adams didn't recognize them, how could Pakenham's opponent, Andrew Jackson, have known of the perils posed by a treaty being negotiated five thousand miles away? He could no more have anticipated the peace terms than he could have sensed an earthquake in the days before it struck. But Jackson's own remarkable instincts did tell him that holding New Orleans—keeping it out of the hands of the British—meant everything to his beloved country.

The British Approach

Admiral Cochrane had begun the process of landing his attack force, but he still had serious reason to be cautious. Some days earlier two men had arrived under a flag of truce, and the admiral received them aboard the HMS *Tonnant*. One of them, a physician named Dr. Robert Morrell, explained they came on behalf of Commodore Patterson. Morrell wanted to attend to the wounded American sailors, while his companion, Thomas Shields, a purser, wanted to negotiate the release of Lieutenant Jones and the other prisoners.

Cochrane suspected they were spies.

The admiral questioned the Americans closely. They were quick to assure him that Jackson's was an enormous and powerful force, that "myriads of Western riflemen . . . were flocking to his standard."[17]

Cochrane remained skeptical of American battle skills after the pathetic failure of the militia outside Washington on August 24, when thousands of ill-trained farmers and shopkeepers had scattered in the face of a British charge and beneath a sky alight with exploding rockets.

But Cochrane asked himself: Was he sending his men to face an army that might be two thousand strong—or did it number twenty thousand, as these men told him? As much as the possibility worried him, he doubted so large a force existed. In any case, he certainly couldn't permit these men to leave the fleet to report to Jackson what they had seen of his ships and soldiers.

"Until the battle was over," Cochrane had told them, "and the fate of the town determined," they were going nowhere.[18] They would be guests of the Royal Navy, waiting out the battle aboard the frigate HMS *Gordon*.

From Pea Island, Cochrane decided to send two of his own men on a spying mission.

He consulted with General John Keane, commander of the army forces, and, on December 20, Captain Robert Spencer of the Royal Navy and Quartermaster Lieutenant John Peddie of His Majesty's army set out for Bayou Bienvenue, a watercourse that led from Lake Borgne to the outskirts of New Orleans. Their task was to determine whether Cochrane's plan was indeed the best route for landing the army.

The men returned the next day from reconnoitering Bayou Bienvenue bearing good news. After spotting Fisherman's Village, a small settlement of a dozen cabins a short distance upstream on the bayou, the two Englishmen had gone ashore. Spencer and Peddie hired as their guides two Spanish fishermen who sold their catch upstream in New Orleans and knew the area well. Having disguised themselves in the blue shirts and the oilskin hats the locals wore, Spencer and Peddie studied the landscape as the fishermen stroked them miles inland. Amazingly, they saw no sentinels, and Spencer and Peddie went ashore and walked to the high road that led into the city. They took in a view of the Mississippi. Within a mere six miles of New Orleans, the two British spies tasted the water of the big river.

Back on Pea Island, they told Cochrane that the plan to land at Bayou Bienvenue was "perfectly practicable," because the bayou was both unobstructed and—this was almost laughable—unguarded ("the enemy had no look-out in that quarter").[19] The bayou was roughly a hundred yards wide and more than six feet deep. Not only could the army go ashore at Bayou Bienvenue, but the advance men had done their job doubly well, returning with more than a dozen fishermen, all with intimate knowledge of Lake Borgne. They would act as pilots for the British barges.

A definite plan was in place.

Bayou Bienvenue

Cochrane gave the order to move. The first of General Keane's force embarked on December 22. The advance guard would be a light brigade consisting of the Fourth Regiment, Eighty-Fifth Light Infantry, and the green-uniformed Ninety-Fifth Rifles. Its commander would be Colonel William Thornton, who had distinguished himself in August at the big victory in Washington.

In addition to regular troops, Thornton took rocketeers armed with rockets. A squad of artillerymen went along, too, with two portable three-pound guns, as did a company of sappers, engineers charged with repairing roads and building bridges. Two other brigades accompanied by heavier armaments would follow.

The first barges shoved off by ten o'clock: the lead expeditionary force of more than 1,600 men was on its way, and after a long row, they entered Bayou Bienvenue in the darkness.

Spotting U.S. pickets on guard a half mile ahead near Fisherman's Village, a party of British infantrymen, stealthy under the cover of night, surprised and quickly overcame the Americans. None of them were able to run back to New Orleans to warn Jackson that the British were on the way.

In the morning, when they resumed their advance after some hours of sleep, a vanguard of troops commanded by Thornton led the string

of barges upstream on Bayou Bienvenue and its extension, Bayou Mazant. When they reached the head of the waterway, they found the
water shallower than expected, and the soldiers had to walk from one
boat to the next, as over an unsteady bridge, to reach land. The sappers went on ahead to clear a path and, where necessary, improvised
bridges over streams. The British force-marched toward their destination, camouflaged by reeds that stood seven feet tall.

At first, progress was slow, but, after almost a mile, the boggy
swampland gave way to firmer ground and a cover of cypress trees. A
mile beyond, open fields came into view.

Over the decades, farmers had reclaimed fertile soil along the
Mississippi. Levees and canals made cultivation possible, and plantations now lined the river, where well-irrigated acreage produced valuable crops. One such property now lay directly in the British path—but
little did Thornton realize that it was a station for Jackson's sentinels.

Under orders from Colonel Thornton, a company of soldiers fanned
out, surrounding the main house of the Villeré plantation. Its owner,
General Jacques Villeré, guarded the coastline elsewhere with his
Louisiana militia; his son Gabriel remained at home, charged by Jackson with watching Bayou Bienvenue. As the British crept closer, Villeré
stood on the house's gallery, smoking a cigar. Deep in conversation
with a younger brother, Major Gabriel Villeré failed to see the first
redcoats as they approached through an orange grove near the house.

When he did, it was too late. He attempted to flee, but the British
quickly took possession of the house, capturing him and easily over-
coming the entire company of thirty militiamen he commanded.

New Orleans was now just seven miles away, an easy two-hour
march along what General Keane regarded as a "tolerably good" road.[20]
Despite Colonel Thornton's argument that they should take the fight

immediately to the Americans, the British made camp. After long nights on the barges, they hoped for a full night's rest. The invasion, months in the making, could wait until tomorrow. This would be their first critical mistake.

A Daring Escape

Though a captive in his own house, Major Villeré refused to resign himself to his fate. Despite being closely guarded, he saw an opportunity and made his move. Managing to get to a window, he leapt out, knocking several surprised British soldiers outside to the ground. He ran for the fence at the edge of a field; to the pop of gunfire and musket balls whistling past his head, he hurdled over the barrier. Before the riflemen could get him in their sights, he disappeared into the dense cypress wood.

The fleeing prisoner understood he was one man pursued by many, but he knew his home terrain well. He raced deeper into the woods, headed for one of the enormous trees he had known since boyhood. He would climb high, he thought, and obscure himself in its dense vegetation. But when he halted at the foot of a great live oak with its netting of Spanish moss, he heard a familiar whimper. There, at his feet, crouched his bird dog, who had dutifully followed her master.

Gabriel Villeré had only moments—he could hear the approaching voices of the British searchers calling to one another—but knew immediately that his dog would betray him. With a heavy heart, he struck the animal with a large stick, killing his friendly traitor. After concealing her body, he ascended into the canopy, and the British proceeded without finding him.

Later that morning, after concluding he had eluded them, the British returned to the plantation. Villeré made his escape. As the Scotsman George Gleig ruefully observed, "The rumour of our landing would, we knew, spread faster than we could march."[21]

"The British Are Below"

At 1:30 p.m. on December 23, 1814, Jackson, at work in his parlor, heard hoofbeats. Three men galloped up to the stoop at 106 Rue Royale and announced that they had important intelligence for the general.

Jackson ordered them admitted.

"What news do you bring, gentlemen?" Jackson asked from his seat.

The breathless Gabriel Villeré, who just hours earlier had escaped the British, had borrowed a horse and hurried to Jackson's headquarters along with two of his neighbors. Though Villeré spoke French, he had Jackson's complete attention as one of the other men translated.

"The British . . . nine miles below the city . . . Villeré"—indicating Gabriel—"captured . . . escaped."

At last Jackson had the information he needed. The long waiting game was over. The world's most powerful army had at last invaded the shores of Louisiana, and after weeks of wondering where and when they would strike, Jackson finally had clarity. He hammered his fist on the table before him as he rose to his full height.

"By the Eternal," he exclaimed, "they shall not sleep on our soil!"

Summoning his staff officers, Jackson ordered that wine be served and, with glass in hand, thanked Villeré for his news. Then he turned to his officers and aides-de-camp.

"Gentlemen," he said simply, "the British are below, we must fight them tonight."[22]

His voice was even, his manner calm, but no one missed the man's absolute determination. Orders were soon flying in every direction. Drumbeats sounded in the streets, and the firing of three cannons signaled to the city a call to arms.

General Carroll and his men were dispatched in the direction of upper Bayou Bienvenue. North of town, under the command of Governor Claiborne, Louisiana militiamen would stand guard over the wide road through the Plain of Gentilly—because Jackson fully expected a British assault on more than one front, he didn't want to leave his back door open. Meanwhile, Edward Livingston relayed to Master Commander Patterson aboard the USS *Carolina* orders to weigh anchor and sail downstream.

Jackson would lead the attack force, which would include the Seventh and Forty-Fourth U.S. Infantry, the Creole battalions, the Choctaws, and a corps of freemen. Together with the marines and the artillery company, Jackson would march south with more than 1,600 men. This assembled army would proceed six miles to the Rodriguez Canal and meet up with Coffee's mounted brigade and the Mississippi dragoons.

With the first stage of his plan prepared, General Jackson could respond to a message received from a lady of New Orleans who wrote on behalf of the women of the city. Alarmed at the rumored British approach, she asked what were they to do if the city was attacked.

"Say to the ladies," Jackson instructed an aide, "not to be uneasy.

No British soldier shall enter the city as an enemy, unless over my dead body."[23]

With that, he ate a small helping of boiled rice, then stretched his lanky frame upon the sofa and closed his eyes for an afternoon nap.[24] With a long and uncertain evening before him, the weary general could use a few minutes' rest. By sunset, the city would be empty of troops— and Jackson would be at the head of his army, marching toward a nighttime fight. The British at their bivouac, just nine miles away, were going to get some unexpected visitors.

CHAPTER 10

The First Battle of New Orleans

Wellington's heroes discovered that they were ill-qualified to contend with us in woods where they must fight knee-deep in water.

—Major Arsène Lacarrière Latour

As Villeré had rushed to Jackson's headquarters, the British took stock of their position in preparation for their attack. Admiral Cochrane remained at the mouth of Bayou Bienvenue at Fisherman's Village, while Keane made the Villeré dwelling house his army's headquarters. The advance guard marched past the house and, bearing right, reached a larger road a short distance on. There the troops halted, taking in a view of more large plantations beyond. These great farms lined the flat, dry ribbon of land all the way to New Orleans.

Though the landscape was dotted with fruit trees, sugarcane was the main crop grown there. Ditches that fed into bayous and swamps to the north drained the fields that, now brown and scruffy, had yielded the year's harvest to machete-wielding slaves and overseers. Bounded as it was on one side by the marshes and, to the south, by the

Mississippi, the site seemed defensible, as good a place to pause before the attack as any. Stacking their guns within reach, Keane's men formed a bivouac in the open fields. Here they would lay out their bedrolls for the night.

The levee—"a lofty and strong embankment, resembling the dykes in Holland, and meant to serve a similar purpose," as George Gleig described it—protected the encampment, since the ground on which they camped was below the level of the water on the other side.[1] Exhausted from their journey through this strange terrain, the British posted a watch, positioning pickets at the periphery of their mile-long camp. Scouting parties dispersed to reconnoiter; some returned having helped themselves at the abandoned cabins and poultry yards they found, carrying hams, cheeses, wines, and other goods. Meanwhile, other soldiers dismantled nearby rail fences made of resinous cypress to build large fires. With smoke swirling into the sky, water was brought from the river.

"Fatigued," General Keane noted, after their "long confinement in the boats," the soldiers set about making an afternoon dinner.[2]

With two brigades of reinforcements soon to land to his rear at Bayou Bienvenue, General Keane planned to wait until the full force from Pea Island caught up. Some of the soldiers took advantage of the warm afternoon, washing up in the river. The relaxed air was broken briefly when, shortly after three o'clock, a bugle warning sent the troops scrambling for their guns. Within minutes, however, the all clear was sounded. A few American cavalrymen had been sighted but they quickly scampered—one of them wounded, the pickets claimed—when fired on by the British advance guard.

A calm set in once again in the camp. Tomorrow they would move on but, as the crisp December night fell, the men warmed themselves around their campfires, more comfortable and better fed than they had been in a week.

British confidence ran so high that Admiral Cochrane and General Keane had ordered the posting of handbills on plantation fences that announced their coming. "LOUISIANANS! REMAIN QUIET IN YOUR HOUSES," the flyers read. "YOUR SLAVES SHALL BE PRESERVED TO YOU, AND YOUR PROPERTY RESPECTED. WE MAKE WAR ONLY AGAINST AMERICANS!"[3]

The British, confident that the people of New Orleans were too newly American to have any sense of patriotism, were sure they would divide and conquer.

Firefight!

Shortly after seven o'clock, one of Keane's lookouts atop the levee spotted a ship in the Mississippi just out of musket range. The British had been relaxed, unworried, laughter ringing out from time to time, but now the easy mood of the evening tensed.

Though silhouetted against the opposite bank, the large vessel defied identification. Might it be a Royal Navy cruiser coming to render assistance?

Or could it be the enemy?

With her sails furled, she wasn't going anywhere. The British on the shore hailed the vessel but got no answer. They tried firing into the air but, once more, all remained quiet on the water. No response.

When the soldiers standing on the levee heard a loud splash, the noise remained a mystery. But aboard the USS *Carolina*, every sailor among the hundred-man crew knew the cause. They had cast a great weight into the sea—that sound had been the bow anchor striking the surface of the Mississippi.

When the anchor struck bottom, Commodore Patterson's men pulled its cable taut. Slowly the eighty-nine-foot vessel came about, her bow pointing into the current flowing toward the sea. She stood steady and ready, her starboard side aligned with the shoreline a few hundred yards away.

In the quiet of the night, the American schooner had just become a floating battery. Armed with three long nine-pound cannons and a dozen twelve-pound carronades, she was perfectly positioned to unleash a broadside. The gunners carefully set their sights on "the [British] fires, like so many landmarks or beacons, enabl[ing] the Americans to point their guns accordingly."[4]

At 7:30 p.m., the onlookers on the shore heard a deep, loud voice, speaking in English. The man's exclamation echoed over the water.

"Now, damn their eyes, give it 'em!"[5]

In the next moment, brilliant muzzle flashes revealed the full outline of the ship. The accompanying thunder of cannons preceded by barely a heartbeat the crash of grapeshot. Well-aimed shot struck the British fires, scattering burning wood and blazing embers; kettles crashed to ground. The cannon fire landed "like so many thunderbolts amongst the astounded troops."[6] Men were knocked to the ground; others were wounded and killed in their sleep.

The calm of the evening, all in a minute, gave way to complete havoc. The British soldiers raced for their arms, looking at the sky and out to sea as the enemy warship continued to pound the camp with regular and accurate fire.

Ground Attack

The king's troops found shelter behind the levee, but their answering muskets did little harm, and the guns of the USS *Carolina* continued to lob deadly iron into the camp. Some soldiers worked to extinguish the fires and to drag wounded men, unable to seek cover on their own, to safety. British artillerists managed to discharge a few rockets in the direction of the ship, but the skyrockets, too, failed to do damage.

After ten minutes the bombardment from the *Carolina* slackened—but Andrew Jackson's second surprise was about to be delivered.

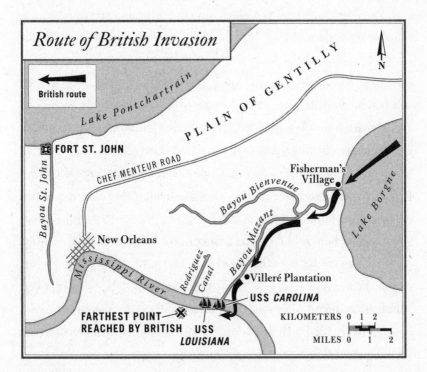

Lying prostrate behind the levee, British soldiers heard the report of muskets from the vicinity of their sentinels; there, with no moon to illuminate their attackers, the advance guard "mistook every tree for an American."[7] As the sporadic gunshots gave way to rapid volleys, a new sense of alarm swept through the British ranks. The realization dawned that the Americans were launching another assault—and this one was coming not from the water but from the land.

Jackson's main force had marched along the river to the Rodriguez Canal; once there, at Jackson's orders, they had moved in near silence to within five hundred yards of the British sentinels and formed a line perpendicular to the river. Two brass fieldpieces were readied, and the troops had waited for the *Carolina* to begin her bombardment.

Now they attacked. With Jackson's line advancing on the stunned British defenders, the artillerymen with their six-pounders began a deadly fire that crashed into the besieged encampment.

Jackson had dispatched Coffee's mounted Tennesseans, together with Beale's Rifles and the Mississippi dragoons, to his left. This substantial force also included Pierre Lafitte and some of his Baratarians.[8] Together, this secondary force had skirted the swamp behind the Villeré plantation and, on hearing the musket fire from the main front, Coffee's vanguard also attacked, driving into the rear of the British right flank.

The tactic was the classic pincer move Jackson favored. To the British, already back on their heels, the effect was frightening, giving them the sense, Lieutenant Gleig reported, that "the heavens were illuminated on all sides by a semi-circular blaze of musketry."[9]

To the battle-hardened British troops, however, this was nothing new. Colonel Thornton ordered his men into action, and two battalions charged the main line of oncoming Americans. Many men fell but the

British penetrated the American line. Catching sight of the American artillery position, they made a bold push for the guns, managing to wound some of the draft horses and upset one of the cannons. But the marines charged with protecting them took to heart General Jackson's words.

"Save the guns, my boys," he called to them, "at every sacrifice!"[10]

Seeing what was unfolding before him, Jackson then spurred his horse and charged into the fray. He was "within pistol shot, in the midst of a shower of bullets, . . . urging on the marines." The fighting was so hot that one of Jackson's officers questioned whether the general wasn't "expos[ing] himself rather too much."[11] But they held the guns and moved forward.

Meanwhile, General Coffee, who had ordered his men to dismount in order "to give them a freer and more certain use of the rifle," attacked the right flank of the British.[12] The fresh fire from these superior marksmen was murderous, made more terrifying by the blackness of the night. Beale's Rifles joined Coffee's men, adding to the pressure on the British.

Having softened up the redcoat ranks with their gunfire, the Americans advanced into the darkness and into their camp. Muzzle fire flashed in the gloom but, even at close range, the darkness and clouds of gun smoke made it nearly impossible to distinguish friend from foe. Shouts of "Don't fire, we are your friends!"[13] rang out as both Americans and British encountered friendly fire in the confusion.

Wary of shooting their own, infantrymen fought hand to hand, bayonet to bayonet, and sword to sword. The British used their guns as clubs, and the Tennesseans who carried tomahawks and hunting knives didn't hesitate to use them. In the darkness, officers lost control of their men, and soon it was each man fighting his own duel in the dark. "No man could tell what was going forward in any quarter," reported Gleig, "except where he himself chanced immediately to stand; no one part of the line could bring assistance to another, because, in truth, no line existed. It was in one word a perfect tumult."[14] The entire assault was a shock to the invaders: as Colonel Thornton observed, "This bold attacking us in our camp is a new feature in American warfare."[15]

As the fighting entered its second hour, the clouds began to break and a quarter moon cast its ghostly light on the field of battle. At first, the direction of the light better illuminated the faces of the American attackers, giving the British a decided advantage. But soon a ground fog rolled in off the river, decreasing visibility again. Finally, with conditions worsening near nine o'clock, Jackson ordered his men to withdraw from the field. They had accomplished enough for one night. Though localized skirmishing continued for some time, most of the Americans marched back upriver, halting at a canal on a nearby plantation. The British retired to their camp.

Counting the Dead

On the morning after, surgeons on both sides worked to save what lives they could. Jackson's surprise attack inflicted serious damage: 24 Americans were dead, 115 wounded, and 74 missing and presumed captured. But enemy casualties were much greater: according to one British source, the toll was more than 500 men. Roughly a square mile in area, the battlefield was tragic to behold, and even a veteran of the French wars like George Gleig was stunned by the carnage. "Not only were the wounds themselves exceedingly frightful, but the very countenances of the dead exhibited the most savage and ghastly expressions. . . . Such had been the deadly closeness of the strife that . . . an English and American soldier might be seen with the bayonet of each fastened in the other's body."[16]

Most of the wounded Americans were carried back to New Orleans, while the injured British were treated at the Villeré plantation, where a makeshift field hospital was established. Doctors amputated limbs and bandaged wounds, while soldiers buried the dead. The wounded British healthy enough to travel were loaded aboard the barges and taken to the fleet. Their beds on land would be needed soon enough; more casualties would surely follow.

General Keane was stunned at the outcome of this first real battle with General Jackson's makeshift army. The Americans had penetrated deeply into the British camp; the British had yielded ground. They had won it back, but what would have happened had Jackson not withdrawn his men? Unable or unwilling to believe that fewer than two thousand Americans could have done such damage to his force of roughly the same size, Keane exaggerated the size of the American force in his report of the battle, more than doubling the actual count.

The intimidation factor of the great Royal Army was beginning to fade; the Americans had held their own. The fight had temporarily halted the advance of the British, and the Americans had demonstrated to their enemy that they could fight the best military in the world. In the hours before the battle, those British who had faced the American militia outside Washington hadn't felt "the smallest sensation of alarm" at seeing American troops nearby. "We held them in too much contempt to fear their attack."[17] A dozen hours later, however, they had been shocked into acknowledging that these American forces, under the command of Andrew Jackson, were a high-caliber opponent.

Most of Jackson's troops were inexperienced; the fresh mix of militiamen and regulars and volunteers had never fought together until that day. Yet the American officers and their men seemed to possess a dangerous mix of military skills that caught the British off guard—initiative, strategic thinking, determination, and fighting techniques. Many of them were superb marksmen, their guns deadly accurate, and even in hand-to-hand combat the American soldier had held his own.

Above all, Andrew Jackson demonstrated he was a man to be reckoned with. In just five hours he had formulated a combined land-and-sea assault plan, assembled a dispersed and diverse force, marched it undetected to the enemy camp, and reduced the king's attackers to near total confusion. Then he and his men had slipped away just as they had come.

Newly aware of how potent their opponents could be, the British recognized the need to exercise caution—meaning that, once again, the Americans had bought themselves time, precious hours and even days to dig in, to establish a solid line of defense at their new camp.

Less than two miles away from the British, Jackson was determined to hold the line, to halt a British march on New Orleans.

December 24, 1814

Under very different circumstances, the British and American peace commissioners met that same day, an ocean away, in Ghent, Belgium. Assembling at a former monastery on the Rue des Chartreux, the teams of negotiators arrived on Christmas Eve afternoon to sign an agreed-upon treaty of peace.

The document actually decided little; it was essentially an agreement to halt hostilities. The first article stated, "There shall be a firm and universal Peace between His Britannic Majesty and the United States," but, amazingly, key issues such as impressment and harassment of trade, the very matters that had led to the American war declaration, were not mentioned.

Henry Clay thought it was a "damn bad treaty," but, like everyone else, he wanted the war to be over.

The American copies of the treaty would cross the Atlantic in a small leather document box; with delays due to stormy weather, it would take thirty-eight days to reach New York. The treaty wouldn't reach President Madison's study in Washington until February 14, 1815. As for New Orleans, the news of the peace would come far too late to avoid the casualties sustained by both sides in the interim. Just as important, the treaty's terms would not be in full force and effect until the governments in both capitals ratified the document.

Thus, the future of the city of New Orleans and the territory of Louisiana—as well as the lives of many men—hung in the balance. The pressure stayed on General Jackson. Now that he knew the route the British assault would take, his job would be to establish a solid defensive line.

CHAPTER 11

The Defensive Line

> It is true the enemy is on our coast and threatens an invasion
> of our territory, but it is equally true, with union, energy, and
> the approbation of Heaven, we will beat him at every point.
>
> **—Andrew Jackson**

"I expect the enemy is pretty sore today," General Jackson observed on the morning after the firefight.[1] Even so, with British reinforcements continuing to step ashore at Bayous Bienvenue and Mazant, a counterattack seemed inevitable.

But when?

Spies reported that, at least for the moment, the British looked to be stationary. But Jackson couldn't just wait—not a minute could be wasted—and he made sure the men around him were anything but idle.

When falling back from the field of battle the night before, the army had marched across several plantation properties toward New Orleans. At 4:00 a.m., Jackson ordered a halt at the Rodriguez Canal, two miles upstream from the British front at the Villeré plantation and six miles short of New Orleans.

This was to be his line in the silty Louisiana soil, and he would make it a breastwork he could defend. The *Carolina* could provide supporting artillery fire from the river and, in the course of the morning, she would be reinforced by the arrival of her sister ship, the *Louisiana*. Commodore Patterson's crew was a motley one—there were Yankees, Portuguese, Norwegians, Spanish, Greeks, Italians, Germans, Arabs, Hindus, and Swedes aboard. As Patterson advised the secretary of the navy, "the crew of the Louisiana is composed of men of all nations, (English excepted) taken from the streets of New Orleans."[2] In other words, this force was diverse enough to be pure American.

General Jackson took Augustin Macarty's mansion for his headquarters. The large house stood on piers, with the main living quarters raised a full story above the Mississippi floodplain. The porch that

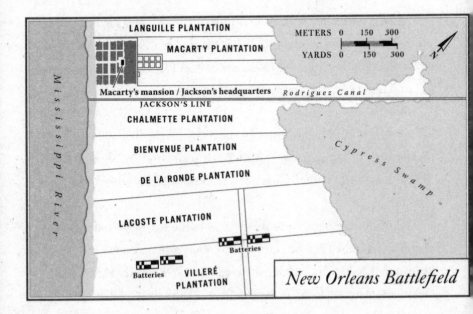

New Orleans Battlefield

swept around the perimeter overlooked the Rodriguez Canal to the east, just a hundred yards away. On the other side of the canal lay another plantation, the property of the Creole family Chalmette, its roughly two hundred acres of open fields mostly given over to the cultivation of sugarcane. From the dormers that peered out of the steep roof of the Macarty house, Jackson, using a telescope, took in a broad view of the more distant British encampment located on two other properties, the Bienvenue and De La Ronde plantations.

Jackson ordered platoons of Mississippi mounted rifles and Louisiana dragoons to patrol the no-man's-land in between the two armies. But the rest of his men were about to become ditchdiggers.

A nearby disused millstream (it had once powered a sawmill), the so-called Rodriguez Canal held no water. Four feet deep and twenty wide, the ditch extended north-south at the boundary of the Macarty plantation. Its strategic value lay in the fact that it ran at a right angle all the way from the levee at the river's edge to a nearly impenetrable wooded swamp at the far edge of the field.

Jackson consulted his chief engineer, Major Arsène Lacarrière Latour, who knew the soils and topography of the region intimately. Latour agreed with Jackson's assessment: Once cleared of weeds and silt, the Rodriguez Canal could be flooded with water from the river to serve as a moat, an obstacle to an oncoming army. And parapets could be raised on the New Orleans side of the canal, ramparts behind which American soldiers and artillery could take cover.

Jackson issued an order to have every shovel in the area commandeered. By the time the morning fog had burned off, Jackson's men were at work, spades in hand, together with slaves from nearby plantations. They moved earth forward from behind the line to form an embankment and used posts taken from nearby fences to prevent the rising mound of soil from falling into the ditch. Other men worked at cutting a sluiceway to permit the flow of water into the canal, and Jackson ordered more channels dug in the levee to flood open land between the armies. Having to march through mud and standing water, Jackson thought, would slow any British attack.[3]

Working in shifts, the army labored through Christmas Day and into the night. The job would be a long one, requiring more than a day or even two or three. But no one knew how much time they had.

Jackson himself supervised. On his horse, he was a constant presence, vigilant and refusing to sleep. One of Rachel's nephews, a captain in the Tennessee militia, soon observed the toll the intense days were taking on the general. "Uncle Jackson," he wrote home, "looks very badly at present, and has broken very much."[4]

His body suffering, Jackson's spirit was strong. When one British prisoner reported to him that Admiral Cochrane had sworn he would take his Christmas dinner in New Orleans, Jackson had a sharp answer.

"Perhaps so," he snapped, "but I shall have the honor of presiding at that dinner."[5]

London's Christmas Gift

On the other side of the line, the British needed some bucking up. The cold, damp weather sat heavily on the exposed soldiers, another hardship after the bitter journey in the barges.

The regular boom of the guns aboard the *Carolina* and now the *Louisiana* continued to endanger life and limb. Even on Christmas Day the British troops had to remain ever-wary of incoming rounds and shrapnel. As one group of officers shared a Christmas dinner made from their dwindling stock of provisions, they heard a loud scream. The men raced outside the little building where they had been eating and found a soldier mortally wounded by a cannonball. "Though fairly cut in two at the lower part of the belly," George Gleig reported, "the poor wretch lived for nearly an hour, gasping for breath."[6]

The risks were constant. Anyone who ventured into the no-man's-land between the two encampments was a target for sharp-eyed American snipers and, once night fell, any exposed Britishers were in danger of periodic hit-and-run volleys from American cavalry and stealthy visits from the Choctaws. Some five dozen Indians armed with tomahawks and bands of Tennesseans with long rifles made deadly work of sneaking up on—and killing—British sentries. The British thought this behavior uncivilized but it had its effect. As one British quartermaster reported, the invaders were robbed of "much time for comfortable rest."[7]

Then, at two o'clock on Christmas afternoon, the British got a gift that lifted their spirits. The Americans were still digging on their side of the battlefield-to-be, but their pickets, stationed forward of the line, heard loud cheering from the British position. When pistol shots rang out and an artillery salvo was fired, everyone snapped to attention.

Were the British attacking?

They were celebrating. In the enemy camp, a name ricocheted from unit to unit: the Honorable Sir Edward Pakenham, major general, had arrived. And the happy news lifted morale instantly.

To the British fighters, "Ned" Pakenham was one of them. He had proved himself on battlefields across Spain and France. Though born to the nobility as the son of an earl, he wasn't afraid to put himself at risk. In helping defeat Napoleon, he repeatedly demonstrated his valor, charging headlong into enemy ranks; his rout of one French force had earned him the nickname Hero of Salamanca. He had been injured in battle many times, including two musket wounds to the neck. The first, it was said, left the legendary fighter with a pronounced tilt to his head; the second, sustained years later, left him with his military posture restored.[8]

A survivor on his own terms, Pakenham was also brother-in-law to the formidable Duke of Wellington, who admired his leadership. "My partiality for him does not lead me astray when I tell you he is one of the best we have," Wellington said of Pakenham. (The Iron Duke himself would not go to America; he was both dubious at the likely outcome—"I don't promise myself much success there," he mused—and otherwise engaged in Paris, where he was wrapping up affairs after being named British ambassador to France.) But on the outskirts of New Orleans, Sir Edward had something new to prove: this campaign was his first independent command and, if he succeeded in taking the city, he carried with him a paper commissioning him as the governor of the captured territory.[9]

Shortly after his arrival, General Pakenham set off for an inspection of the front to see for himself the nature of the landscape and the position of his enemy. Almost immediately, he began to question the decisions made by General Keane and Admiral Cochrane; soon he was furious, recognizing the dangerous position he had been handed.

He and his new command were in a box, with a narrow path of attack that was confined by the river on one side and the swamp on the other. Dead ahead there was an American force busily digging itself in. Behind lay a narrow path of retreat. The source of supply was the fleet, moored sixty miles away, with only small open boats to deliver food, men, and munitions. Communications were poor.

In short, as Pakenham saw it, the first fight with the Americans had left the British with an "ominous result," a position of real "jeopardy."[10] One of his officers reported that Pakenham was so angry that his cursing was overheard by men of all ranks.

Still, he had a job to do: he would have to extricate his force; he had to devise and execute a plan that he thought would work. He convened a meeting of the advisers he'd brought with him, together with Keane and Cochrane and their officers.

Sitting in the parlor of the Villeré house—the owner was with his Louisiana militiamen, awaiting the battle on other side of the line—Pakenham didn't mince words. "Our troops should have advanced to New Orleans immediately [on December 23]," he told them. That failure, he said, was an "error."[11] If they had marched straight on, rather than pausing for the night, the city might already be theirs.

Keane and Cochrane shifted the subject to the fight of December 23, attempting to portray the battle as a British victory. Keane claimed that he and his men had held their ground and "repulsed" the attacking Americans who, after attacking, had "thought it prudent to retire [from the field of battle]."

Pakenham disagreed. He saw the night battle quite simply as a "defeat."[12]

That brought the discussion around to their present position.

Pakenham told the officers around him that he was considering a full withdrawal. A better plan could be made, he believed. The entire operation could begin afresh. This fine British force could be deployed elsewhere and odds of a big victory increased.

At this, Admiral Cochrane exploded.

The seasoned navy veteran would have none of it. Cochrane rejected Pakenham's argument: he didn't see defeat—far from it. And the very suggestion that he, his men, and his plan had failed made him immensely angry.

The now-furious Cochrane challenged Pakenham: if the general's army couldn't do the job of taking New Orleans, he threatened, Cochrane's sailors and marines of the Royal Navy would storm the American lines and move on New Orleans.

"The soldiers could then," he taunted Pakenham caustically, "bring up the baggage."[13]

For a moment, the men were at an impasse.

Pakenham was taken aback by Cochrane's outrage, but he knew he needed the admiral's willing cooperation. Under these circumstances, there could be no wholesale rethinking of the strategy, and he realized he had no choice but to relent. As the guns of the *Carolina* and the *Louisiana* continued to send cannonballs into the British encampment, Pakenham resigned himself to trying to make the best of what he recognized was a wretched situation.

He would begin by destroying the *Carolina*.

A Shattering Surprise

On December 27, Andrew Jackson awakened from his first sustained sleep in three days. Following a quiet day of supervising the digging on the American side, the general, to his dismay, found that the British had decided to begin this new day with a barrage of artillery fire shortly after seven o'clock.

Jackson hurried to the dormer windows on the top floor of the Macarty mansion. He saw that the British objective was neither his army nor the line at the Rodriguez Canal. Instead, the enemy cannons

bombarded the USS *Carolina,* which had annoyed them with its guns
for several days.

Billowing smoke revealed the position of the British guns, dug in
downstream on the levee. Standing near them was General Edward
Pakenham himself, commanding an artillery battery that, as far as
Jackson knew, hadn't even existed just the day before. And the guns
were new to the battle, too, longer and with greater range than the
ones his men had faced four days before.

A corps of officers had arrived with Pakenham, one of whom was
artillery commander Colonel Alexander Dickson. Regarded as one
of the ablest gunners in the Royal Army, he had been Wellington's
artillery commander and fought with Pakenham at Salamanca, Spain.
He had immediately taken charge of the guns that, after arriving on
the bayous in boats and barges, had been dragged along the path toward the river by horses. Cochrane promised larger guns would follow
but, as of Christmas Day, the Royal Artillery had on hand a pair of
nine-pounders, four six-pounders, four three-pounders, and two five-
and-a-half-inch howitzers.

Dickson and his men had positioned them to destroy the *Carolina.*
Wishing to keep their strategy secret—as well as to avoid drawing fire
from the *Carolina*—the guns had been brought to the levee after dark
on Christmas night. Colonel Dickson ordered that the guns be spaced
out over a distance of several hundred yards, and trenches were dug
into the rear of the levee to protect the guns from returning fire. The
barrels were set just above grade, and the carriages rested on lengths
of wood repurposed from nearby fencing to prevent the heavy iron
weapons from sinking into the soft ground. With their work nearly
completed before dawn on December 26, the redcoats camouflaged
the guns with bundles of sugarcane stalks left on the fields after the

harvest. The British withdrew before daylight; they would wait a day before firing, since needed artillery rounds were still arriving on the bayous.

After sunset, the British had gone back to work. They made their final preparations and, at 2:00 a.m., the gunners lit fires to heat the nine-pound balls. The artillerymen had their orders: General Pakenham wished them to commence fire at daylight.

On the morning of December 27, with the firing under way and the booms of the British guns filling his ears, Jackson issued an order that the *Louisiana,* presently moored less than a mile upstream from the *Carolina,* sail out of range. The *Carolina* returned the British fire with her twelve-pounder, the only gun aboard with the range to hit the British position from the ship's mooring on the far side of the Mississippi.

Jackson watched helplessly as deadly accurate British gunnery began to take its toll. Within a half hour, a cannonball baked in a fire as hot as a blacksmith's furnace crashed through the deck of the *Carolina*. It came to rest deep in the ship's main hold, beneath the control cables, a spot difficult for the crew to reach. The hot shot soon ignited a fire whose flames spread rapidly and, within minutes, the uncontrollable blaze was consuming the schooner from within.

More hot shot struck the ship. With several fires threatening to envelop the vessel, the crew had no alternative but to abandon ship. As nine o'clock approached, with flames licking closer and closer to the powder magazine belowdecks, the crew, some of them Lafitte's pirates, managed to roll two of the ship's cannons overboard before they clambered into the *Carolina*'s boats, pushed off, and rowed madly for shore.

When the powder in the hold exploded, windows rattled miles away in New Orleans. Shattered and flaming remnants of the schooner, sent skyward by the blast, hissed into the water and fell to earth as far away as the opposite side of the Mississippi. In the momentary quiet that followed, ash and debris continued to rain down—and the soldiers on the American line heard shouts and cheers from the British side.

Then the enemy fire resumed and, with knowing dread, Andrew Jackson observed that the British had shifted the trajectory of their cannon fire toward the last of the American warships. The USS *Louisiana,* though more than a mile upstream, had just become the target.

Her crew had unfurled her sails, but the *Louisiana,* aided by no more than a whisper of wind and fighting the Mississippi current, could make no headway upstream; that was her only escape route. To the men across the river, British and American alike, the outcome seemed inevitable—but one option remained to save her from the British fire that was now breaking over her quarterdeck. If the wind could not deliver the ship to safety, then manpower would have to do the job.

The *Louisiana*'s boats went over the side, followed by her sailors as they clambered into position at their oars. As if to emphasize the importance of their errand, a shell smashed into the deck of the immobilized ship.

With great ropes tethered to the ninety-nine-foot sloop, the sailors strained at their oars. Other men standing in the shallow water near the shore pulled on ropes, too, but once the cables were taut, the scene seemed frozen, with the little boats, like children tugging on their mother's apron strings, striving to pull the immobilized *Louisiana* to safety.

At first: nothing. Then, slowly, almost imperceptibly, the mother ship began to move. Despite continued fire, fortune was with the Americans and the oarsmen managed to pull the *Louisiana* the half mile needed to get out of the range of the British ordnance.

This time the Americans cheered and, with the cessation of British artillery fire, the day's hostilities came to an end.

A British Assault

The assault on Patterson's little flotilla had blown up one ship and driven the other out of range. Although that action made a direct attack on Jackson's line more feasible, General Pakenham still lacked clear knowledge of his opponent's power and position. The persistent American snipers and militia cavalry patrolling the area between the armies had limited British reconnaissance, a problem that, Pakenham knew, he must correct.

From their position, all the British could see of the American force were the unimpressive cavalry patrols, which, Dickson reported, consisted of men wearing "a kind of blanket dress." The volunteer soldiers had been issued no uniforms, but were dressed in woolen shirts, homemade trousers, and hats of wool or raccoon skin. With long hair and scruffy, unkempt beards, these woodsmen carried "long muskets or rifles."[14]

On December 28, Pakenham organized his force to advance for the purpose of "reconnoit[ering] the enemy's position, or to attack if . . . practicable."[15] He wanted to get closer, to get a better sense of how large Jackson's force was, to try softening up the defenses. The Americans still had to prove themselves to the war-hardened Pakenham.

A frosty morning mist had burned off when four British regiments,

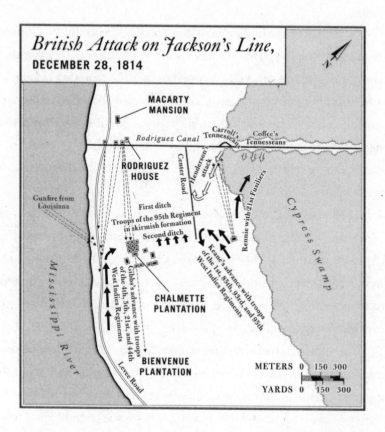

British Attack on Jackson's Line,
DECEMBER 28, 1814

MACARTY MANSION

Rodriguez Canal   Carroll's Tennesseans   Coffee's Tennesseans

RODRIGUEZ HOUSE

Center Road

Henderson's attack

Gunfire from Louisiana

First ditch

Troops of the 95th Regiment in skirmish formation

Second ditch

Keane's advance with troops of the 1st, 85th, 93rd, and 95th West Indies Regiments

Rennie with 21st Fusiliers

Cypress Swamp

Gibbs's advance with troops of the 4th, 5th, 21st, and 44th West Indies Regiments

CHALMETTE PLANTATION

Mississippi River

Levee Road

BIENVENUE PLANTATION

METERS 0   150 300

YARDS   0   150 300

commanded by General Keane, advanced along the edge of the swamp. Four other regiments stepped off along the levee road, led by General Samuel Gibbs, who had arrived with Pakenham as his second in command. Artillerists supported both columns, prepared to bombard the Americans with mortars and rockets.

As the redcoats moved closer to the American line, the rising sun in a clear sky revealed a breastwork before them that, in some places, had reached five feet in height. The American line spanned the terrain from the riverbank to the cypress swamp. When Edward Livingston had brought Jean Lafitte to inspect the line of defense a few days earlier, the privateer had immediately spied a vulnerability. "Lafitte thinks our line to afford complete protection ought to be extended *through* the first wood, to the cypress swamp," Livingston told Jackson.[16] Out of respect for Lafitte's understanding of the local terrain and impressed by his grasp of military tactics, Jackson acted upon the suggestion at once, ordering the line to be extended deep enough into the swampy perimeter that any skirting the end of the defense was a practical impossibility.

Accompanying his men on horseback, Pakenham was surprised to see the muzzles of at least five big guns protruding through the crude crenellations along the top of the parapet. The built-up ramparts were clearly still a work in progress, varying greatly in height and thickness along a line that seemed to bend back on itself near the cypress swamp to follow its boundary.

Jackson's men had constructed redoubts for four artillery batteries. Since the ground softened to a soggy mix of mud and groundwater at a depth of three feet, the general had once again adopted someone else's idea, one that may have been suggested by a ditch-digging slave. The suggestion was to bring bales of unshipped cotton, warehoused in the city, to fill and stiffen the muddy hollows. Jackson ordered it done, and girdled by iron rings, the bales were buried beneath a layer of dirt, with wooden platforms for the guns mounted on top. Two of the cannons were good-size twenty-four-pounders. Two of the gunnery crews were Baratarians, who had arrived that very morning, "red-shirted, bewhiskered, rough and desperate-looking men, all begrimed with smoke and mud."[17]

As the British approached, the outnumbered American pickets in the fields fired volleys but quickly retreated. Pakenham's columns marched forward and soon came within half a mile of the Rodriguez

Canal. The oncoming British troops made an impressive sight in their colorful uniforms of red, gray, green, and tartan, marching to the beat of drums and the call of bugles. To the novice soldiers on the American side this was their first real look at the mighty British war machine on the march. Even as rockets began exploding overhead and British artillery lobbed shells and deadly iron toward the American line, the disciplined British "veterans moved as steadily and closely together as if marching in review."[18]

When the American gunners began returning fire, however, their aim proved deadly: "Scarce a bullet passed over, or fell short of its mark," Gleig recorded, "but all striking full into the midst of our ranks, occasioned terrible havoc."[19] Master Commander Daniel Patterson and the men aboard the *Louisiana,* moored on the opposite bank of the Mississippi, fired a broadside that swept the line of redcoats along the levee. Over the next several hours, the ship's guns would maintain a constant fire, bombarding the British with eight hundred shots, now that the enemy was back in their range.

Hearing the screams of their wounded, the British column hesitated and then stopped. At the order of their officers, the men by the levee sought shelter in ditches, behind tall reeds, finding whatever cover they could.

The British column advancing along the swampland on the other side of the field fared better. They had to deal with fire from the Americans' left flank, manned by Tennesseans under the command of Generals Coffee and Carroll, but they were out of range of the *Louisiana.*

Seeking to get a better understanding of the situation, Pakenham dismounted and moved forward on foot for a better look at the American batteries and battlement. One thing was clear immediately: his limited artillery was inadequate in the face of such fire. He sent back word that work should begin immediately on an earthwork to bring forward his own guns.

Meanwhile, the *Louisiana* continued to bombard the troops closer to the levee, and the land guns mounted on the ramparts maintained a steady fire, aiming in particular at the small British artillery installations.

As the fight unfolded, Jackson received an uninvited visitor, one bringing news from Governor Claiborne.

In the city, he was told, there was talk of surrender: The residents knew about the British approach and their recent attacks, and had heard rumors of the enemy's sheer numbers and military power. Jackson, eager to return to his spyglass and the fight before him, listened with growing impatience to talk of the state legislature and the concern that he might not prevail in the battle now raging outside.

Finally, he had had enough.

"Return to . . . your honorable body," he said firmly, "and say to them from me, that if I was so unfortunate to be beaten . . . and compelled to retreat through New Orleans, they would have a *warm session.*"[20]

"Warm session"?

Jackson later elaborated on his meaning. If he could not defend it, he would burn the city, take up a position up the river, and cut off supplies to the British, thereby forcing them to leave the country. Quite simply, the British were not going to march victorious into any city that he was defending. Nor were any treasonous legislators with a doubtful allegiance to the United States of America going to raise the white flag.

With that, he went back to fighting his battle.

On the British side, Pakenham learned that his handful of artillery pieces were out of action, their carriages shot away. The American cannoneers got high marks for their marksmanship, and Pakenham, seeing that the attack on his left was going nowhere beneath the shower of iron from the *Louisiana*, decided to order a withdrawal.

The British soldiers, accustomed to prevailing in their battles, admitted to shame and indignation as they fell back. Their morale wasn't aided by the fact that the American gunfire required a stealthy withdrawal, one that could not be completed until after dark, leaving many redcoats lying in the field waiting for sunset. A humiliating retreat had followed a proud march into battle, and Pakenham's force slowly countermarched two miles back from the American line, making camp just beyond range of all but the largest of the enemy's cannons.

Whatever the attack's failures—surely Ned Pakenham hadn't led them to the easy victory they expected—the general had managed to get a good look at the enemy position. The deadly American guns, Pakenham resolved, would be his next objective. If he was to succeed in overrunning the American line, the enemy artillery would have to be silenced first and, with only four-, six-, and nine-pound guns at hand, Pakenham ordered that the two eighteen-pounders already dragged to Villeré's plantation be brought forward. And he ordered another eight guns to be brought from the fleet.

As Pakenham made his plans, Jackson supervised the installation of another gun at the center of his ramparts, this one a thirty-two-pounder. He knew the British would be back and better prepared, and he was going to be ready.

The New Year's Day Artillery Fight

Aside from a few minor skirmishes, the opposing armies maintained their distance for three days. Jackson waited for the enemy to make the next big move, since his force, still smaller than Pakenham's, was bet-ter protected behind the earthworks. But Jackson tolerated no idleness.

His aide-de-camp Major Latour observed that despite Jackson's evident fatigue, "the energy manifested by General Jackson spread, as it were, . . . and communicated itself to the whole army. . . . If he ordered it to be done . . . immediately a crowd of volunteers offered themselves to carry his views into execution."[21]

Jackson's directives continued to radiate in all directions. At his orders, the city of New Orleans was scoured for needed guns and ammunition, since many freshly recruited militiamen had arrived without weapons. At the front, the commanding general hadn't less-ened the pressure to reinforce the earthworks, and the excavation continued without letup. From the British line, one soldier reported, "We could plainly perceive great numbers of men continually at work upon [the American ramparts], mostly blacks . . . but their white people also (the army, we conclude) were constantly employed upon it."[22] After noting that troops at the far end of the defensive line, clos-est to the swamp, had been badly outnumbered by the force Pakenham led several days earlier, Jackson sent more men to strengthen that flank, including more Tennesseans and Choctaws.

Aware that there was a chance his major line of defense could be overrun by Pakenham's superior force, Jackson ordered his engineers to design and construct two secondary lines to the rear; one was a mile and a half west of the Rodriguez Canal, the other almost two miles closer to New Orleans. Jackson added more artillery batteries to the main front so a baker's dozen guns protruded through the de-fensive wall, ranging from a small brass carronade near the swamp to the big thirty-two-pounder near the center.

Nor had Jackson neglected the opposite bank of the river. A team of 150 slaves worked to complete a parapet lining a canal there. From the *Louisiana,* Commodore Patterson's men brought more cannons ashore—a twenty-four-pounder and two twelve-pounders—and dug them in at the right bank post. They were reinforced there by Brigadier General David Morgan and 450 Louisiana militiamen laboring at the earthworks.

But the British had been busy, too, readying to put in place a new strategy for a new year.

Silent Marching

At nightfall on New Year's Eve, half the British army advanced in near silence. They passed the position of their pickets, stopping just six hundred yards from the Rodriguez Canal. With two regiments on guard duty, the rest of the soldiers stacked their arms and went to work with the spades, picks, and sledges they carried.

Speed was of the essence: Pakenham's men were constructing new gun emplacements and had only a few hours before the sun would rise, exposing them to the guns of the watching Americans. As the men mounded up earth, sculpting a small version of the American embankment behind which their gunners could take cover, Admiral Cochrane's sailors dragged ten eighteen- and four twenty-four-pound carronades forward. They had rowed their heavy loads (the bigger guns weighed more than two tons) from the fleet at Ship Island and dragged them to the camp, using country carts designed for moving sugar barrels. Now they used the last of their strength to position the iron guns and their heavy carriages behind the new earthworks. They aimed them at the American camp.

As the sky brightened in the early hours, the American lookouts watched nervously. General Jackson and his men had heard the British at work in the darkness, and were anxious to see what the enemy had been up to. But the arrival of morning brought no clarity; a dense fog rolled in, completely concealing the field of battle.

Dread mounted as the fog lingered, leaving the Americans in uncomfortable anticipation of an attack. Interrogations of British deserters had revealed that Pakenham had called for major troop reinforcements. Once they arrived, everyone assumed he would attack, and it was possible that the sound in the night had been that of the fresh troops preparing. Then, just as the blanket of thick morning mist burned off around eight o'clock, the ominous calm gave way to the deafening din of artillery. The British were firing their newly advanced cannons at the American line. In particular, the British artillery aimed for the Macarty house, where they knew General Jackson made his headquarters.

The guns hit their mark, and the shrill scream of rockets overhead accompanied the sounds of the house's destruction. "Bricks, splinters of wood and furniture, rockets and balls," Major Latour reported, "were flying in all directions."[23] In the minutes that followed, more than a hundred cannonballs, rockets, and shells crashed into the plantation house. Its porches were "beaten down, and the building made a complete wreck." Miraculously, no one was hurt, and Jackson, as was his habit, had quickly departed—not to flee, but to fight. According to his adjutant Major Reid, it was Jackson's practice, "on the first appearance of danger . . . instantly to proceed to the line."[24]

From the front, Jackson could look upon the result of the enemy's overnight labors as the British bombardment continued: There were three new gun emplacements, crescent-shaped batteries that offered the gunnery crews protection both from the American line and from guns fired across the Mississippi. Including three mortars and two howitzers, twenty-two guns had been positioned by the English on crude wooden platforms. In the interests of speedy installation, the British had brought forward barrels of sugar found at plantations they'd ransacked as a substitute for sandbags. Rolled into place upright, the hogsheads became a protective parapet atop the batteries.

Jackson also took in another ominous sight: Some two hundred yards to the rear of the British guns stood the brightly uniformed infantry. Again, two columns had been formed into battle array, one on either side of the field, ready to attack. Less obvious was a third, smaller party, hidden in the dense cover at the edge of the swamp.[25]

There was little Jackson's men could do but hope their guns would hold off the invasion. And at the order of Jackson's chief artillerist—"*Let her off!*"—the American guns were soon returning fire.[26]

The British had more guns than the Americans, but from their lower elevation on the plain, their aim was skewed, often shooting high above their marks, sending their loads soaring over the American line. Other shots thudded harmlessly into the soft earth of the embankment, though one arching round hit an American powder carriage; the explosion was so loud, the gunnery paused briefly and a distant cheer was heard from the British line. Another almost hit its mark when it grazed the Baratarian Dominique You, a gun commander and half brother of Jean Lafitte. Furious, he swore an oath even before binding up his wound: "I will pay them for that!"[27]

Meanwhile, General Jackson rode back and forth along the line encouraging his men. "Don't mind these rockets, they are mere toys to amuse children," he told them, calming the inexperienced soldiers and rallying the seasoned.[28] His encouragement worked and the earthworks held; a few of the American guns were eventually silenced, but the parapet was little damaged by the English artillery. The Americans' fire proved better directed and, within an hour, several of the enemy guns had been put out of commission.

On the other side of the line, General Pakenham watched as his options faded. The hogsheads of sugar were ineffective; cannonballs penetrated them as if the barrels were empty. The supply of ammunition was dwindling, and his artillery fire began to slow, then became irregular; finally, by midafternoon, the British had retired from the field. "When the batteries have silenced the enemy's fire and opened his works, the position will be carried as follows . . ." read Pakenham's written orders from the night before.[29] But that had not happened. It was British artillery that had been silenced; no hole had been torn in the American line. No attack had been possible.

"We retired, therefore, not only baffled and disappointed, but in some degree disheartened and discontented," Gleig observed. "All our plans had as yet proved abortive."[30] The British fighters still had nothing to show for the hardships they had suffered over the course of the preceding days—not to mention weeks.

A New Plan

The redcoats' morale was at low ebb. To retreat was not in the nature of the Royal Army; however, as the year 1815 began, Wellington's veterans had been forced to retrace their own steps for the second time in a week. Having to laboriously drag their ordnance back to their own lines after dark on New Year's Day only added to the sense of insult. British casualty counts were at least twice the American losses.

Dysentery was taking hold in the camp, and rations were poor, the army having exhausted the resources of the surrounding plantations. The men subsisted on "maggoty pork and weevily biscuit."[31] The coffee supply had been depleted. The round-the-clock harassment by American snipers and artillery continued, and the rate of desertion was rising. The siege was lasting far longer than the invaders had expected, and the easy and glorious victory they anticipated had not come to pass.

Andrew Jackson and the Americans had proved formidable foes, but Sir Edward Pakenham was undeterred. He had faced the finest armies in Europe. He had delivered the decisive blow in victories that won Great Britain, Wellington, and himself great honor. And here, on the American Gulf Coast, his enemy was little more than a ragtag array of volunteers. They ranged from dandily dressed New Orleans gentlemen to the "dirty shirts," men armed with "duck guns." This band was led by a broken-down country lawyer whose only claim to military fame was the defeat of some underequipped Indians.

Certain he could still defeat the Americans, Pakenham summoned his officers to a brief meeting: Ned had a plan. To capture New Orleans, his army had to accomplish one simple thing: blast through Jackson's fortification. To do that, he explained, they must hurl the army, with even greater force than before, at their opponents—but this time they would do it after pummeling the enemy into near submission *with its own guns.*

The key was a direct attack on the American line on the west bank. Once the guns across the river had been captured, they could turn Patterson's cannons back on Jackson's army, catching the Americans in a cross fire between the west bank artillery and Pakenham's Chalmette batteries. Then the main force of the ever-enlarging British army would drive through the American earthworks in the biggest attack yet.

To do so, however, boats from the bayous and Lake Borgne would have to be taken overland to the Mississippi since there was no waterway linking the bayou to the river. Pakenham proposed rolling the boats on timbers, but Admiral Cochrane suggested an alternative: his men could extend the waterway from the Villeré canal to the levee. Initially, Pakenham had his doubts, but Cochrane got the nod.

The excavation of the waterway would take days, so crews of soldiers and sailors went to work on January 2, in four six-hour shifts. By Friday, January 6, it was done. And, on the American side, the ramparts had grown taller, thanks to the continued exertions of men with shovels.

That same day, Pakenham's spirits got a real lift. More reinforcements arrived, adding two full regiments to an army that now exceeded eight thousand men. And these men were superb soldiers. One of Pakenham's generals sang their praises: "Two such corps would turn the tide of a general action. We were rejoiced!"[32] Ammunition for the guns was brought forward, some of it in the knapsacks of the arriving infantry. The work of preparing cartridges was undertaken; more than four hundred men spent their days packing powder and shot. The notion of an imminent victory, of shared spoils after the capture of the city, began once again to take hold among the invaders.

On Saturday, January 7, Pakenham confidently issued his orders. William Thornton was to lead the west bank attack force. Using vessels floated into the Mississippi via the newly dug canal, his two regiments, together with 200 sailors and 400 marines, would embark at midnight. He and his 1,300 men were to land at daylight and capture the American force on the right bank.

On firing a rocket to signal their success, the main attack on the works overlooking the Rodriguez Canal could begin. Pakenham had reason to feel optimistic. After all, he had the finest fighting force in the world and, if his scouts had it right, a considerable advantage in both men and artillery. What didn't he have? Andrew Jackson and the American commitment to victory.

The Quiet Before the Tumult

On the night of January 7, General Jackson retired early. The intelligence of the preceding hours, gained from prisoners captured on the river, led him to one conclusion: the British attack was imminent; almost certainly it would come with dawn the following day.

He had seen for himself through his spyglass that the British camp was a den of activity. Major Latour told him that the British were bundling sugarcane stalks and making scaling ladders, to be used, they supposed, to bridge the moat and climb the American earthworks.

The overextended general understood very well that a few hours' rest could only help him do his duty: the past week had been enervating, as changeable as the weather.

After the fight on the first, there was good news on January 2: some three thousand new militiamen, most from Kentucky, would soon arrive to join Jackson's melting-pot army. Every man mattered in this tough fight and, as Jackson watched for the Kentuckians on the third, he wrote to Secretary of War James Monroe: "I do not know what may be [the Britishers'] further design—Whether [they will] redouble their efforts, or . . . apply them elsewhere."[33]

On the fourth, the Kentuckians did arrive, but they were poorly armed (fewer than one in ten carried a rifle) and so badly clothed the men visibly shivered as they walked through New Orleans. A frustrated General Jackson observed, "I have never in my life seen a Kentuckian without a gun, a pack of cards, and jug of whiskey."[34]

His anticipation of another British attack elevated his impatience with everyone around him. When he discovered that promised shipments of ammunition had not arrived from the city, he summoned Governor Claiborne, the man charged with providing munitions. Jackson warned the intimidated Claiborne, "By the Almighty God, if you do not send me balls and powder instantly, I shall chop off your head, and have it rammed into one of those fieldpieces."[35]

On the sixth, he had the Kentuckians with guns take positions at the Rodriguez Canal; the others would reinforce the secondary lines of defense.

All week long, Jackson configured his troops with care. He chose the 430 men of the Seventh Regular Infantry to anchor his right, shoulder to shoulder with 740 Louisiana militiamen. Next came the Forty-Fourth Regiment, numbering 240 men, with the Kentuckians (500 in number) and the largest corps of all, 1,600 of his fellow Tennesseans, at the far left. The 230 Mississippi dragoons remained to the rear, with a mix of others completing the left bank army. The total came to almost 5,000 men. Across the river were roughly 1,000 troops, including some Kentuckians and more Louisiana militia.[36] What Andrew Jackson had was a collection of Americans of all colors, creeds, and ethnic groups, melted into one fighting force, coming together to make military history.

All but two of his cannons were embedded in the earthworks; only a new, not-yet-finished redoubt, with two 6-pounders, sat forward of the main line, giving it a commanding view of both the levee road and the front of the earthworks. The other eleven guns—a mix of 6-, 12-, 18-, and 24-pounders—plus the big 32-pounder, were arranged in batteries at intervals along the main line. They were manned by a mix of navy gunners, Louisiana militiamen, and Baratarians.

The ramparts themselves, the work of a fortnight and more of tedious, backbreaking labor, remained as varied as the men charged with defending them. At the base, the earthen wall ranged from fourteen to twenty feet in thickness; its height, too, depended upon where on the line a man stood. In some places, the ramparts reached just five feet, in others perhaps twice that, but the elevation was enhanced by the four-foot depth of the muddy canal at the foot.

Jackson ordered the ramparts constantly manned and, as night fell on January 7, he rode the line. He and the men could hear hammering and digging sounds in the near distance but Jackson offered encouraging words, talking to gunners and soldiers, officers and infantry, the volunteers and the regulars. By order and by example, in every way he knew how, Jackson had readied his army, in mind and body, to defend New Orleans. The array of troops he had managed to assemble was truly remarkable: Tennesseans and Kentuckians on the left, battalions of Indians and Africans in the middle, dragoons from Mississippi in reserve, and a blending of regulars and militias from a mix of places distributed such that the length of earthworks was lined with American guns.

After dining lightly, Jackson took to his sofa to try to sleep. Several of his aides lay on the floor, still in uniform, their guns and sword belts at their sides. On previous evenings, the night watch in the camp had been entrusted to alternating companies of soldiers, but on this Saturday night the entire army had been instructed to bed down with their weapons within reach.

A few hours later, Jackson awoke in the darkness. The time was one o'clock, and he heard footsteps in the hall.

"Who's there?" he called.

The sentry admitted a courier with a message from Commodore Patterson. Late the previous day, standing on the shore opposite the Villeré plantation, he had seen enemy forces loading cannons in the barges. He assumed that he and his west bank position would be their target. The navy man asked Jackson to send reinforcements to the opposite side of the river in case the British attacked there.

Anxious and impatient, the general required only a moment to consider the matter before turning Patterson down. Time was too short for more men to reach Patterson—Jackson had already dispatched four hundred Kentuckians to reinforce Patterson and Brigadier General Morgan, the Louisiana militiaman posted with him. And nothing Patterson said persuaded Jackson that the major attack would be anywhere but on his own side of the Mississippi.

"I have no men to spare," he told the messenger.[37] Patterson and Morgan were on their own. Jackson had no idea of the misstep he had just made, but he was uninterested in going back to sleep. Turning, he addressed the aides around him.

"Gentlemen, we have slept enough. Rise. The enemy will be upon us in a few minutes."[38]

They would indeed, and not only in the way Jackson expected.

The Ursuline Nuns

Jackson enjoyed one advantage over Pakenham. As he and his officers dressed for battle, many of the devout women of New Orleans knelt just five miles away, praying that he and his soldiers would save the city.

The word of imminent battle had reached the households of New Orleans. Many women—wives and sisters and mothers of soldiers—feared not just for the men they loved as they prepared to fight the enemy. Rumors spreading dread of what a mob of conquering British soldiers might do to the women and to New Orleans if the city fell had been circulating, too. Determined to lend their voices and entreaties, female residents had made their way on the night of January 7 to the Ursuline convent.

The women joined the sisters in a vigil at the Chapel of Our Lady of Consolation. There the nuns had moved their most honored icon to a prominent place over the altar. It was a wooden sculpture of Our Lady of Prompt Succor. Five years earlier the large carved statue had arrived from France: dressed in a sweeping golden robe, her head adorned with a great crown, Mary held the child Jesus in her arms. Another statue of Our Lady of Prompt Succor was said to have miraculously defended the nuns in the past; in one of the great fires that had swept New Orleans, the flames had approached the convent but had been turned away by a sudden change in the wind's direction when a nun placed a statue of Our Lady in the window. The convent was one of the few buildings in the city that survived the fire.

Now, the people of New Orleans were hoping for more divine intervention. With the great statue of a wordless Blessed Virgin looming over the nuns and the women of the city, the nearly inaudible whispers of petitioners sent skyward pleas, "implor[ing] the God of battles to nerve the arm of their protectors, and turn the tide of combat against the invaders of their country."[39]

During the night, more and more women thronged to the chapel.

Within its walls, some wept, while others called out for divine intervention. Vows were made, including one by the Mother Superior, Sainte Marie Olivier de Vézin, who had previously offered General Jackson the services of the Ursuline sisters in caring for the wounded.

In the early hours of January 8, she made a fresh promise, this time to God. If the Americans prevailed in the day's battle—and that remained a mighty *if*—a solemn mass of Thanksgiving would be held in celebration and remembrance every year into the distant future.

In not so many hours, the outcome would be known.

CHAPTER 12

Day of Destiny

These d——d Yankee riflemen can pick a squirrel's eye out as
far as they can see it.

—Anonymous British prisoner of war

A flagstaff stood at the center of the American line, defiantly
flying the American colors. On January 8, 1815, the question of the day was, *Would it still wave at sunset?*

General Edward Pakenham, like Jackson, had also retired to his
bed the night before, but he'd risen a little later, at five o'clock. In the
predawn darkness he and his army, once again, had advanced toward
the Americans; now, with the sky in the east just gaining the vague
reddish tinge of dawn, he listened. From his position near the middle
of the Chalmette Plain, the British commander wanted nothing more
than to hear the sounds of William Thornton's guns echoing across
the Mississippi.

The new waterway at the Villeré plantation had broken through
to the river two days before, making possible the planned launch of
Thornton and his men the previous night. But, to his acute regret,
Pakenham would learn soon after waking that the wished-for gunfire

would be delayed. Nor would he see a rocket fired from the opposite shore, the agreed-upon signal for success in breaching Patterson's works.

Colonel William Thornton and his entire mission were running late, very late indeed.

Thanks to the failure of Admiral Cochrane's design for a temporary lock between the river and the bayou, most of the British ships had grounded in the canal. The hastily constructed dam at the near end of the canal extension had given way, permitting the water in the lock to run off toward Lake Borgne. That meant only a few of the craft in the planned forty-seven-boat flotilla reached the river's shallows before the larger barges grounded in the mud of the canal. Royal Navy sailors had set to work to drag more boats to open water, but less than two-thirds of the boats, many of them small, had made it through. When Thornton's amphibious force finally departed, it had shrunk to fewer than five hundred men.

Worse yet, given all the delays in maneuvering the boats through the makeshift canal, they sailed eight hours late.

Standing poised to order the main attack, his men in readiness, Pakenham, an experienced military tactician, understood exactly what the delay at the watercourse meant for the battle. "Thornton's people," a resigned General Pakenham said to a trusted officer beside him, "will be of no use whatever to the general attack."[1] With the night move across the water badly delayed, the general faced a momentous decision. Attack head on, or wait for Thornton's men to breach the flank?

Observing Pakenham's agitation—and knowing how crucial Patterson's guns might be to the success or failure of the day's fighting—one of his adjutants, Captain Harry Smith, suggested a rapid retreat in the last moments before sunrise. "We [will be] under the enemy's fire so soon as discovered," he warned. There might be time to reset the plan and return another day.

After almost a fortnight of delays and setbacks, Pakenham rejected the idea.

"I have twice deferred the attack," he replied. "We are strong in numbers now comparatively. It will cost more men, [but] the assault must be made."

Smith tried once more, again urging delay, but Pakenham's mind was made up.

"Smith, order the rocket to be fired."[2]

With a whistling message skittering across the sky, the British marched forward.

"That is their signal for advance, I believe," said General Andrew Jackson, hearing the hiss and bang of the first rocket. It shot skyward from the edge of the swamp, followed by a second, this one from the other side of the field.[3]

Since 4:00 a.m., Jackson's men had been awake, armed, and ready behind their earthworks. Suddenly alert, as after the crack of the pistol shot signaling the start of a horse race, the American artillerists stood by, their loggerheads red-hot and ready to fire their guns. The soldiers peered over the ramparts. The rifles and muskets had been loaded. In that moment, every heart began to beat more rapidly.

But to the Americans' surprise, the enemy remained unseen. A thick morning fog hugged the ground, obscuring the oncoming army.

The British Ranks

Pakenham's orders, written and issued the night before, divided his forces on the Chalmette Plain into three brigades.

Under the command of General Samuel Gibbs, the main attack was to come from the British right. At the vanguard would be the Forty-Fourth Infantry, an Irish regiment ordered to collect the three hundred bundles of sugarcane and sixteen ladders from an earthen redoubt partway to the American line. On reaching the canal, they were to throw the cane stalks into the ditch and then raise the scaling ladders. Two regiments of infantry, along with three companies of rifles, were charged with protecting the column's right from any counterattack and to provide cover as the Forty-Fourth approached the ditch. If all went well, the larger body of Gibbs's brigade would follow the Forty-Fourth. Crossing the ditch on the canes and scaling the ladders over the earthworks, they would penetrate the previously unbreakable American line and be face-to-face with American forces.

But this plan would fall apart, when whether intentionally or unintentionally, the Forty-Fourth would leave the canes and ladders behind, realizing perhaps that running full speed into the teeth of lethal American fire would amount to a suicide mission. Carrying ladders instead of pointing guns, they would be easy targets for Jackson's skilled marksmen.

Barely a half hour before dawn, a dismayed General Gibbs discovered the blunder. Without the ladders, Gibbs's men had no way to scale Jackson's wall. Knowing this, Gibbs instantly ordered the regiment to retreat some five hundred yards and bring the ladders forward, but, when first rocket's report echoed, the men with the heavy ones were still well behind the van and moving "in a most irregular and unsoldier-like manner."[4]

The outraged General Gibbs bellowed at Thomas Mullins, the leader of the Forty-Fourth, threatening to hang him from the "highest tree in that swamp."[5] But, the error made, it could not be undone, and Mullins's crucial failure would become the subject of debate for generations of historians.[6] (Mullins himself faced a court-martial back in England; though convicted of having neglected orders, he was cleared of the charge of having done so willfully.)

Whatever the cause of the mistake, the British plan to scale the earthworks had been foiled and, for Mullins's men, the consequences

Battle of New Orleans, JANUARY 8, 1815

on January 8 were awful. "In less time than one can write it, the 44th Foot was literary swept from the face of the earth," recorded Quartermaster E. N. Burroughs. "No such execution by small arms has ever been or heard of."[7]

On the opposite flank, a smaller force of companies commanded by Lieutenant Colonel Robert Rennie was to advance along the riverbank. Their objective was to overrun Jackson's new forward redoubt—at any cost. Pakenham needed its two guns, with their line of sight across the field, to be silenced, thereby preventing a slaughter of British troops as they reached the Rodriguez Canal and clambered up the earthworks.

A third force—consisting of General Keane, in command, and the Ninety-Third Highlanders and Ninety-Fifth Rifles—was to move on the center of the earthworks. Pakenham left in reserve the latest arrivals, the Seventh Fusiliers and the Forty-Third, led by General John Lambert.

The British drew closer, marching in rank and file to bugle and drum, but, before the forms of the men themselves could be distinguished, the brilliant red hues of their uniforms permitted the American gunners to gauge the distance. As Jackson's men aimed their guns, strains of "Yankee Doodle" were heard behind the American ranks. The Yankees gave three cheers and then blasted the entire line of redcoats with a round of fire.

The oncoming British, still marching through the low-lying fog, saw "cannon-balls tearing up the ground and crossing one another, and bounding along like so many cricket-balls through the air."[8]

Truly, the fight had begun.

The Bloodiest Parade

From the ramparts, the entire field of battle was visible to General Jackson. To his left, a British column, some sixty men across and marching in close ranks, walked out of the mist near the swamp. The sky was suddenly alight with a shower of rockets and, on the opposite side of the field, an even larger British force emerged, advancing en masse. For the American officers watching from behind the earthwork, two-thirds of the Chalmette Plain appeared suddenly to be occupied by a very determined enemy. It was a relentless red wall of British soldiers marching toward them.

As they charged the American gun emplacements, the Twenty-First Regiment looked down the huge barrel of the biggest American cannon, the thirty-two-pounder. Charging forward, advancing in double-quick time, George Gleig and his men failed to reach the gun position before the weapon discharged. Packed with musket balls, the load "served to sweep the center of the attacking force into eternity."[9]

Although the Twenty-First fell into disarray, the troops behind continued to push forward.

On the left, Colonel Rennie's force advanced rapidly, making for the crescent-shaped battery. Despite intense rifle and artillery fire, some of which came from across the river where Patterson's guns were now in action, the British closed rapidly on their objective. Rennie led the British attackers. He took a shrapnel wound in the calf, but that didn't stop him. He managed to leap through a gun embrasure a moment after its cannon fired, calling to his men, "Hurra, boys, the day is ours!"[10]

An instant later, on the exposed rear of the unfinished gun emplacement, Rennie fell. A musket ball entered his skull just above the eyebrows, lodging in his brain. He'd become an easy target for the marksmen in Captain Beale's Rifles, and the same volley that killed him took the lives of several men around him. Seeing the danger, the others in his company turned and fled.

When the main British force approached the center of the American line at a distance of two hundred yards, rifle fire erupted: the enemy walked into "a sparkling sheet of fire."[11] Farther along the line, the charging British soldiers met with the same shower of musket balls. Jackson's forces, crowded behind the parapets, took turns: One man in front fired, then fell back to reload, making way for the next soldier to empty his gun into the mass of oncoming humanity. Some riflemen fired as quickly as they could reload; others sighted carefully from the top of the breastwork, took deliberate aim, then shot.[12]

Standing high on the parapet with a panoramic view of the field, Jackson surveyed the battle unfolding beneath him. He offered repeated exhortations.

"Stand to your guns, don't waste your ammunition," he cried.

"See that every shot tells!"

"Give it to them, boys; let us finish the business today!"[13]

He was the backbone.

As the battle continued, supplies were running low, and tempers were running high. Jackson moved along the line but stopped at gun battery number three, under the command of the Baratarian Dominique You. A short, barrel-chested man, the pirate had impressed the general. ("If I were ordered to storm the gates of hell, with Captain Dominique as my lieutenant," Jackson said, "I would have no misgivings of the result.")[14]

Now, however, with eyes swollen from the smoke in the air, You stood by a silent twenty-four-pounder.

"What! What! By the Eternal, what is the matter?" Jackson demanded. "You have ceased firing!"

You looked up at Jackson. "Of course, general, of course!" he explained. "The powder is good for nothing—fit only to shoot blackbirds with, and not redcoats!"

Jackson turned to an aide. Before galloping off, he ordered, "Tell the ordnance officer that I will have him shot in five minutes as a traitor, if Dominique complains any more of his powder."[15]

Just minutes into the battle, according to one Kentucky rifleman, "the smoke was so thick that everything seemed to be covered up in it."[16] But the woodsmen, armed with .38-caliber long rifles (the barrels were forty-two inches long), kept firing with deadly accuracy. Half-hidden in the dense cypress vegetation, they loaded their guns with balls and buckshot. Their fire was nearly constant and, according to one Louisiana merchant watching down the line, "the whole right of the British column was mowed down by these invisible riflemen."[17]

General Keane's column had also fallen under intense fire, and Keane himself, with wounds in the neck and thigh, had been carried from the field. With him gone, the resolution of his men wavered and they began to fall back even as General Lambert's forces advanced to reinforce the charge.[18]

Some British troops had reached the Rodriguez Canal and tried to scale the earthen parapet. But firm footholds proved hard to find in the slippery mud and, without ladders, those who began the climb found the soft earth gave way, sending them sliding back down. From above, "a murderous discharge of musketry [caused] . . . a dreadful loss of men and officers."[19]

The immense battle was being fought across the breadth of the plain but, to the veteran British fighters, their enemy seemed close to invisible. From below, it appeared to the attackers as if the Americans, "without so much as lifting their faces above the rampart, swung their firelocks by one arm over the wall, and discharged them directly upon [our] heads."[20]

Even to a seasoned infantry officer who earned honors fighting Napoleon, this field of battle was overwhelming: "The echo from the cannonade and musketry was so tremendous . . . [that it] seemed as if the earth was cracking and tumbling to pieces, or as if the heavens were rent asunder by the most terrific peals of thunder that ever rumbled; it was the most awful and the grandest mixture of sounds."[21]

"And the flashes of fire looked as if coming out of the bowels of the earth."[22]

On the British right, General Gibbs went down. As Gibbs was carried from the field, Pakenham, together with his staff, galloped forward from his post well back from the front line. After removing his hat, the commanding general rode into midst of the battle.

The men around him were "falling and staggering like drunken men from the effects of the fire."[23] Some were advancing, others retreating, but they responded to Pakenham's desperate urging. "For shame," he called to them, "recollect that you are British soldiers!"[24] The troops had begun to re-form when a musket ball slammed into the general's knee. When another rifleman shot his horse dead, Pakenham fell to the ground but, despite an arm that hung limp from still another wound, he demanded the mount of a junior officer. The general needed the help of an aide-de-camp to mount the animal and, just as he was attempting to settle into the saddle, an artillery round whistled in.

A deadly iron ball ripped into Pakenham's groin. This time, his spine mangled by the grapeshot, the general collapsed into the arms of his aide-de-camp.

He, too, was carried to the rear, and the bearers laid their commanding general down beneath a great live oak tree in the center of the field, just out of firing range. The surgeon summoned to his side could do nothing, but the dying Pakenham was able to utter one last command. For the ear of John Lambert, the only British major general left standing, Pakenham whispered, "Tell him . . . to send forward the reserves."

Pakenham had fallen, well short of New Orleans, and would die quietly on the battlefield within the hour. General Gibbs, though in evident agony, survived into the next day, before joining Pakenham in death.[25]

Barely two hundred yards away, Jackson's men suffered miraculously few casualties behind their protective parapet. And in the convent, the nuns prayed on.

On the West Bank

The attack across the river—Pakenham's best hope, his only hope—occurred altogether too late. Pakenham himself was beyond hearing, but more than an hour into the attack, the sound of gunfire could finally be distinguished across the water.

The *pop, pop, pop* of a musketry volley was followed by the boom of artillery. Colonel Thornton's force was attacking the forward line of Captain Morgan's Louisiana militia.

Far behind schedule at launch, Thornton's mission had been

further delayed by the boatmen's complete failure to anticipate the strong Mississippi currents. Once the British boats were well launched into the river, the driving waters carried them far downstream from the intended landing place. By the time they reached the opposite shore, the redcoats had a four-mile march north toward their objective—and it would be a trek accompanied by the sounds of the battle already begun across the river at the Chalmette Plain. To their chagrin, Thornton and his men could also see Patterson's guns just ahead, firing freely at the wave of attacking redcoats across the river.

More determined than ever, however, Thornton's band of soldiers, sailors, and marines attacked the breastwork manned by the advance guard of Louisiana militia. Unlike the great berm that loomed over the Chalmette battlefield, the west bank ramparts proved to be no great obstacle to the British. At first, artillery fire slowed their advance, but, noting the Americans' right flank was poorly protected, Thornton ordered his troops to sweep left and attack there. Seeing that they would soon be overrun, many of the militia troops simply fled.

Patterson, watching from his redoubt a few hundred yards away, recognized that the tide ran against him. Before the British force could reach him, he ordered his men to spike the guns. A length of iron rod was hammered into the vent, or touchhole, at the rear of each gun. The guns would not fire again until the spikes were removed, a time-consuming and laborious process. Then the Americans retreated.

The west bank battle was over; the British now controlled the position. Yet there were no true winners: Thornton was wounded in the fight and Patterson had walked away unscathed. The British had the guns but the artillery had been rendered entirely useless—Jackson's men at the Rodriguez Canal would not be fired upon by Patterson's guns, this day or any other. The fight would become a postscript to the terrible tragedy that had befallen General Pakenham's force on the opposite bank.

There, as the only British major general still standing, Lambert by default had become the ranking officer of the New Orleans mission. He had watched as the regiments Pakenham had sent into battle were shredded by Jackson's firepower. His two regiments remained largely intact; they had been held in reserve that morning. But he had no doubt he was left to shoulder a great defeat, that his job now was to begin to plan his exit. In the coming hours, he would order Thornton—against the recommendations of Admiral Cochrane—to abandon the hard-won west bank and rejoin the main British force.

A Flag of Truce

The guns had quieted across the field by the time a flag of truce reached Jackson at midday. With the outcome of the battle no longer in doubt, he had retired to his quarters at the Macarty house. Before doing so, he walked the entire length of the American line and, in the company of his staff, he stopped at each command. He addressed the men and their officers, offering "words of praise and grateful commendation." To his troops, he seemed the most erect, warm, and relaxed version of himself, the proud victor.[26]

The enemy's courier brought him a request for a cease-fire so the British could bury their dead. The signer was General Lambert—a name unknown to Jackson—but the two men soon agreed to terms.

Though it was the official end of the battle, a more poignant surrender had occurred earlier when, on the left of the American earthworks, some Kentucky riflemen noticed a white flag waving. The

Kentuckians held their fire and, as word moved up the line, the din of gunshots ceased. In the quiet, a fresh gust of wind cleared the dense gun smoke, and the Americans could see the bearer of the white handkerchief. A British officer, he held the makeshift pennant high on a sword or a stick. Some said he was a major, and epaulets decorated his shoulders.

He stepped over the breastwork and was quickly surrounded by Americans. One of the Tennesseans, "a private all over begrimed with dust and powder," demanded his sword. The enemy officer hesitated until an American officer ordered, "Give it up!"

In the next moment, holding the weapon in both hands, the man who represented the Crown handed his sword to a humble American soldier, executing a polite bow as he did so.[27]

No one on the Chalmette Plain remained in doubt as to the victor in the Battle of New Orleans.

The Bloodied Field

With the roar of artillery in the distance, the women gathered at the Cathedral of St. Louis had continued to pray. The doors were open as usual to the people of the town, but this morning's High Mass was said to "a congregation of shuddering women."[28] Their fears were fed by the sounds of war.

"The cannon [fire] . . . seemed like one continued peal of tremendous thunder," wrote one lady of the city. She and her neighbors listened in horror. "We were prepared to run . . . knowing that if [the British] got the upper hand . . . our lives would be destroyed."[29] Instead, many sought spiritual solace in the pews beneath the cathedral's twin towers. The service was conducted by the Very Reverend William Dubourg, the vicar apostolic. He offered up the holy sacrifice of the Mass to the accompaniment of collective prayers of the citizenry at the cathedral and the pious sisters of the Ursuline convent, all seeking the success of General Jackson and the troops on the Chalmette Plain. According to one later account, a courier entered the chapel in the middle of the Mass, crying, "Victory is ours!"[30] Were the community's supplications being answered?

On the Chalmette Plain, the firing had stopped. Long before any official word arrived from the front, rumors of a big victory traveled up the riverbank, neighbor to neighbor. The people of New Orleans ran into the streets; in place of distant gunfire, cheers of joy echoed. When a messenger from the battlefield arrived, riding a worn-out-looking horse, he hurried about, asking surgeons, apothecaries, and anyone with a cart to come to the field of battle. There were wounded to be tended, too many to count—most of them British.[31]

Back at the Rodriguez Canal, said one soldier, the scene was "a sea of blood." The illusion resulted from hundreds of red uniforms obscuring the stubble of last year's sugarcane crop. The letting of blood had indeed been great, leaving an unfathomable number of dead and dying soldiers prostrate on the Chalmette Plain. In some places the bodies were so numerous that it seemed possible to walk without ever touching the ground for a distance of perhaps two hundred yards.[32]

The lines of attack could easily be read in the array of dead. The terrible carnage was at its worst near the center of the field, but other broad bands of slain soldiers commemorated the British assaults near the levee and by the swamp.

There were rows and stacks of bodies even before the field

surgeons began their work. Some corpses had no heads, while others were missing arms or legs. The lifeless faces were a distillation of fear and pain; the dying men's expressions had been frozen as they screamed or cried. Oddly, some looked to have been laughing.

There were stirrings amid the corpses. Wounded men moaned and screamed and called out for help but, as the astonished Americans watched from the ramparts, hundreds of the British got to their feet, men who had "fallen at our first fire upon them, without having received so much as a scratch."[33] Some of the cowards ran for the British line; others surrendered. Said Jackson later, "I never had so grand and awful an idea of the resurrection as on that day."[34]

No two accounts of the battle, whether written that week, that month, that century, or in the many decades since, would agree on the exact casualty count, but all agreed it was stunningly high. According to one British infantry captain, "three generals, seven colonels, seventy-five officers, . . . a total of seventeen hundred and eighty-one officers and soldiers, had fallen in a few minutes."[35] Some writers elevated the number—General Keane reported 2,030, other sources have said 3,000. Jackson initially gave Monroe an estimate of 1,500, a number he later revised to 2,600.

The American losses on the Chalmette Plain on January 8 amounted to no more than a dozen dead. More would be killed on the west bank and in skirmishes in the days following, but the battle, indisputably, was a far greater disaster for the British. General Jackson's earthworks and his unlikely melding of men had held. The city of New Orleans no longer feared a British invasion.

For the nation, the meaning was larger, too. Against all odds, General Jackson had preserved the mouth of the Mississippi for America. At the center of the muddy earthworks, atop its staff, untouched by British hands and overlooking the Chalmette Plain, the Stars and Stripes still waved.

General Jackson and his multiethnic, multigenerational army made up of people from every American social class and occupation had come together to do what Napoleon had failed to do: destroy the finest fighting force in the world. Thanks to Jackson's military instincts, his impeccable planning, and his ferocious leadership, America had prevailed in the most important fight of its young life.

The boy becomes a man: a brutish British officer is about to strike young Andy Jackson. The boy survived, scarred and angry, to resist another British attack, this one at the Battle of New Orleans thirty-five years later.

Hoping to expand America westward, President Thomas Jefferson sent James Monroe to Paris to negotiate the Louisiana Purchase in 1803. Pictured here, Monroe (left) and Robert R. Livingston (center) complete negotiations with French foreign minister Comte Talleyrand. Monroe would later go on to be involved in the territory's defense in his positions as secretary of war and secretary of state during the War of 1812.

Captain James Barron of the USS *Chesapeake* formally surrenders, offering his sword to the captain of the victorious HMS *Leopard* in June 1807. The unprovoked attack by the British warship on the American frigate helped set the stage for the War of 1812.

After the War of 1812, Jackson became known for his military demeanor, as captured in this image of him with his hand gripping his sword, his eyes fixed on his adversary. Major General Andrew Jackson was a confident and natural leader of men in battle.

JOHN VANDERLYN, THE HISTORIC NEW ORLEANS COLLECTION

Jackson's beloved wife, Rachel Donelson Jackson (1767–1828), was the only person to whom Jackson could confide his innermost fears and doubts. Born into a well-established Nashville family, Rachel was a partner to the roughhewn Jackson in his rise to prominence.

JOHN CHESTER BUTTRE/ THE HISTORIC NEW ORLEANS COLLECTION

In 1812, James Madison (1751–1836) was an unpopular president; in 1817, after Jackson's big victory in New Orleans, Madison left office riding a wave of popular acclaim. In the face of daunting odds, he had led his country into its second war of independence.

Known as Chief Red Eagle to his fellow Creeks, William Weatherford (ca. 1781–1824) was born of mixed parentage, with a Scots father and a Native American mother. A courageous and resourceful opponent, Red Eagle had, by the time of the surrender (pictured here), won Andrew Jackson's grudging respect.

The signing of the Treaty of Ghent on Christmas Eve 1814 appeared to bring the War of 1812 to a close. John Quincy Adams shakes hands with a uniformed British minister as Albert Gallatin (to the right of Adams) and Henry Clay (seated) look on.

With the powerful Royal Navy patrolling the coast, American goods accumulated on the docks. At the port of New Orleans, that meant millions of dollars in bales of cotton.

Dashing and dangerous, Jean Lafitte (1780–1823) was a privateer, smuggler, and entrepreneur. Along with his brothers and the other Baratarian pirates, many of them superb cannoneers, Lafitte lent his deep knowledge of the waters around New Orleans to the cause of saving New Orleans from the British.

The wellborn Louise d'Avezac (1785–1860) married a prominent New Orleans lawyer, Edward Livingston (1764–1836). As Mrs. Livingston, she offered the transplanted New Yorker entrée into New Orleans society— and, in turn, Livingston, appointed an adjutant to General Jackson in 1814, helped Jackson win the support of the city's powerful Creole class in the defense of the city.

A trusted aide to Jackson during the early days of the war, Thomas Hart Benton (1782–1858) played a role in the gunfight that almost killed the general in Nashville in 1813. Much later, as a powerful senator from Missouri, Benton proved to be a congressional ally of then president Andrew Jackson.

A stalwart friend and sometime business partner of Jackson's, General John Coffee (1772–1833) proved his military skills again and again, leading his cavalry brigade of fellow Tennesseans against the Creeks and the British alike.

JOHN COFFEE.

Perhaps the lowest point in the nation's history, August 24, 1814, was the day the British set fire to the public buildings in Washington, DC, leaving both the President's House and the Capitol smoking ruins. The humiliation of that moment proved to be a great motivation for Jackson and his men.

The bombs bursting over Baltimore on the night of September 13, 1814, signaled a change in America's fortunes. The British failure to take the city in Maryland, together with other losses at Plattsburgh, New York, and New Orleans, assured that the United States would remain independent.

The five American gunboats on Lake Borgne were besieged by a flotilla of British barges. In less than two hours, on December 14, 1814, the vastly larger British forces captured the outgunned American ships under the command of Lieutenant Thomas ap Catesby Jones.

A veteran of the fight with the Tripoli pirates, Master Commander Daniel Todd Patterson (1786–1839) was the senior officer of the U.S. Navy at the New Orleans station. He and Jackson would collaborate by putting the limited naval resources in Patterson's command to very good use to defend the city.

Long before Jackson set foot in New Orleans, Governor William C. C. Claiborne (1775–1817) sought the general's help. Appointed by President Jefferson as the first Louisiana territorial governor, Claiborne had been duly elected to that office with Louisiana's statehood in 1812.

JAMES BARTON LONGACRE, THE HISTORIC NEW ORLEANS COLLECTION

Young Samuel Houston (1793–1863) fought with his fellow Tennesseans against the Creeks; despite sustaining wounds at the Battle of Horseshoe Bend, he rose to fight again. A longtime ally of Jackson's, he later became governor of Tennessee and the first president of the Republic of Texas.

PHOTOGRAPH © LIBRARY OF CONGRESS

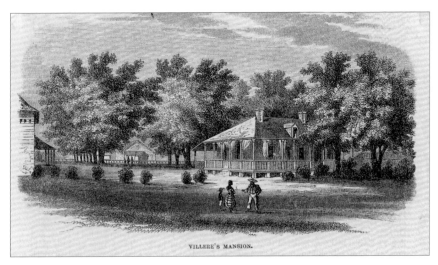

VILLERE'S MANSION.

When the British arrived to attack New Orleans, their officers established headquarters at the mansion on the Villeré plantation, just downriver from the encampment of Jackson's army.

VIEW OF THE RODRIGUEZ CANAL—JACKSON'S LINES.

Jackson set thousands of his men to hard labor to transform the Rodriguez Canal into a tall embankment lined with gun emplacements. Before that, the canal was little more than a drainage ditch.

A much-honored soldier who had fought bravely in Europe under the command of his brother-in-law the Duke of Wellington, General Edward "Ned" Pakenham (1778–1815) was dispatched by London to lead the enormous British force to victory in New Orleans. After capturing Louisiana, he was to become the territory's British governor—but General Jackson had different ideas.

GOUPIL & CO., THE HISTORIC NEW ORLEANS COLLECTION

Also a veteran of the French wars, Vice Admiral Sir Alexander Forrester Inglis Cochrane (1758–1832) commanded the British expeditionary force in the Gulf of Mexico. The greedy Cochrane looked both to improve his fortunes and to avenge the death of a brother killed in the American Revolution.

LIBRARY OF CONGRESS

In what is today's Alabama, Jackson prepares to fight on Indian turf. Whether his opponent was Indian or British, Jackson was unafraid to ride into the heat of battle.

Painted by Jean Hyacinthe de Laclotte, a Louisiana militiaman who fought in the January 8, 1815, battle, this vivid view of the events of the day was based on sketches Laclotte made as the battle unfolded.

The flag still waves—with Jean Lafitte and three freemen of color celebrating in the foreground while a dead General Pakenham, left, falls from his horse.

EUGENE LOUIS-LAMI, LOUISIANA STATE MUSEUM

In a historical exaggeration, this image portrays Jackson conferring with an aide near battlements consisting almost entirely of cotton bales.

DENNIS MALONE CARTER, THE HISTORIC NEW ORLEANS COLLECTION

This commemorative print, made ca. 1820, puts a lot of the battle's elements together in one composition. Along with General Jackson, it is thought to portray General William Carroll and Edward Livingston in the foreground, the redcoats and the U.S. infantry, and navy ships in the river at the horizon line.

For Major General Sir Edward Pakenham, the Battle of New Orleans ended in death. He sustained several wounds in the first hour before a musket ball severed his spine. His men laid him at the base of a massive live oak tree, where he quietly bled to death as both sides fought on.

The Ursuline nuns of New Orleans prayed for victory, asking Our Lady of Prompt Succor—an honorific title the sisters used for the Blessed Virgin—to save their city from the invaders. In this late-nineteenth-century composite, an image (lower right) commemorates the Battle of New Orleans.

F. CHAMPENOIS, THE HISTORIC NEW ORLEANS COLLECTION

Jackson stood tall in the memories of American schoolboys for generations, as suggested by this 1922 illustration for a children's magazine, *The Youth's Companion*.

LIBRARY OF CONGRESS

JACKSON'S TRIUMPH AT NEW ORLEANS.

The victorious general waves to the crowd from his open carriage in a mid-nineteenth-century image bearing the title *Jackson's Triumph at New Orleans* from an illustrated magazine.

A photograph of Andrew Jackson just before his death. When he saw it, a furious Jackson dismissed the likeness; he said it made him "look like a monkey."

CHAPTER 13

The British Withdraw

We, who only seven weeks ago had set out in the surest confidence of glory, and, I may add, of emolument, were brought back dispirited and dejected.

—**George Gleig,** *A Narrative of the Campaigns of the British Army at Washington and New Orleans*

General Jackson took nothing for granted. He watched the British camp like a hawk from the top of the Macarty house and, on his orders, American artillerymen kept up a constant barrage of round shot and mortar shells. He wanted the British to know their American enemy was both vigilant and determined.

Jackson considered ordering a ground attack on his wounded foe, but to come out from behind his ramparts to fight the British—they were still a far larger and better-trained force—and to do so in an open plain? He and his counselors decided that such a battle need not be fought and that to undertake it might even provoke the enemy to renew their attack.[1]

Such worries seemed all the more real when Jackson got word from Fort St. Philip, sixty miles downstream on the Mississippi, that five of Admiral Cochrane's gunships were firing on the fortification. American gunners managed to keep the British vessels out of cannon range, but the British still bombarded the fort with long-range mortar shells. That the British still had designs on New Orleans seemed hard to deny, but after nine days of indecisive artillery exchanges (the British fired more than a thousand rounds, killing just one American and wounding seven) Cochrane's ships sailed away on the night of January 17. Fort St. Philip was pockmarked but intact.[2]

Jackson might have prepared a trap for the enemy's land force. If General Lambert's army wasn't going to advance, the troops would have to retreat from the Chalmette Plain. The American woodsmen with their long rifles could have made the wounded enemy run a hellish gauntlet as they retraced the narrow path through swampland to the shore before embarking, one barge at a time, to be relayed across Lake Borgne. But as Jackson wrote to James Monroe, that also seemed an unnecessary "risque."[3]

Finally, Jackson's patience paid off. On January 19, he awoke to find "the enemy [had] precipitately decamped."[4] The British had stoked their nighttime campfires to lull the American pickets into thinking all was as usual. Then, at midnight, the army wordlessly began an all-night march through the mud, back along the Bayou Bienvenue to the Fisherman's Village. Nine days had been required to improvise a roadbed along the creek, stiffening the muddy morass with reeds and tree limbs.

Finally, the British were truly gone. Even the late General Pakenham had departed. Disemboweled and submerged in a hogshead of rum, the remains of the British commander had begun the journey home to Ireland, there to be interred in the family vault in County Meath, a few miles from Dublin.

Contrary to widespread expectations—his own, Parliament's, Admiral Cochrane's, and others'—General Pakenham would never be the governor of Louisiana.

A Celebration in New Orleans

Jackson made his way back to the city he had saved. On January 20, returning for the first time in nearly a month, he marched his army into the heart of New Orleans.

The streets were lined with "the aged, the infirm, the matrons, daughters and children," recorded one adjutant. "Every countenance was expressive of gratitude—joy sparkled in every feature, on beholding fathers, brothers, husbands, sons, who had so recently . . . repell[ed] an enemy [who came] to conquer and subjugate the country."[5]

The men of New Orleans and the other defenders were welcomed home, as Jackson's aide Major Reid saw it, in "a scene well calculated to excite the tenderest emotions."[6] The sense of relief in the city was enhanced by the disparity in casualty totals on the battlefield: British dead and wounded exceeded a thousand, but there were remarkably few American widows and orphans.

A man of simple religious faith, Jackson wished to give thanks to the "Ruler of all events," as he put it. He wrote to the Abbé Dubourg at New Orleans's cathedral, requesting that Dubourg organize a "service of public thanksgiving" for "the signal interposition of Heaven in giving success to our arms against the enemy."[7]

On January 23, the people of the city gathered once again at the Place d'Armes, the city's main square. A triumphal arch had been erected and festooned with evergreens and flowers. A dense throng of people packed the streets and the nearby levee. A battalion of New Orleans militiamen lined the path to the entrance of the cathedral. Spectators filled the balconies and windows overlooking the square. Eighteen young women lined the approach from the arch to the church, one for each of the eighteen states. Wearing white dresses and blue veils, the girls held flags and baskets. Everyone awaited the arrival of the victorious general.

An artillery salvo announced his coming, and his appearance on horseback produced a deafening cheer from the crowd.

Jackson dismounted, stepping onto the raised floor of the arch. Two girls placed a laurel crown on his head. On a path strewn with flowers, Jackson progressed to the cathedral's entrance, where he was met by the abbé and his college of priests, all dressed in sacramental vestments. They entered the church, accompanied by the reading of an ode composed for the occasion. Its last couplet proclaimed, "Remembrance, long, shall keep alive thy fame / And future infants learn to lisp thy name."[8]

The Abbé Dubourg welcomed Jackson, thanking the man he called the city's "deliverer." He compared him to George Washington; he was among the first to do so but very far from the last. The cathedral could not accommodate the crowd of more than ten thousand people, but those admitted saw Jackson take a seat near the altar to the accompaniment of organ music. After the chanting of the hymn "Te Deum," the Mass, lit by a thousand candles, came to a close as Jackson accepted the honors and his crown humbly. He told the hushed crowd, "I receive it in the name of the brave men who . . . well deserve the laurels which their country will bestow."[9]

With the ceremonies concluded, the crowd escorted Jackson to his quarters, but only after the general, hearing reports of the sisters' all-night vigil on the eve of the battle, visited the Ursuline convent to thank them for their prayers.[10] "By the blessing of heaven, directing the valor of the troops under my command, one of the most brilliant victories in the annals of war was obtained," he said.[11] That night, Jackson suspended the curfew, and the city of New Orleans would celebrate until dawn.

Unfinished Business

Despite the aura of victory, Andrew Jackson remained watchful. As his aide Major Reid observed, "[The enemy] had now retired; yet, from their convenient situation, and having command of the surrounding waters, it was in their power at a short notice, to reappear."[12] Just in case, Jackson left infantry regulars at the Rodriguez Canal, and he stationed Tennessee militiamen and Kentucky rifles near the landing place at the Villeré plantation.

The British might find another target. "I have no idea that [the] enemy will attempt Fort Bowyer," Jackson noted in a letter. "Still you cannot be too well prepared or too vigilant—[Admiral] Cochrane is sore, and [General] Lambert crazy; they may in this situation attempt some act of madness."[13]

Jackson's hunch proved dead right: Fort Bowyer was in the British sights.

As far as Admiral Cochrane was concerned, the American war wasn't over, since no messenger from Ghent had yet reached American shores. And there was Fort Bowyer, just up the coast. A smaller navy force had failed to capture the fortification back in September, but now the admiral had sixty ships at his disposal and many thousands of troops. So, with what was now General Lambert's army back aboard, the fleet set sail on January 27.

Destination: Mobile Bay.

Though the fort was surely a lesser target than New Orleans, this opportunity to regain lost prestige could hardly be passed by. And General Lambert wanted to dispel "the sullen carelessness [and] indifference" evident in his men after the beating they had taken at the Chalmette Plain.[14]

On Wednesday, February 8, Cochrane's armada landed three regiments of some five thousand men several miles from Fort Bowyer. Although the American commander, Colonel William Lawrence, ordered his guns to fire on the British, they would not be deterred: by Saturday, the muzzles of four eighteen-pounders, two six-pounders, a pair of howitzers, and eight mortars were pointed at the fort. The British were ready.

Before opening fire, however, Captain Harry Smith, under a flag of truce, carried a demand from his commanding officer, General Lambert, to Colonel Lawrence.

His message in short: *Surrender your fort.*

Looking out at his powerful enemy from the confines of the highly flammable wooden fort, Lawrence asked for time. He wanted two hours to consider the offer, which included a promise that, if he declined to accept Lambert's terms, he could evacuate the women and children inside Fort Bowyer. He had watched helplessly for the preceding three days. With only 360 men in his command, he faced overwhelming odds.

Lawrence saw no alternative but to surrender. To fight would be to waste lives in an unwinnable battle, and his officers seconded his decision. At noon, on February 12, 1815, Lawrence and his men marched out of Fort Bowyer, accompanied by twenty women and sixteen children. They laid down their arms and yielded the fort to the British.

When he heard what happened, Jackson expressed to Monroe his mortification at the handover. It had occurred without a shot being fired but, worse yet, the capitulation of Fort Bowyer cleared the way for the British to enter Mobile Bay and besiege Mobile.

The news took Jackson back in time: Months before, he had foreseen a British strategy that began with Mobile. Now, it seemed, the sequence of events he feared most was about to unfold. Could this signal a new offensive cycle?

In a matter of hours, however, the momentum shifted for good when, the next day, the British frigate HMS *Brazen* sailed into view. Fresh from an Atlantic crossing, she brought word of the Treaty of Ghent. Cochrane and his generals were ordered to end hostilities and prepare to sail home.

Yet for Andrew Jackson, the war would be over only when he knew for certain it was over; he could never take Admiral Cochrane's word for that.

The Slow Pace of Peace

On the evening of February 14, 1815, a messenger carrying a leather document box arrived at the borrowed home in Washington occupied by James Madison. Eager hands opened the cast brass lockset to reveal a thick sheaf of papers.

A cover letter from Henry Clay explained the contents. Accompanied by many position papers prepared in the negotiation process, there was the all-important Treaty of Ghent, sealed and signed and very official. The treaty was brief (just eleven articles) and to the point, beginning with its most basic assertion: "There shall be a firm and universal Peace between His Britannic Majesty and the United States."

Mr. Madison submitted the document to the Senate without delay. It was read aloud three times to the assembled body, and some senators wondered at the absence of any reference to impressment and the harassment of neutral trade, two of the main reasons for declaring war two and a half years earlier. Nor was there mention of navigation of the Mississippi. Nevertheless, when the key question was asked in proper parliamentary fashion—"Will the Senate advise and consent to the ratification of this treaty?"—the resulting vote was for ratification, thirty-five yeas, no one opposed. On February 17, a second copy arrived in Washington from London, this one bearing the signature of the prince regent.

The men of the government could finally relax: Mr. Madison's War was over.

A thousand miles away, however, in his headquarters on Rue Royale in New Orleans, General Jackson still awaited the news. Not that rumors hadn't reached him—on February 19, a clipping from a London newspaper appeared that reported the war had ended—but Jackson continued to refuse to lower his guard until he got the official word from Washington. Even after Edward Livingston returned from a further negotiation with Admiral Cochrane over prisoner exchanges with news that the HMS *Brazen* had brought word of a peace treaty, Jackson suspected the reports of a peace deal were merely a "stratagem."[15]

To many in the city, the hero of New Orleans began to seem like their jailer with his insistence that the draconian restraints of martial law remain in place. With the war over to their satisfaction, merchants resented the general's tight rein on commerce. Militiamen wanted to be released from duty to return to their civilian lives but, despite their pleas, Jackson continued stubbornly to insist that he needed formal notification from the secretary of war.

A woman's touch, however, eased some of the tension.

Nine months had elapsed since the surrender of the Creek chief William Weatherford, an event that had prompted Andrew Jackson's last visit home. Rachel had, in turn, postponed her December trip to New Orleans after the British arrived on the city's doorstep. When news of the January 8 victory reached Rachel, she decided the couple had been separated long enough. Though winter travel posed worrisome dangers, Mrs. Jackson set out, along with other Tennessee officers' wives, for New Orleans.

Several weeks later, the general welcomed his wife; throughout their long marriage, he would always mourn their separations. She arrived with their adoptive son Andrew Jr. on whom the general doted. The moment was one of pure delight for Jackson.

As for Rachel, her arrival amounted to more than a reunion with the man she loved: having never visited a city larger than provincial Nashville, New Orleans was a grand revelation to her. The Jacksons were the guests of Edward Livingston and his stylish wife. Louise Livingston took a liking to the unaffected Mrs. Jackson, despite her visitor's dowdy clothes and an unfashionably sunned complexion, the result of managing their plantation in her husband's absence.

The Jacksons became the guests of choice around town at "balls, concerts, plays, theaters, [etc.]," even though, Rachel allowed, "we don't attend the half of them."[16] But one they did go to was a great ball to celebrate George Washington's birthday.

The site of the February 22 gala was the French Exchange where, for three days, preparations had been under way for the grand evening.

Flowers abounded, as did colored lamps that, from the rear, illuminated transparencies painted on varnished glass. One read, "Jackson and Victory: they are but one." Jackson, taking an advance look at the decorations, took note of it. He inquired lightly, "Why did you not write 'Hickory and Victory: they are but one'?"[17]

Supper was served and dancing followed. When the hero took the floor with Rachel in his arms, the crowd was transfixed. To some observers, the savior of the city and his lady looked mismatched. The slim and girlish divorcée that Jackson had married twenty-one years before had aged into a rather stout, round woman; the poorly nourished Jackson looked more haggard and angular than ever.

To one Creole gentleman still smarting over Jackson's refusal to lift his martial law decree, the sight invited a snide remark. "To see these two figures, the general a long, haggard man, with limbs like a skeleton, and Madame la Generale, a short, fat dumpling, bobbing opposite each other like half-drunken Indians, to the wild melody of *Possum up de Gum Tree,* and endeavoring to make a spring into the air, was very remarkable."[18] Though some made fun, the ladies of the city raised a subscription to purchase jewels for presentation to the well-liked Mrs. Jackson.

At last, on March 8, 1815, having received "persuasive evidence" of ratification of the treaty, Jackson released the reins. He dismissed the Louisiana militia and, after official word arrived, on March 13, he issued orders for Generals Carroll and Coffee to march their commands without delay back home. He expressed his thanks and admiration.

"Farewell, fellow soldiers. The expression of your general's thanks is feeble," he said in his closing address, "but the gratitude of a country of freemen is yours—yours the applause of an admiring world."[19]

Finally, the Hero of New Orleans could go home. In early April, accompanied by a small band of devoted officers and men, he and Rachel began a slow progress northward. They were feted in Natchez and other towns on the way and, as they neared Nashville, an ever-larger throng of Volunteers escorted the victor and his wife. The state's politicians, wishing to share in Jackson's newfound radiance and renown, would give yet another banquet, but his desired stopping place was the Hermitage.

When his adoring public delivered him to his home, Andrew Jackson addressed his friends and neighbors, both in welcome and in farewell. For most of the last eighteen months, Jackson had been a stranger, a warrior and traveler away from home, and the time had taken a toll. He looked more sinewy than ever, carrying perhaps 145 pounds on his six-foot-one-inch frame.[20] But his blue eyes remained as penetrating as ever, his posture still ramrod straight, despite the hardships of the war.

During his months away he had become accustomed to addressing crowds; his Tennessee apprenticeship as a regional politician and judge may have prepared him for greater things, but it had been the trial that was the Battle of New Orleans that made him not merely a public man but a national figure, a man whose name and accomplishments had been celebrated in newspapers and taverns across the country.

But his homecoming in Nashville meant a great deal to him. "Your friendship and regard," he told the crowd, "is a rich compensation for many sacrifices and many labors."

Jackson's rhetorical style, once wooden and strident, had become the voice of a wise elder. In that manner, and cherishing the warm welcome, he explained what the events just ended signified.

"The sons of America," he went on, "have given a new proof how impossible it is to conquer freemen fighting in defense of all that is dear to them. Henceforward we shall be respected by nations who, mistaking our character, had treated us with the utmost contumely and outrage. Years will continue to develop our inherent qualities, until, from being the youngest and the weakest, we shall become the most powerful nation in the universe."[21]

Andrew Jackson, once and for all, had evened an old score. This time it had been the British who left the battle bloodied and defeated. The Union was intact. He had proved himself to the powers in Washington. A war that could have ended in partition instead closed with the rise of an army of new American heroes with Andrew Jackson at its head. Thanks to the scarred orphan, never again would America be invaded by a foreign power, and the enemy it defeated would one day become an ally.

General Jackson's War

Back in the summer of 1812, a Federalist pamphleteer had dismissively nicknamed the conflict "Mr. Madison's War."[22] Madison's political opposition didn't want to go to war and, once it was declared, they wanted to tar him with it. But in 1815, with the return of peace and Jackson's big triumph, the stain rapidly faded. The press coverage helped: the *Niles' Weekly Register* spoke for many Americans that February and March: "The last six months is the proudest period in the history of the republic," its columns asserted. "[We] demonstrated to mankind a capacity to acquire a skill in arms to conquer 'the conquerors of the conquerors of all' as Wellington's invincibles were modestly styled." Furthermore, the *Register*'s editors concluded, "Who would not be an American? Long live the republic! . . . Last asylum of oppressed humanity! Peace is signed in the arms of victory!"[23]

The brilliance of the victory in New Orleans overshadowed the dark humiliation of the burning of the public buildings in Washington; in time, with the blurring of memory, the nation's recollections of the war would center on Andrew Jackson. Mr. Madison's War would become General Jackson's War. He was remembered as having restored America's honor.

The end of the war and its best moments—a handful of sea battles won by U.S. warships, the rocket's red glare that illuminated a giant flag in Baltimore (memorialized by the barrister Francis Scott Key), and, most of all, the Battle of New Orleans—provided Americans with a new sense of nationhood. In Europe, particularly among the inhabitants of Great Britain, a new recognition emerged that their American cousins couldn't be regarded merely as poor relations; one had to respect a people who stood up and defended themselves against the British Empire. Once dismissed by George Gleig as "an enemy unworthy of serious regard,"[24] the American military—whether regular or militia, army or navy or marines—had become a force to be reckoned with.

General Andrew Jackson had melded a largely amateur force into an army, one that had vanquished a sophisticated force perhaps twice its size. His attack on December 23 had been a masterstroke, one that stunned the British and bought Jackson and the defenders of New Orleans essential time. The general had marshaled his limited naval resources to harry the British from the Mississippi. He had improvised a brilliant defensive strategy. He had exercised restraint and discipline.

He deployed his men in a way that took advantage of their strengths as riflemen and minimized their weaknesses. His tactics forced General Pakenham's well-drilled force to confront American strengths on U.S. terms.

Despite a lack of formal military training, Jackson proved himself to be the ablest general in the war. Significantly, he was also a man capable of inspiring other men to do their duty. That mix of confidence and resolution boded well for a future foray into the realm of politics. As both a general and a politician, he pursued fixed goals because he had a vision for his country.

He wasn't a complicated man, but he possessed—and was possessed by—an extraordinary certainty. He was a man who could be fired by anger. Jackson hadn't been much of a student; his mother's forlorn wish for him to join the ministry died even before she did. His intelligence was not book-learned; he operated on instinct and experience. His orientations were the essential verities: duty to country (at first that meant region but, with the life-changing events in Louisiana, it became nation); duty to God; and duty to family, not only, in the narrow sense, to his relations but also to his neighbors, whom he regarded as his brothers and his sisters, and to his men and those who voted for him, whom he regarded as children given unto his care.

Jackson's unyielding belief in the Republic and his instinct for democratic values help explain why later historians would refer to his time as the Age of Jackson.

Epilogue

The Hero's Return: January 1840

> The instrument chosen by the Lord to get His will done, as Gideon was chosen in Biblical times, was General Andrew Jackson.
>
> —**Wilburt S. Brown,** *The Amphibious Campaign for West Florida and Louisiana,* 1969

As the year 1839 drew to a close, Andrew Jackson faced a decision. He held an invitation in his hand: with the twenty-fifth anniversary of the big battle just weeks away—the "silver jubilee" the organizers called it—the city he had saved invited him to return to celebrate his greatest military triumph.

The old man was honored, of course; he acknowledged that he had "sacrificed both property and health in the salvation of New Orleans."[1] He believed January 8 meant as much to American history as July 4, and his role in the victory was perhaps his greatest pride, despite having gone on to serve two terms as the nation's seventh chief executive (1829–37) and to dominate his era, a common man, as Jackson saw himself, captaining the ship of state through enormous changes.

But traveling all the way to New Orleans? That looked like a problem.

For one thing, his health was poor. He had spent the last five months of his presidency confined to his bed after almost dying following another of the periodic lung hemorrhages that plagued him (the lead ball from his 1806 duel remained embedded in his lung). In contemplating a long trip, he feared the physical challenges of a jarring ride in winter weather.

Another problem was that, despite his fame and considerable landholdings, he had little cash to spare. "I am out of funds," he confided to his namesake nephew, Andrew Jackson Donelson. Some years hadn't been good on Jackson's plantation, and Andrew Jr. had grown into a spendthrift, a constant drag on his famous father's finances. But the general, whatever his health and circumstances, remained a proud man. "I cannot bear to borrow or travel as a pauper," he admitted.[2]

At seventy-two, Jackson was no longer young—but the opportunity to return to the Crescent City did bring back powerful memories. The tall earthworks at the Battle of New Orleans had truly elevated him; that was one reason he insisted on being called *general* rather than *president*.

His defeat of the British had gained him respect in Washington, where, in February 1815, Congress had ordered a medal be struck—featuring his profile, dressed in his high-collared uniform—to honor his "splendid achievement." Almost overnight, he had unexpectedly become a national figure, his fame exploding far beyond the bounds of New Orleans and the Southwest. In the nation's cultural center, Philadelphia, a printmaker had produced a commemorative engraving; Jackson's likeness, with his arched brows, the crest of hair atop his tall forehead, and his imperious expression, became recognizable across the land. Jackson entrusted Major John Reid with his correspondence and other papers in order that his aide might write an account of the battle. Although Reid died before completing *The Life of Andrew Jackson, Major-General in the Service of the United States,* the book, bearing the bylines of both Reid and John Henry Eaton, appeared in 1817. It would be the closest thing to an account of his part in the War of 1812 by Jackson himself.

In the twenty-five years since the Battle of New Orleans, Jackson had seen vast changes. The once-unpopular President James Madison had emerged from the Second War of Independence a much-honored man. His successor, James Monroe, rode a wave of new prosperity and goodwill into an "era of good feelings," as one Boston newspaper put it after Monroe's inauguration in 1817.[3] The westward boom that Jackson had foreseen brought soaring land values, rapid population growth, and the appearance of new and substantial towns. New states joined the Union, including Indiana, Mississippi, Illinois, Alabama, and Missouri. Foreign trade and shipping blossomed.

Jackson continued to do his bit—and then some—after the war. His defeat of the Creeks had already cleared a great swath of territory for settlement, but in 1818, pursuing the Seminoles at President Monroe's orders, he wrested Florida from Spain, and then served as its territorial governor. Jackson had emerged as the most important leader of his region. In 1823, as a U.S. senator from Tennessee, he had been positioned to run for the presidency. Though he won the most electoral votes in the four-man race of 1824, his lack of a plurality meant the contest was decided in the House of Representatives, where John Quincy Adams prevailed. The vote left a sour taste in Jackson's mouth: another of the candidates, the former Ghent negotiator Henry Clay, had thrown his support to Adams and soon thereafter been named secretary of state. To Jackson, the deal was a dirty one—and he labeled Clay the "Judas of the West."

The 1828 election ended differently when changes in voter eligibility (property requirements for suffrage were eliminated in most states, quadrupling the electorate) helped Jackson prevail. He had a gift for intuiting what the common man wanted, but his victory also seemed preordained: His friend Edward Livingston had spoken for many when he told Jackson, back in 1815, "General, you are the man. You must be President of the United States."[4] Barely a dozen years later, Livingston's prognostication came true.

Andrew Jackson was far from the only person whose prospects had been changed by the battle. Edward Livingston, for one, had prospered. He had become a Louisiana congressman (1823–29) and a U.S. senator (1829–31). His friendship with the general proved lasting, and during Jackson's presidency, Livingston had been a key confidant as secretary of state (1831–33) and minister to France (1833–35).

Thomas Hart Benton, Jackson's former subordinate in the Tennessee militia and an opponent in the 1813 gunfight that left Jackson gravely wounded, had resurfaced as a powerful U.S. senator from Missouri (and a valuable Jackson ally) during Jackson's presidency.

In contrast, Governor William Claiborne continued to have an uneasy relationship with his varied Louisiana constituency; he died young, at just forty-two years of age, in 1817.

Some of the military men who served with Jackson had risen in the ranks, but others floundered. Daniel Todd Patterson's service in New Orleans gained him a captaincy and, for a time, the ship he commanded was the legendary USS *Constitution* (the frigate had gained its nickname, "Old Ironsides," during Mr. Madison's War). At the time of his death, in 1839, Patterson was commander of the Washington Navy Yard.

Thomas ap Catesby Jones remained in the U.S. Navy, gaining a minor place in American literature after he crossed paths with a navy deserter named Herman Melville, who would memorialize him as Commodore J—— in *Moby-Dick; or, The Whale* (1851).

The militia general William Carroll returned to civilian life and was twice elected governor of Tennessee. John Coffee returned to real estate speculation, often in partnership with his friend Andrew Jackson.

The least likely of Jackson's men, the Baratarian pirates, had won his respect and appreciation for their artillery skills and, in his general orders after the Battle of New Orleans, he acknowledged as much: "The general cannot avoid giving his warm approbation of the manner in which [the privateers] have uniformly conducted themselves while under his command. . . . The brothers Lafitte have exhibited the same courage and fidelity, and the general promises that the government shall be duly apprised of their conduct."[5] In February 1815, they received their pardons but the life of the straight and narrow proved difficult. Jean Lafitte resumed privateering, eventually from a new base of operations at the port of Galveston in Spanish Texas. Lafitte died in 1823 of wounds sustained in a ship-to-ship battle but his legend lived on: the swashbuckler would fire the imaginations of novelists and scriptwriters. His brother Pierre, once more a pirate, operated out of an island base between Cuba and Mexico. He died of fever in 1821 and was buried in a convent churchyard in northeastern Yucatán.

Some of Jackson's fellow fighters in the Indian wars had gone on to fame and fortune. Sam Houston's enduring popularity won him the governorship of Tennessee before he went west to Texas. There he would serve as both president of the short-lived Republic of Texas and as governor of the state of Texas after it joined the Union.

Davy Crockett became a U.S. congressman and later died at the Alamo, but not before writing his colorful, if rather folkloric, *A Narrative of the Life of David Crockett, of the State of Tennessee* (1834). At the time of his death a decade after the Battle of Horseshoe Bend, William Weatherford—Jackson's worthy Red Stick opponent, once known as Red Eagle—had become a planter, horse breeder, and owner of three hundred black slaves, residing on a farm near the site of Fort Mims.[6]

On the other side of the line, Sir John Lambert and John Keane—unlike the deceased generals Pakenham and Gibbs—made it back to Europe alive. Both joined the Duke of Wellington in defeating Napoleon once more, this time at the Battle of Waterloo, on June 18, 1815. Both Lambert and Keane went on to serve in Jamaica, administering the civil government of the colony. Lambert died a general, in 1847, but Keane, raised to a peerage after service in India, died a baron, in 1844.

When Alexander Forrester Inglis Cochrane retired from the Royal Navy, in 1824, he was commander of the Plymouth navy headquarters; he died in Paris, in 1832.

Colonel William Thornton became a lieutenant general and received a knighthood in 1836. Subject to delusions—perhaps a consequence of head wounds sustained years earlier—he shot himself in 1840. Captain Nicholas Lockyer recovered from the several wounds he sustained on Lake Borgne and served a long career in the Royal Navy, dying aboard the ship he captained, the HMS *Albion,* at age sixty-five in 1847.

The Ursuline nuns who had prayed for victory on January 8, 1815, rose from their knees after the firing stopped and, hospital cots at the ready, welcomed the wounded to their school. They nursed men from Kentucky and Tennessee, and even British soldiers. One novice, Sister Sainte Angèle Johnston, was fondly remembered by her patients. Most of the nuns spoke only French; Sister Angèle, a native of Baltimore, was one of the few who spoke English. "Wait until the little sister . . . comes," one wounded soldier said to another. "She will understand you and give you what you want."[7]

In the years after the war, the Ursuline nuns remained true to the promise that Mother Superior Olivier de Vézin had made to the Almighty. To this day, on January 8, the Ursuline nuns conduct an annual Mass of Thanksgiving in honor of Our Lady of Prompt Succor and the Battle of New Orleans.

Remembering the Battle of New Orleans

In the months and years after the battle, there was much hand-wringing in Great Britain concerning the great defeat at New Orleans. Cochrane and Keane got the blame—Wellington himself thought an attack via Lake Borgne foolhardy, a violation of his cherished principle that an army must always be in contact with its base. Wellington also believed Cochrane's greed for plunder distorted his military judgment and preparations.

On the American side, military historians have argued over how Bayou Bienvenue could have been left open to the British (a court-martial convened on the matter in 1815 exonerated young Gabriel Villeré). A case has been made repeatedly that Jackson's force was vulnerable and that, had Admiral Cochrane and General Keane listened to the pleading of Colonel Thornton on December 23, 1814—he is said to have argued for immediately marching on New Orleans as the British had at Washington—then Jackson might have lost the Battle of New Orleans. As with all such hypotheticals, however, no firm conclusion can ever be reached.

Jackson's failure to properly defend the west bank raises another what-if. Many military historians believe that, given only slightly altered circumstances, the capture of Patterson's position could have been catastrophic to the American cause.

Some analysts blame the failure of the British campaign on the lack of secrecy; their attack on the Americans was not a surprise. The explanation for that has been alternately assigned to loose British lips and to Jackson for his cultivation and use of intelligence sources. In the same way, the debate continues to swirl about troop numbers: Did the British have five thousand effectives? Six thousand? Nine thousand? Or many more? The Americans certainly had fewer, but there is no agreement as to how many on that side, either.

In the end, though, everyone understood—then and now—that Jackson was the man of the hour, the man who met his moment standing atop his earthworks. He was ready to fight to the last man, to give his own life, and to burn the city of New Orleans before surrendering it to the British.

He made a series of decisions that have come to be seen as wise, even profound, in the eyes of most commentators: his double-time march on Pensacola; his flexible approach to defending the city of New Orleans; his surprise attack on December 23; his choice to shift from offense to defense; his decision before the big day to make his stand at the Rodriguez Canal and then to remain safely behind his ramparts after January 8, 1815.

On the other hand, his stubbornness alienated the populace of New Orleans after the victory at the Chalmette Plain. And he failed to designate a second in command: he might have died, for example, in the cross fire on December 23; if he had, could anyone else have held his army together? Yet his single-mindedness in leadership won the allegiance of his troops through a mix of intimidation and fatherly affection. They would fight heroically, despite the rockets zooming crazily overhead, rather than risk the wrath of Old Hickory.

On reading the accounts in most textbooks, the student comes away with the sense that the War of 1812 ended in a draw. Furthermore, if weights were assigned to the gives and the takes as specified in the Treaty of Ghent, Lady Justice's scale would likely find they balance, more or less, as the two sides come out about even. No territory changed hands; Great Britain made no promises regarding impressment; the world went back to the peaceable business of trade.

But General Jackson knew better: he had saved New Orleans; if he had not, the postwar history of his nation would have been different indeed.

The General's Last Stand

At the Hermitage, Andrew Jackson lived the life of a recluse, old and infirm, rarely leaving home and avoiding public appearances. He and his family worried that a simple cold—and the accompanying cough— could endanger his life. Yet the general's old determination still burned and, in December 1839, he decided that neither his fragile health nor his straitened finances could be allowed to stand in the way of a trip to New Orleans for the silver jubilee.

He saw a higher purpose: the journey, he believed, would forward the cause of democracy. As he told President Martin Van Buren, "My whole life has been employed to establish and perpetuate our republican system [and] if I should die in the effort, it cannot end better than endeavoring to open the eyes of the people to the blessings we enjoy."[8]

Jackson borrowed against the sale of his cotton crop to defray the costs; he simply had to make the journey.

On Christmas Eve, he left Nashville in a carriage, with his traveling companion, his nephew, Major Donelson. The roads were rough, snow-covered in places, and four long days were required to travel the 125 miles to the mouth of the Cumberland River. There he boarded the *Gallatin*, a steam-powered packet boat headed down the Ohio River.

If Jackson had had his way, he would have been accompanied by Rachel, but the stresses of the 1828 election a dozen years earlier had cost him dearly. So many insults were cast at both husband and wife that Rachel remarked to a friend just before ballots were cast, "I would rather be a doorkeeper in the house of God than live in that palace in Washington." Just days after the close of the hard-fought electoral battle, Rachel Jackson was indeed summoned by her Lord, stricken with an intense pain in her left arm, shoulder, and chest. Suddenly, the president-elect was in mourning for the love of his life.

As the *Gallatin* steamed south—the ship was named after Albert Gallatin, one of the men who had negotiated the Treaty of Ghent and, later, served as President John Quincy Adams's minister to the Court of St James's—Jackson observed many signs of how, in his lifetime, his nation had changed, shifting from a largely agricultural society to one increasingly based on industry. The advent of new technology meant that regularly scheduled steamboats made his march home from Natchez, back in the spring of 1813, seem like a quaint historical oddity. More than a thousand steamers now plied the Mississippi, making travel more rapid, predictable, and comfortable.

The general and his entourage arrived in New Orleans right on schedule, on the morning of Wednesday, January 8. The convoy had grown to five steamboats and, on stepping ashore at ten o'clock, Jackson, ignoring his illnesses and age, impressed the crowd of an estimated thirty thousand people.

Hatless, his hair a striking silver, and looking heartier than he felt, the general saluted the spectators as he rode in a carriage, part of a procession to the familiar confines of the Place d'Armes. For many hours, he would endure receptions, a service in the cathedral, speechifying, a reunion with officers from the army that defended the city, and fireworks.

Although the exhausted Jackson excused himself from a scheduled trip to the Chalmette Plain, even his political enemies cheered him that day. As one opposition newspaper reported, "[We] forgot the politician and thought only of the man—welcom[ing] him as the 'Hero of New Orleans' and the fearless defender of his country."[9]

If the Battle of New Orleans had made the man—and rising to the challenge as he did can certainly be said to have been Jackson's most essential rite of passage—then he did the same for his nation. He saved not only New Orleans from the British but preserved the Union.

But Andrew Jackson had stood in Pakenham's path. If he had not, the entire Gulf Coast might have been returned to Spain or remained in British hands.

With the celebrations in New Orleans concluded, Jackson returned to his stateroom aboard the *Vicksburg* and the steamship began its voyage upstream. Back at the Hermitage, Jackson would live five more years before dying quietly, on June 8, 1845. A year later the sculptor Clark Mills would be commissioned to execute an equestrian stature of Jackson and, in 1853, the twelve-foot-tall likeness of Jackson astride a rearing horse was dedicated. It stood—and stands today—at the center of Jackson Square, as the Place d'Armes was renamed in honor of the general.

His legacy was large and, like the War of 1812 and the Battle of New Orleans, subject to debate. Saving New Orleans made Andrew Jackson a national hero and, with his nation still mourning George Washington, Jackson inherited the great man's mantle. General Washington led the first fight with the British—but Andrew Jackson's success at New Orleans preserved his nation's hard-fought independence.

AFTERWORD

Presidential Memory

The more I learn about Jackson, the more I love him.

—President Franklin Delano Roosevelt, 1936

Since the release of the hardcover edition of this book last year, I have followed closely the debate raging over Andrew Jackson's legacy. I myself fall in the category of Jackson admirer, though I acknowledge that some of his decisions in life, politics, and battle were wrong. Despite his flaws, no clear-eyed evaluator can dispute Jackson's patriotic motivations and the significance of his legacy even today. In fact, in some ways Old Hickory is more relevant than ever; President Donald Trump sees enough importance in Jackson to return his portrait to the Oval Office.

Our forty-fifth president is not the only one who looked up to Jackson. Some of our finest leaders saw in him someone to emulate. While this generation of Americans feels compelled to evaluate him by the standards of today, iconic presidents of America's past saw in him primarily someone to admire.

After the Battle of New Orleans, Andrew Jackson's countrymen adored him. They knew he saved the nation and thought of him, along with George Washington, as a defining national figure. In one way, Jackson was even more their man than the founders; unlike the presidents up to that point, Jackson inherited no land or family reputation. He owed no allegiance to what he called the "aristocracy of the union," and the common people claimed him as their own. Birth registries across the county offered one sign of that status. In years to come, for every baby named, say, "George Washington Smith," another would be christened "Andrew Jackson Jones."

In 1828, his admirers elected him president in a landslide—his 178 electoral votes more than doubled incumbent John Quincy Adams's 83. On March 4, 1829, a great crowd gathered to cheer as he took the oath of office; in the view of one watcher, he was "the People's President" on "the People's Day."[1] So enthusiastic was the crowd that the celebration got a bit out of hand at the White House, ending in broken furniture, smashed crystal, and men clambering out windows. Forced to escape to a hotel, this new president was dubbed "King Mob" by one Supreme Court justice.[2]

The more refined members of the judicial branch may have disapproved, but Jackson had a mandate and acted on it. Thanks to his fiscal policies, the nation had no debt (for the only time in history) for one year of his presidency. He vetoed more legislation than all his predecessors combined. A firm believer in America's "Manifest Destiny," he pursued territorial expansion as if it were a moral duty. When a national controversy over tariffs threatened the Union (South Carolina claimed they could "nullify" the tariffs), everyone believed

President Jackson's threat to "hang the first man I can lay my hand on engaged in such treasonable conduct, upon the first tree I can reach."[3] All talk of secession faded.

Since then, Jackson's reputation has fluctuated as his politics and bluster have come in and out of favor, but he shows no signs of being forgotten. From the nineteenth century into the twenty-first, the seventh president has influenced many of America's presidents, who have turned to him for inspiration both in war and in politics.

Theodore Roosevelt

Theodore Roosevelt encountered Jackson's legacy early in life. Suffering from a case of unrequited love as a senior at Harvard, he buried his sorrows at the library. A voracious reader who would read a book a day throughout his life, he decided, in 1879, to write a book of his own. The topic? The War of 1812.

After a few months, he set the project aside—the woman he loved, Alice Lee, finally consented to be his wife—but he returned to his manuscript after his marriage. On publication, in 1882, *The Naval War of 1812* quickly sold out three printings. It became a standard reference on the war and, at twenty-three, Roosevelt gained recognition as a serious historian.

One figure stands especially tall in his book. Roosevelt wasted little ink on the U.S. Army in 1812, 1813, and 1814; as he put it, "the war on land had been for us full of humiliation."[4] But he found General Jackson mesmerizing. "The only military genius," Roosevelt concluded, "that the struggle developed was Andrew Jackson."

Yet young Roosevelt also recognized how complex a man Andrew

Jackson had been. In 1882, he wrote, "In after-years [Jackson] did to his country some good and more evil; but no true American can think of his deeds at New Orleans without profound and unmixed thankfulness." An advocate of military preparedness and, above all, strong leadership, Roosevelt could not help but admire how Jackson managed his unlikely army of frontiersmen, pirates, Creoles, and blacks. "Even their fierce natures quailed before the ungovernable fury of a spirit greater than their own; and their sullen, stubborn wills were bent at last before [Jackson's] unyielding temper and iron hand."

As president years later, Roosevelt pursued his policy of the Square Deal, which echoed Jackson's desire to fight for common people in the face of moneyed interests. He saw political equity in associating his name with the strong-willed Jackson (Roosevelt, after all, was a proponent of "speak softly and carry a big stick"). Later still, in his post-presidential autobiography, Roosevelt disparaged Jackson as "King Andrew." But he would be far from the last president to honor, even with mixed feelings, the Jackson legacy.

Harry S. Truman

At age ten, Harry Truman first chanced upon Andrew Jackson. Harry was recuperating from a bout with diphtheria; for months his legs and arms had been paralyzed and his mother had been forced to move him about in a baby carriage. But as the symptoms faded, Truman regained his strength and he devoured a four-volume set of *Great Men and Famous Women*, a gift from his mother.

The subjects ranged from Goethe to Grover Cleveland, Hannibal to Robert E. Lee. Truman quickly found favorites, one of them Andrew Jackson. For Truman, the Tennessean became a lifelong hero.[5]

Unlike Theodore Roosevelt, who was the son a wealthy New York family, Harry Truman came from rough-and-ready stock. His father (nicknamed "Peanuts") worked at different times as a mule trader, farmer, and night watchman, and, despite his father's lack of military experience, Harry saw a connection between Jackson and John Truman. "My father was a fighter," Harry Truman would say, "and if he didn't like what you did, he'd fight you. He was an Andrew Jackson descendent."[6] Though the families weren't directly related, they did share Scotch-Irish ancestry and undeniable frontier toughness.

When, at twenty-four, Truman joined the Freemasons, he reveled in knowing that Jackson, too, had been a member. In business selling men's clothing, Truman spent more time reading books about Jackson (according to his partner's recollections) than he did serving his customers.[7] That business would fail but while serving as a judge in Missouri in the thirties, Truman commissioned an equestrian statue of Jackson that still stands in front of the courthouse. The former clothier was so concerned about the correctness of the likeness that he took measurements of a surviving Jackson uniform. As president, he positioned a bronze model of that Jackson statue on a table in his office for all visitors to see.

When he posed with Franklin Roosevelt after the latter had invited him to be his running mate, in August 1944, they stood in shirtsleeves beneath a tree planted by then president Andrew Jackson on the White House's South Lawn. "Give 'em Hell" Harry could hardly have known that less than a year later he would become the nation's thirty-third president when FDR died in office.

President Truman would be a tough fiscal conservative in the vein of his favorite president. He wanted, as Jackson had done, to reawaken "the people again to the fact that they control the government."[8] He chose to stand with average men and women. "Jackson wanted sincerely to look after the little fellow who had no pull," Truman once said, "and that's what a president is supposed to do."[9]

He was a plain speaker, at least partly in honor of the tradition of backcountry politics he shared with Andrew Jackson. And the general public knew it, too. Thousands gathered in Washington for his first inaugural, in 1949; another ten million people watched what was the first inauguration broadcast on television.

To the end, Jackson was a living presence for Truman. When he chose not to run for reelection in 1952, he named Andrew Jackson (and others) as a precedent for a two-term presidency. Over a century after his death, Jackson's legacy lingered.

Continuing Influence

Other presidents also paid homage, making trips to Jackson's Hermitage, as many did to Washington's Mount Vernon. When Teddy's cousin Franklin Delano Roosevelt visited, in 1934, he was a first-term president. He and his wife, Eleanor, were heading for the Little White House in Warm Springs, Georgia, but Jackson and the Hermitage left a strong impression. To the tune of "Hail to the Chief" (played on Jackson's pianoforte), he was greeted by a descendant of Rachel Jackson's. Despite his disabilities—only steel braces, his cane, and an aide at his elbow permitted FDR to stand—he honored the general's toughness by touring the Hermitage without his wheelchair.[10]

In the next presidential campaign, Roosevelt and his New Deal programs were under siege. He saw a parallel to Jackson's battles while in office. As Roosevelt confided to his vice president, "It is absolutely true that [Jackson's] opponents represented the same social outlook and the same element of the population that ours do. The more I learn about Andy Jackson, the more I love him."[11]

Perhaps Jackson's many ailments were another connection for the usually wheelchair-bound Roosevelt, but, having won a second term, he ordered the construction of a replica of the Hermitage's facade on the White House lawn to serve as a reviewing stand for his 1937 inauguration. In March 1941, as FDR pondered war with the Axis powers, he spoke to his radio audience from the deck of the USS *Potomac* and once again invoked the memory of Jackson. He compared the approaching war—just nine months later the Japanese would attack Pearl Harbor—to the "responsibility [that] lay heavily upon the shoulders of Andrew Jackson."[12]

Although John F. Kennedy did not visit the Hermitage, he counted Jackson as a Democratic forefather, describing him rather ambiguously as "both a picture of dignity and a master of profanity."[13] Lyndon Baines Johnson did make it to Hermitage, Tennessee, arriving, in March 1967, for a celebration of Jackson's two hundredth birthday. Just a year away from what was shaping up to be a hard-fought reelection campaign, Johnson spoke in his Hermitage speech of the "Jacksonian revolution." He also mentioned Jackson had been a slaveholder as he described the goals of his own Great Society agenda. "We are still striving," Johnson told the crowd, "to involve the poor, the deprived, the forgotten American, white and Negro, in the future of their society." In closing, he cited Jackson's "rugged confidence," probably a reference to the anti-war opposition Johnson faced, a major factor in his unexpected decision not to pursue another presidential term in 1968.[14]

Perhaps it was inevitable that Ronald Reagan, a man who knew star power firsthand, chose to pair portraits of Washington and a youthful-looking Andrew Jackson in the Oval Office. He, too, would attend a Jackson birthday party, and in a Nashville speech, in 1982, he aligned Jackson's legacy with his own vision for smaller government. "Our federal government has become so bloated and fat that Jackson wouldn't recognize it," Reagan told his audience. He reminded them of the kind of leader his long-ago predecessor had been. "It was Jackson," said Reagan, "who reminded us that 'One man with courage makes a majority.'"[15]

More presidents than we have space for visited the Hermitage; in the future, more will do the same. We will also see Jackson's stock continue to rise and fall. Recently there's been discontent at celebrating a man with Jackson's history regarding Native Americans, as well as controversy over the plan, advanced during the Obama administration, to replace Jackson on the twenty-dollar bill with Harriet Tubman, a decision more recently postponed.

Although his era was very different from ours, the desire of so many presidents, Republican and Democratic, to relate to him speaks to his importance. Whatever his flaws, the general rose above humble roots to command an army and, later, to captain his country. His leadership remains inspiring. His presence in the public mind, in the writings of historians, and in the eyes of presidents demonstrates the man's immortality. In short, the Hero of New Orleans remains an indisputable, if debated, American icon long after he vanquished an unbeatable foe on the Chalmette Plain.

—Brian Kilmeade, May 2018

ACKNOWLEDGMENTS

As someone who first fell in love with American history by learning about the local history where I grew up, I have a tremendous amount of appreciation for the enthusiasm that scholars, researchers, and reenactors bring to their study of the people and events who helped shape their corner of the world and the nation at large. This project was no exception. The dedication of the men and women in Louisiana and Tennessee who assisted us with our reconstruction of the Battle of New Orleans as well as the character of Andrew Jackson is a testament to their field.

This book could not possibly have happened without our superlative team at Sentinel, headed by Adrian Zackheim. He proved once again that he is a man of tremendous vision and appreciation for the impact of dynamic, meaningful stories; it is truly an honor to be able to develop these books under his guidance and expertise. Will Weisser can best be described as a high-octane executive who fuels all the books we have produced at Sentinel, and his involvement is essential and deeply appreciated. Bria Sandford, likewise, is one of the most outstanding individuals with whom I have ever had the pleasure of working. She keeps an unimaginable number of plates spinning and does so without ever breaking her stride or her smile. She is both gracious and tenacious, a delight and a powerhouse; it was her suggestion for the title, after many long and agonizing conversations as a team, that was the breakthrough that allowed this story to find its way.

Bob Barnett, our tremendous agent, has built a reputation as one of the most respected people in the business—and for good reason. He not only represents the book but also truly cares about its development and success in a way that goes above and beyond a simple business transaction. I am continually awed by and grateful for his involvement in our work, and his support for everything it takes to make each book all it can be.

It's always great working with the award-winning writer Don Yaeger, whose humor, talent, and experience make these projects so much better and so much more fun. And with Don comes his longtime cohort Tiffany Yecke Brooks. Without her incredible contribution, this book would simply not be the same. *(Here's the big secret in my opinion, Don: Tiffany likes history more than sports.)*

The research component of this project was staggering in its magnitude—primary documents, secondary documents, tangential documents that proved essential, and in-person tours of numerous sites. Thankfully, we were blessed with historian after historian who responded to our requests for information with amazing enthusiasm and humbling brilliance. In New Orleans, world-class historian Douglas Brinkley was able to share his tremendous knowledge as well as steer us to the great people at the Historic New Orleans Collection and the Jean Lafitte National Historical Park's visitors' center. Thank you, too, to Ron Drez, who does as much as anyone in this country to keep American history alive. And a huge thanks to Ron Chapman, who gave us way too much of his personal time taking us through the Chalmette

Battlefield and giving us tours of downtown. His passion, knowledge, and book (*The Battle of New Orleans: "But for a Piece of Wood"*) helped bring this story to life.

In Tennessee, I'd like to spotlight the great help from Tom Kanon, a talented archivist with the Tennessee secretary of state's office. His guidance was essential in helping us develop a fuller picture of the character of Andrew Jackson. Additionally, the entire staff at the Hermitage, Andrew and Rachel Jackson's home, was unbelievably welcoming, helpful, and incredibly knowledgeable. I would especially like to thank Marsha Mullin, vice president of museum services and chief curator. Your dedication to preserving Jackson's legacy is humbling, and your knowledge is astounding. Thank you for giving us such valuable insight while also showing true southern hospitality.

And to Hugh Howard, whose depth of knowledge never fails to astound me, thank you for your suggestions and guidance in getting us started and keeping us on track with what felt, at times, like an overwhelming number of sources.

The key to the success of any book is the promotion and marketing, and most of that falls on the shoulders of George Uribe and his company, Guestbooker. George and the outstanding Victoria Delgado Chism have headed the promotion, working tirelessly to make *Thomas Jefferson and the Tripoli Pirate*s an enormous success and a *New York Times* bestseller. Their work to ensure past successes helped lay the path for future ones.

The entire Fox News family has been outstanding in all they have done to support my work on this project as well as to help spread its important message. I would like to spotlight all those who built and sustain Fox News Channel today. Special thanks to Rupert Murdoch, Suzanne Scott, Jay Wallace, and Jack Abernathy for supporting my passion for American history and for launching the one-hour TV special in conjunction with the publication of the book. I'm grateful to John Finley for putting together an amazing team, including Brian Gaffney, Jennings Grant, and Carrie Flatley, leading up to the special's release, and I owe tremendous thanks to Paul Guest and Amanda Muehlenkamp, social media mavens who worked around the clock to get the word out about this book. And nothing gets done without the legal team, of course, so I am indebted to them for all of their behind-the-scenes help, especially Dianne Brandi, the legal eagle who keeps us on the straight and narrow.

Steve Doocy and Ainsley Earhardt were great allies in the monumental process of getting this book out, all while Ainsley had the additional challenge of writing and promoting her children's book. Their support for the project was truly appreciated.

I also am thrilled to spotlight the incredible support of the staffs of my two programs: on TV, *Fox & Friends,* and on the radio, *The Brian Kilmeade Show.* I have the pleasure of working with such great people on a daily basis, and they are consistently looking to bend their schedules so that I can develop and promote projects like this. To Vice President Lauren Petterson, how you oversee thirty hours of weekly programming and still support me in all my extra work is beyond me. Gavin Hadden, you are a positive, patriotic EP—thank you. I would also like to single out the ceaseless support from my other star TV producers: Sean Groman, Brian Tully, A. J. Hall, Andrew Murray, Lauren Peikoff, Chris White, Kelly McNally, Kelly May, Stephanie Freeman, and Lee Kushnir.

On the radio, I constantly need flexibility for interviews, specials, and appearances, and my support team is endlessly patient and professional. Led by Alyson Mansfield, who helps me beyond radio as my coordinating producer, Eric Albeen, Peter Caterina, and Aaron Spielberg round out the radio A team.

Finally, to my wife and children, I can never thank you enough. My wife, Dawn, the most patient and supportive woman in the world, I know this book took time away from our family. I am forever grateful for your willingness to shoulder more of the responsibilities while I am researching, writing, or traveling for what has become, during its production, a kind of second full-time job. To Bryan, Kirstyn, and Kaitlyn, I deeply appreciate your understanding and even your enthusiasm for this work. May you someday be as blessed as I am to have a family that encourages you to similarly pursue your interests and passions.

Andrew Jackson and the Miracle at New Orleans is a story of a highly factionalized society coming together at a time of crisis and uniting their skills, valor, and spirit for the sake of preserving this nation. I can think of no message more timely or important. Jackson led the way, but it was the willingness of the ordinary citizens—soldiers, militiamen, civilians, outlaws—who carried out his vision. Despite the vast differences in language, ethnicity, national origin, race, social class, and countless other factors, the people who defended New Orleans recognized that what united them was stronger than what divided them. This story is a testament to Americans' willingness to reach out across lines and come together to protect our beautiful liberty. Perhaps no moment in American history better encapsulates our national motto: *E pluribus unum*. Out of many, one.

NOTES

PROLOGUE

1. Parton, *Life of Andrew Jackson*, vol. 1 (1861), p. 89.
2. Quoted in Groom, *Patriotic Fire*, p. 37.

CHAPTER 1: FREEDOMS AT RISK

1. Andrew Jackson to Thomas Monteagle Bayly, June 27, 1807.
2. Parton, *Life of Andrew Jackson*, vol. 1 (1861), p. 133.
3. Benton, *Thirty Years' View* (1854), vol. 1, p. 736.
4. Andrew Jackson, Proclamation to the Tennessee Militia, March 7, 1812.
5. "Jackson's Announcement to His Soldiers," November 14, 1812.
6. Thomas Jefferson to Robert R. Livingston, April 18, 1802.

CHAPTER 2: HOW TO LOSE A WAR

1. Henry Clay, speech to Senate, February 22, 1810.
2. Thomas Jefferson to William Duane, August 4, 1812.
3. William Eustis to Henry Dearborn, July 9, 1812.
4. John Randolph, speech to Congress, December 10, 1811, in *Annals of Congress,* 12th Congress, 1st Session, p. 447.

5. Quoted in Groom, *Patriotic Fire,* p.166.

6. Andrew Jackson to Willie Blount, July 3, 1812.

7. Andrew Jackson, quoted in Remini, *Andrew Jackson and the Course of American Empire* (1977), p. 170.

8. "The Departure from Nashville, a Journal of the Trip Down the Mississippi," in Jackson, *Correspondence of Andrew Jackson,* vol. 1. (1926), pp. 256–71.

9. John Armstrong to Andrew Jackson, February 5, 1813.

10. James Madison to Robert R. Livingston and James Monroe, April 18, 1803.

11. John Armstrong to Andrew Jackson, February 5, 1813.

12. Andrew Jackson to John Armstrong, March 15, 1813.

13. "Jackson's Announcement to His Soldiers," November 14, 1812.

14. Andrew Jackson to Felix Grundy, March 15, 1813.

15. Andrew Jackson to James Wilkinson, March 22, 1813.

16. Andrew Jackson to James Madison, March 15, 1813.

17. Andrew Jackson to Rachel Jackson, March 15, 1813.

18. *Nashville Whig,* quoted in Remini, *Andrew Jackson and the Course of American Empire* (1977), p. 180.

19. Parton, *Life of Andrew Jackson,* vol. 1 (1861), p. 382.

CHAPTER 3: THE MAKING OF A GENERAL

1. Groom, *Patriotic Fire* (2006), p. 38.

2. Charles Dickinson, May 21, 1806, in *Correspondence of Andrew Jackson,* vol. 1 (1926), p. 143.

3. Parton, *Life of Andrew Jackson,* vol. 1 (1861), p. 387.

4. Thomas Hart Benton to Andrew Jackson, July 25, 1813.

5. Parton, *Life of Andrew Jackson,* vol. 1 (1861), p. 394.

6. Griffith, *McIntosh and Weatherford* (1988), p. 111.

7. Andrew Jackson to the Tennessee Volunteers, September 24, 1813.

8. Reid and Eaton, *Life* (1817), p. 33.

9. Crockett, *Narrative of the Life of David Crockett* (1834), p. 88.

10. John Coffee, Official Report, November 3, 1813, in Parton, *Life of Andrew Jackson,* vol. 1 (1861), p. 437.

11. Parton, *Life of Andrew Jackson*, vol. 1 (1861), p. 439.

12. Andrew Jackson to Rachel Jackson, November 4, 1813.

13. Quoted in Remini, *Andrew Jackson and the Course of American Empire* (1977), p. 193.

14. Andrew Jackson to Willie Blount, November 11, 1813.

15. Crockett, *Narrative of the Life of David Crockett* (1834), p. 92.

CHAPTER 4: A RIVER DYED RED

1. John Borlase Warren to Lord Melville, November 18, 1812.

2. Matthew D. Cooper, quoted in Owsley, *Struggle for the Gulf Borderland* (1981), p. 69.

3. Colonel William Martin to Andrew Jackson, December 4, 1813.

4. Reid and Eaton, *Life* (1817), p. 84.

5. Andrew Jackson to the First Brigade, Tennessee Volunteer Infantry, December 13, 1813.

6. Andrew Jackson to Rachel Jackson, December 29, 1813.

7. Andrew Jackson to Willie Blount, December 29, 1813.

8. See Pickett, *History of Alabama*, vol. 2 (1851), pp. 324–25, and Griffith, *McIntosh and Weatherford* (1988), pp. 129–31.

9. Reid and Eaton, *Life* (1817), p. 136.

10. "Report of Jackson to Governor Blount," March 31, 1814.

11. John Coffee to Andrew Jackson, April 11, 1814.

12. Andrew Jackson, "General Order," March 24[?], 1814.

13. Andrew Jackson to Rachel Jackson, April 1, 1814.

14. Reid and Eaton, *Life* (1817), p. 165. Variant versions of Jackson and Weatherford's meeting are found in Pickett, *History of Alabama*, vol. 2 (1851), pp. 348–52, and in Royall, *Letters from Alabama* (1830), pp. 17–19, as recounted by one of Jackson's subalterns in 1817 to Anne Royall, whom some consider to be the first American woman journalist.

15. Reid and Eaton, *Life* (1817), p. 166.

16. Ibid., pp. 166–67.

17. Major John Reid, quoted in James, *Life of Andrew Jackson* (1933), p. 172.

18. Attributed to Andrew Jackson in Woodward, *Woodward's Reminiscences of the Creek* (1939), p. 102.

19. John Armstrong to James Madison, May 14, 1814.

20. Andrew Jackson to Rachel Jackson, August 5, 1814.

21. *American State Papers,* Military Affairs, vol. 1, p. 379.

22. Ingersoll, *Historical Sketch of the Second War,* vol. 1 (1853), pp. 197–200.

CHAPTER 5: THE BRITISH ON OFFENSE

1. Crété, *Daily Life in Louisiana* (1978), p. 61.

2. *Times* (London), April 27, 1814.

3. Albert Gallatin to James Monroe, June 13, 1814.

4. Henry Clay to James Monroe, August 18, 1814.

5. Letter fragment of August 13, 1814, cited in James, *Life of Andrew Jackson* (1933), p. 184. See also letter of August 8, 1814, reprinted in Latour, *Historical Memoir* (1816, 1999), pp. 184–85.

6. Andrew Jackson to Robert Butler, August 27, 1814.

7. Andrew Jackson to William C. C. Claiborne, August 30, 1814.

8. Andrew Jackson to Robert Butler, August 27, 1814.

9. Although the story of the Lafitte-Lockyer encounter has been told many times in different ways (including by Lafitte himself many years later in his less-than-reliable *Journal*), perhaps the best and most authoritative version appeared shortly after the Battle of New Orleans in Latour, *Historical Memoir* (1816, 1999), pp. 24ff. See also James, *Life of Andrew Jackson* (1933) and "Napoleon, Junior" (1927).

10. Walker, *Jackson and New Orleans* (1856), p. 41.

11. Edward Nicholls to Jean Lafitte, August 31, 1814, in Latour, *Historical Memoir* (1816, 1999), appendix III, pp. 186–87.

12. Jean Lafitte to Jean Blanque, September 4, 1814, in ibid., appendix V, p. 189.

13. Jean Lafitte to William C. C. Claiborne, September 4, 1814, in ibid., p. 191.

CHAPTER 6: JACKSON UNLEASHED

1. Tatum, "Major H. Tatum's Journal" (1922), p. 55.

2. Andrew Jackson to James Monroe, September 17, 1814.

3. Kouwenhoven and Patten, "New Light on 'The Star Spangled Banner'" (1937), p. 199.

4. James Madison, "A Proclamation," September 1, 1814.

5. Latimer, *1812: War with America* (2007), p. 331.

6. Andrew Jackson to John Rhea, October 11, 1814.

7. Andrew Jackson to James Monroe, October 10, 1814.

8. Reid and Eaton, *Life* (1817), p. 221.

9. Charles Cassiday to Andrew Jackson, September 23, 1814.

10. González Manrique to Andrew Jackson, November 6, 1814.

11. "From Our Ministers at Ghent," *Niles' Weekly Register,* October 15, 1814.

12. Adams, *Memoirs of John Quincy Adams,* vol. 3 (1874), p. 45.

13. Albert Gallatin to James Monroe, August 20, 1814.

14. Albert Gallatin to William Crawford, April 21, 1814.

15. Henry Clay to James Monroe, October 26, 1814, in *Papers of Henry Clay,* vol. 1 (1959), p. 996.

16. James Monroe to Andrew Jackson, October 10, 1814.

CHAPTER 7: TARGET: NEW ORLEANS

1. Edward Codrington to his wife, November 12, December 10, 1814, quoted in Mahon, "British Command Decisions" (1965), p. 54.

2. Carter, *Blaze of Glory* (1971), pp. 87–88.

3. Alexander F. I. Cochrane to Earl Bathurst, July 14, 1814, reprinted in Crawford, ed., *Naval War of 1812* (2002), p. 131.

4. [Gleig], *Narrative of the Campaigns of the British Army* (1821), p. 240.

5. Adams, *War of 1812,* p. 223.

6. Andrew Jackson to James Monroe, November 20, 1814.

7. Andrew Jackson to Rachel Jackson, November 15, 1814. The medicament prescribed was a mix of calomel and the Mexican herbal jalap, which, like

other purgatives in a time of primitive medicines, tended to induce vomiting or diarrhea.

8. Andrew Jackson to Rachel Jackson, February 21, 1814.
9. Walker, *Jackson and New Orleans* (1856), p. 13.
10. Ibid., p. 15.
11. Reilly, *British at the Gates* (1974), p. 210.
12. Hatcher, *Edward Livingston* (1940), p. 123.
13. Hunt, *Memoir of Mrs. Edward Livingston* (1886), pp. 52–53; James, *Life of Andrew Jackson* (1933), p. 204.
14. Andrew Jackson to James Brown, February 4, 1815.
15. Tatum, "Major H. Tatum's Journal" (1922), pp. 96–97.
16. Latour, *Historical Memoir* (1816, 1999), p. 48.
17. Tatum, "Major H. Tatum's Journal" (1922), p. 99.
18. Latour, *Historical Memoir* (1816, 1999), p. 59.

CHAPTER 8: LOSING LAKE BORGNE

1. [Gleig], *Narrative of the Campaigns of the British Army* (1821), p. 247.
2. Daniel Patterson to Andrew Jackson, quoted in McClellan, "Navy at the Battle of New Orleans" (1924), p. 2044.
3. Latour, *Historical Memoir* (1816, 1999), p. 50.
4. Andrew Jackson to James Monroe, December 10, 1814.
5. B. E. Hill, quoted in Latimer, *1812: War with America* (2007), p. 376.
6. Lossing, *Pictorial Field-Book of the War of 1812* (1868), p. 1026.
7. Alexander Cochrane, quoted in Carter, *Blaze of Glory* (1971), p. 123.
8. Thomas ap Catesby Jones to Daniel T. Patterson, March 12, 1815, reprinted in Latour, *Historical Memoir* (1816, 1999), p. 213.
9. Ibid., p. 214.
10. Carter, *Blaze of Glory* (1971), p. 126.
11. Thomas ap Catesby Jones to Daniel T. Patterson, March 12, 1815, reprinted in Latour, *Historical Memoir* (1816, 1999), p. 214.

CHAPTER 9: THE ARMIES ASSEMBLE

1. Walker, *Jackson and New Orleans* (1856), p. 153.
2. Quoted in Parton, *Life of Andrew Jackson,* vol. 2 (1861), p. 56.
3. Tatum, "Major H. Tatum's Journal" (1922), p. 106.
4. Heaney, *Century of Pioneering* (1993), p. 380n16.
5. Andrew Jackson to W. Allen, quoted in Remini, *Andrew Jackson and the Course of American Empire* (1977), p. 254.
6. Tatum, "Major H. Tatum's Journal" (1922), p. 105.
7. "Jackson's Address to the Troops in New Orleans," December 18, 1814.
8. [Gleig], *Narrative of the Campaigns of the British Army* (1821), p. 260.
9. Aitchison, *British Eyewitness at the Battle of New Orleans* (2004), p. 61.
10. [Gleig], *Narrative of the Campaigns of the British Army* (1821), pp. 261–62.
11. Ibid., p. 262.
12. Walker, *Jackson and New Orleans* (1856), pp. 138–39n.
13. Andrew Jackson to James Monroe, December 27, 1814.
14. Latour, *Historical Memoir* (1816), p. 71.
15. Andrew Jackson to Major Reynolds, December 22, 1814.
16. Earl Bathurst to Edward Pakenham, October 24, 1814.
17. Walker, *Jackson and New Orleans* (1856), p. 111.
18. Thomas Shields and Robert Morrell to Daniel T. Patterson, January 14, 1815, reprinted in Latour, *Historical Memoir* (1816, 1999), p. 219.
19. Keane, "A Journal of the Operations Against New Orleans," reprinted in Wellington, *Supplementary Despatches,* vol. 10 (1863), p. 395.
20. Ibid., p. 397.
21. [Gleig], *Narrative of the Campaigns of the British Army* (1821), pp. 277–78.
22. Walker, *Jackson and New Orleans* (1856), pp. 150–51; see also James, *Life of Andrew Jackson* (1933), p. 820n55.
23. Walker, *Jackson and New Orleans* (1856), p. 161.
24. Ibid., p. 157.

CHAPTER 10: THE FIRST BATTLE OF NEW ORLEANS

1. [Gleig], *Narrative of the Campaigns of the British Army* (1821), p. 279.
2. Keane, "A Journal of Operations Against New Orleans," reprinted in Wellington, *Supplementary Despatches,* vol. 10 (1863), pp. 396–97.
3. Parton, *Life of Andrew Jackson,* vol. 2 (1861), p. 84.
4. Cooke, *Narrative of Events* (1835), pp. 190–91.
5. Ibid.
6. Ibid.
7. [Gleig], *Narrative of the Campaigns of the British Army* (1821), p. 286.
8. Davis, *Pirates Lafitte* (2005), pp. 214–15.
9. [Gleig], *Narrative of the Campaigns of the British Army* (1821), p. 286.
10. Walker, *Jackson and New Orleans* (1856), p. 171.
11. Latour, *Historical Memoir* (1816, 1999), p. 83.
12. Thomson, *Historical Sketches of the Late War Between the United States and Great Britain* (1817), p. 351.
13. Cooke, *Narrative of Events* (1835), p. 195.
14. [Gleig], *Narrative of the Campaigns of the British Army* (1821), p. 292.
15. Quoted in Groom, *Patriotic Fire* (2006), p. 141.
16. Ibid., p. 294.
17. [Gleig], *Subaltern in America* (1833), p. 219.

CHAPTER 11: THE DEFENSIVE LINE

1. Andrew Jackson to William Claiborne, December 24, 1814.
2. Daniel Patterson to the secretary of the navy, December 29, 1814, reprinted in Latour, *Historical Memoir* (1816, 1999), p. 233.
3. *Historical and Archaeological Investigations at the Chalmette Battlefield* (2009), pp. 48–49.
4. John Donelson, quoted in Parton, *Life of Andrew Jackson,* vol. 2 (1861), p. 102.
5. Walker, *Jackson and New Orleans* (1856), p. 213.

6. [Gleig], *Narrative of the Campaigns of the British Army* (1821), pp. 301–2.

7. Surtees, *Twenty-Five Years in the Rifle Brigade* (1833), p. 356.

8. Walker, *Jackson and New Orleans* (1856), p. 201.

9. Brands, *Andrew Jackson* (2005), pp. 272–73.

10. Cooke, *Narrative of Events* (1835), p. 203.

11. Remini, *Battle of New Orleans* (1999), p. 89.

12. General Keane to General Pakenham, December 26, 1814, reprinted in James, *Full and Correct Account of the Military Occurrences of the Late War,* vol. 2 (1818), p. 531.

13. Walker, *Jackson and New Orleans* (1856), p. 212.

14. Dickson, "Artillery Services in North America in 1814 and 1815" (1919), p. 98.

15. Smith, *Autobiography,* vol. 1 (1902), p. 228.

16. Edward Livingston to Andrew Jackson, December 25, 1814.

17. Walker, *Jackson and New Orleans* (1856), p. 226.

18. Ibid., p. 227.

19. [Gleig], *Narrative of the Campaigns of the British Army* (1821), p. 309.

20. Andrew Jackson to John McLean, March 22, 1824.

21. Latour, *Historical Memoir* (1816, 1999), p. 12.

22. Surtees, *Twenty-Five Years in the Rifle Brigade* (1833), p. 363.

23. Latour, *Historical Memoir* (1816, 1999), p. 95.

24. Reid and Eaton, *Life* (1817), pp. 326–27.

25. Smith, *Autobiography,* vol. 1 (1902), n.p.

26. Walker, *Jackson and New Orleans* (1856), p. 257.

27. Remini, *Battle of New Orleans* (1999), p. 109.

28. Walker, *Jackson and New Orleans* (1856), p. 257.

29. Edward Pakenham, Orders, December 31, 1814, reprinted in Wellington, *Supplementary Despatches,* vol. 10 (1863), p. 398.

30. [Gleig], *Narrative of the Campaigns of the British Army* (1821), p. 318.

31. Walker, *Jackson and New Orleans* (1856), p. 238.

32. Smith, *Autobiography,* vol. 1 (1902), p. 233.

33. Andrew Jackson to James Monroe, January 3, 1815.

34. Buell, *History of Andrew Jackson,* vol. 1 (1904), p. 423.

35. Nolte, *Fifty Years* (1854), p. 219.

36. The numbers vary greatly, depending upon the source, among them Roosevelt, *Naval War of 1812* (1889), pp. 225–26.

37. Jackson's Manuscript Narrative, Library of Congress, quoted in James, *Life of Andrew Jackson* (1933), p. 241.

38. Parton, *Life of Andrew Jackson,* vol. 2 (1861), p. 188.

39. Edward Livingston, quoted in ibid., p. 228. See also Heaney, *Century of Pioneering* (1993), pp. 237–38.

CHAPTER 12: DAY OF DESTINY

1. Smith, *Autobiography,* vol. 1 (1902), p. 235.

2. Ibid., pp. 235–36.

3. Buell, *History of Andrew Jackson,* vol. 2 (1904), p. 12; Reid and Eaton, *Life* (1817), p. 338.

4. Parton, *Life of Andrew Jackson,* vol. 2 (1861), pp. 192–94.

5. Quoted in Groom, *Patriotic Fire* (2006), p. 196.

6. Reilly, *British at the Gates* (1974), p. 296.

7. Quoted in Carter, *Blaze of Glory* (1971), p. 254.

8. Cooke, *Narrative of Events* (1835), p. 231.

9. [Gleig], *Subaltern in America* (1833), p. 262.

10. Walker, *Jackson and New Orleans* (1856), p. 335; Cooke, *Narrative of Events* (1835), p. 253.

11. Cooke, *Narrative of Events* (1835), p. 235.

12. Anonymous, "A Kentucky Soldier's Account" (1926), reprinted in Hickey, ed., *War of 1812* (2013), p. 671.

13. Walker, *Jackson and New Orleans* (1856), p. 327.

14. Quoted in Remini, *Battle of New Orleans* (1999), p. 210.

15. Gayarré, *Historical Sketch of Pierre and Jean Lafitte* (1964).

16. Anonymous, "A Kentucky Soldier's Account" (1926), reprinted in Hickey, ed., *War of 1812* (2013), p. 670.

17. Nolte, *Fifty Years* (1854), p. 221.

18. John Lambert to Earl Bathurst, January 10, 1815, reprinted in Latour, *Historical Memoir* (1816, 1999), pp. 312–13.

19. Cooper, *Rough Notes of Seven Campaigns* (1914), p. 139.

20. [Gleig], *Narrative of the Campaigns of the British Army* (1821), p. 326.

21. Cooke, *Narrative of Events* (1835), p. 234.

22. Ibid.

23. Ibid., p. 252.

24. Parton, *Life of Andrew Jackson,* vol. 2 (1861), pp. 196–97.

25. The stories of Pakenham's death vary. Among the choice versions are General Lambert's account—see John Lambert to Earl Bathurst, January 10, 1815, reprinted in Latour, *Historical Memoir* (1816, 1999), pp. 312–13; Parton, *Life of Andrew Jackson,* vol. 2 (1861), pp. 196–98; and Walker, *Jackson and New Orleans* (1856), p. 331.

26. Walker, *Jackson and New Orleans* (1856), p. 340.

27. Anonymous, "A Kentucky Soldier's Account" (1926), reprinted in Hickey, ed., *War of 1812* (2013), p. 672.

28. Arthur, *Story of the Battle of New Orleans* (1915), p. 239.

29. Mrs. Henry Clement, quoted in Clement, *Plantation Life on the Mississippi* (1952), pp. 135–36.

30. Heaney, *Century of Pioneering* (1993), p. 238.

31. Walker, *Jackson and New Orleans* (1856), pp. 346–47.

32. Anonymous, "A Kentucky Soldier's Account" (1926), reprinted in Hickey, ed., *War of 1812* (2013), p. 673.

33. Parton, *Life of Andrew Jackson,* vol. 2 (1861), pp. 208–9.

34. Ibid., p. 208.

35. Cooke, *Narrative of Events* (1835), p. 239.

CHAPTER 13: THE BRITISH WITHDRAW

1. For a fuller description of this deliberation, see Nolte, *Fifty Years* (1854), pp. 224–25, and Parton, *Life of Andrew Jackson,* vol. 2 (1861), pp. 234–36.

2. Brown, *Amphibious Campaign* (1969), p. 160, and Reid and Eaton, *Life* (1817), p. 361ff.

3. Andrew Jackson to James Monroe, January 19, 1815.

4. Ibid.

5. Latour, *Historical Memoir* (1816), p. 197.

6. Reid and Eaton, *Life* (1817), p. 367.

7. Andrew Jackson to Abbé Dubourg, January 19, 1815.

8. Arthur, *Story of the Battle of New Orleans* (1915), p. 236.

9. Andrew Jackson's reply to the Reverend W. Dubourg, in Reid and Eaton, *Life* (1817), p. 407.

10. Heaney, *Century of Pioneering* (1993), p. 239.

11. Quoted in Drez, *War of 1812* (2014), p. 347n252.

12. Reid and Eaton, *Life* (1817), p. 365.

13. Andrew Jackson to James Winchester, January 30, 1815.

14. [Gleig], *Narrative of the Campaigns of the British Army* (1821), p. 349.

15. Andrew Jackson address, February 19, 1815, reprinted in Latour, *Historical Memoir* (1816), p. xc.

16. Rachel Jackson to Robert Hays, March 5, 1815.

17. Nolte, *Fifty Years* (1854), p. 238.

18. Ibid., pp. 238–39.

19. Andrew Jackson address, March 14, 1815.

20. Reid and Eaton, *Life* (1817), p. 392.

21. Parton, *Life of Andrew Jackson,* vol. 2 (1861), pp. 330–31.

22. John Lowell, "Mr. Madison's War," in Boston *Evening Post,* July 31–August 10, 1812.

23. *Niles' Weekly Register,* February 18 and March 14, 1815.

24. [Gleig], *Narrative of the Campaigns of the British Army* (1821), p. 374.

EPILOGUE

1. Andrew Jackson to Andrew Jackson Donelson, December 10, 1839.

2. Ibid.

3. *Columbian Centinel,* July 12, 1817.

4. Hunt, *Memoir of Mrs. Edward Livingston* (1886), p. 52.

5. Andrew Jackson, "General Orders," January 21, 1815.

6. Griffith, *McIntosh and Weatherford* (1988), p. 252.

7. Heaney, *Century of Pioneering* (1993), p. 239.

8. Andrew Jackson to Martin Van Buren, December 23, 1839, quoted in Remini, *Andrew Jackson and the Course of American Democracy* (1984), p. 456.

9. *Nashville Union*, January 22, 1840.

AFTERWORD

1. Margaret Bayard Smith, *The First Forty Years of Washington Society* (1906), p. 296

2. Joseph Story to Mrs. Story, March 7, 1829.

3. Remini, *Andrew Jackson and the Course of American Democracy* (1984), pp. 233–37.

4. Here and after, quotations have been drawn from Roosevelt, *The Naval War of 1812* (1882).

5. David McCullough, *Truman* (New York: Simon & Schuster, 1992), p. 43.

6. Merle Miller, *Plain Speaking: An Oral Biography of Harry S. Truman* (New York: Berkley, 1974), p. 67.

7. Jon Meacham, *American Lion: Andrew Jackson in the White House* (New York: Random House, 2008), p. 257.

8. Ralph E. Weber, ed., *Talking with Harry: Candid Conversations with President Harry S. Truman* (Wilmington, DE: Scholarly Resources Books, 2001), p. 124.

9. Harry S. Truman, *Where the Buck Stops: The Personal and Private Writings of Harry Truman* (New York: Warner Books, 1989), p. 295.

10. Mary French Caldwell, "Another Breakfast at the Hermitage: Part II: 1934," *Tennessee Historical Quarterly*, vol. 26 (fall 1967), p. 249–50.

11. Franklin Delano Roosevelt to John Nance Garner, quoted in Elliott Roosevelt, ed., *F.D.R.: His Personal Letters*, vol. 1 (New York: Duell, Sloan, and Pearce, 1950), p. 433.

12. Franklin Delano Roosevelt, "Radio Address from the USS *Potomac* for Jackson Day Dinners," March 29, 1941.

13. John F. Kennedy, "The Heritage of Andrew Jackson" (1960), p. 1.

14. Lyndon Baines Johnson, "Remarks at the Hermitage at Ceremonies Marking the 200th Anniversary of the Birth of Andrew Jackson" (March 15, 1967).

15. Ronald Reagan, "Address Before a Joint Session of the Tennessee State Legislature in Nashville," March 15, 1982. Jackson's words regarding courage may—or may not—have been uttered by him, but an early biographer, James Parton, attributed them to him in his *Life of Andrew Jackson*.

FOR FURTHER READING

The stories recounted in this book have been told multiple times; the accounts often vary in their particulars, with higher or lower troop numbers, discrepancies of dates, and many variant details. To tell this story in the most accurate way possible, we have proceeded with great care, working from the earliest sources where possible, quoting and citing the individuals who were actually on the scene. Prominent among them, of course, was Andrew Jackson. You will see him quoted often, in quotations drawn from the two main editions of his papers unless otherwise specified.

Throughout the text, you will find the narrative enhanced by the voices of many historical figures. Although the quotations have been precisely rendered from original sources, odd spellings, capitalization, and punctuation—none of which were standardized circa 1815—have been modernized for the twenty-first-century reader.

Adams, Henry. *History of the United States of America During the Administrations of James Madison*. New York: Charles Scribner's Sons, 1890.

_____. *The War of 1812*. Edited by Major H. A. DeWeerd. Washington, DC: Infantry Journal, 1944.

Adams, John Quincy. *Memoirs of John Quincy Adams, Comprising Portions of His Diary from 1795 to 1848*. Vol. 3. Philadelphia: J. B. Lippincott, 1874.

Aitchison, Robert. *A British Eyewitness at the Battle of New Orleans: The Memoir of Royal Navy Admiral Robert Aitchison, 1808–1827*. Edited by Gene A. Smith. New Orleans: Historic New Orleans Collections, 2004.

Ambrose, Stephen. "The Battle of New Orleans." In *To America: Personal Reflections of an Historian*. New York: Simon & Schuster, 2002.

Arthur, Stanley Clisby. *The Story of the Battle of New Orleans*. New Orleans: Louisiana Historical Society, 1915.

Bassett, John Spencer. *The Life of Andrew Jackson*. Garden City, NY: Doubleday, Page, 1911.

Benton, Thomas Hart. *Thirty Years' View*. 2 vols. New York: D. Appleton, 1854.

Brands, H. W. *Andrew Jackson: His Life and Times*. New York: Doubleday, 2005.

Brooks, Charles B. *The Siege of New Orleans*. Seattle: University of Washington Press, 1961.

Brown, Wilburt S. *The Amphibious Campaign for West Florida and Louisiana, 1814–1815*. Tuscaloosa: University of Alabama Press, 1969.

Buell, Augustus C. *History of Andrew Jackson: Pioneer, Patriot, Soldier, Politician, President*. 2 vols. New York: Charles Scribner's Sons, 1904.

Carpenter, Edwin H., Jr. "Arsène Lacarrière Latour." *Hispanic American Historical Review*, vol. 18, no. 2 (May 1938), pp. 221–27.

Carter, Samuel, III. *Blaze of Glory: The Fight for New Orleans, 1814–1815*. New York: St. Martin's Press, 1971.

Channing, Edward A. *The Jeffersonian System*. New York: Harper & Brothers, 1906.

Claiborne, John F. H. *Life and Times of Gen. Sam. Dale, the Mississippi Partisan*. New York: Harper & Brothers, 1860.

Clay, Henry. *The Papers of Henry Clay*. Vol. 1. Lexington: University of Kentucky Press, 1959.

Clement, William Edwards. *Plantation Life on the Mississippi*. New Orleans: Pelican, 1952.

Cooke, John Henry. *A Narrative of Events in the South of France, and of the Attack on New Orleans, in 1814 and 1815*. London: T. & W. Boone, 1835.

Cooper, John Spencer. *Rough Notes of Seven Campaigns in Portugal, Spain, France and America During the Years 1809-10-11-12-13-14-15*. Carlisle, UK: G. & T. Coward, 1914.

Crawford, Michael J., ed. *The Naval War of 1812: A Documentary History*. Vol. 3. Washington, DC: Naval Historical Center, 2002.

Crété, Liliane. *Daily Life in Louisiana: 1815–1830*. Baton Rouge: Louisiana State University Press, 1978.

Crockett, David [Davy]. *A Narrative of the Life of David Crockett, of the State of Tennessee*. Philadelphia: E. L. Carey and A. Hart, 1834.

Davis, William. *The Pirates Lafitte: The Treacherous World of the Corsairs of the Gulf*. Orlando, FL: Harcourt, 2005.

Dickson, Alexander. "Artillery Services in North America in 1814 and 1815." *Journal for the Society of Army Historical Research,* vol. 8, no. 32 (April 1919), pp. 79–112.

Dictionary of American Biography. New York: Charles Scribner's Sons, 1928–58.

Drez, Ronald J. *The War of 1812, Conflict and Deception: The British Attempt to Seize New Orleans and Nullify the Louisiana Purchase*. Baton Rouge: Louisiana State University Press, 2014.

Eaton, John Henry. *Memoirs of Andrew Jackson, Late Major-General and Commander in Chief of the Southern Division of the Army of the United States.* Boston: C. Ewer, 1828.

Fernandez, Mark. "Edward Livingston, America, and France: Making Law." In *Empires of the Imagination: Transatlantic Histories of the Louisiana Purchase,* edited by Peter J. Kastor and François Weil. Charlottesville: University of Virginia Press, 2009.

Gallatin, Albert. *The Writings of Henry Gallatin.* Vol. 1. Philadelphia: J. B. Lippincott, 1879.

Gayarré, Charles. *Historical Sketch of Pierre and Jean Lafitte: The Famous Smugglers of Louisiana.* Austin, TX: Pemberton Press, 1964.

_____. *The Story of Jean and Pierre Lafitte.* New Orleans: Press of T. J. Moran's Sons, 1938.

[Gleig, George Robert]. *A Narrative of the Campaigns of the British Army at Washington and New Orleans.* London: John Murray, 1821.

_____. *A Subaltern in America; Comprising His Narrative of the Campaigns of the British Army, at Baltimore, Washington, &c. &c., During the Late War.* Philadelphia: E. L. Carey & A. Hart, 1833.

Griffith, Benjamin W., Jr. *McIntosh and Weatherford, Creek Indian Leaders.* Tuscaloosa: University of Alabama Press, 1988.

Groom, Winston. *Patriotic Fire: Andrew Jackson and Jean Laffite at the Battle of New Orleans.* New York: Alfred A. Knopf, 2006.

Hatcher, William B. *Edward Livingston: Jeffersonian Republican and Jacksonian Democrat.* Baton Rouge: Louisiana State University Press, 1940.

Heaney, Jane Frances. *A Century of Pioneering: A History of the Ursuline Nuns in New Orleans, 1727–1827.* Edited by Mary Ethel Booker Siefken. New Orleans: Ursuline Sisters of New Orleans, Louisiana, 1993.

Hickey, Donald. *Glorious Victory: Andrew Jackson and the Battle of New Orleans.* Baltimore: Johns Hopkins University Press, 2015.

_____. *The War of 1812: A Forgotten Conflict.* Urbana: University of Illinois Press, 1989.

_____, ed. *The War of 1812: Writing from America's Second War of Independence.* New York: Library of America, 2013.

Historical and Archaeological Investigations at the Chalmette Battlefield. New Orleans: U.S. Army Corps of Engineers, 2009.

Hume, Edgar Erskine, ed. "Letters Written During the War of 1812 by the British Naval Commander in American Waters." *William and Mary Quarterly,* vol. 10, no. 4 (October 1930), pp. 279–301.

Hunt, Charles Havens. *Life of Edward Livingston.* New York: D. Appleton, 1864.

Hunt, Louise Livingston. *Memoir of Mrs. Edward Livingston: With Letters Hitherto Unpublished.* New York: Harper & Brothers, 1886.

Inskeep, Steve. *Jacksonland.* New York: Penguin, 2015.

Jackson, Andrew. *Correspondence of Andrew Jackson.* Edited by John Spencer Bassett. 7 vols. Washington, DC: Carnegie Institution, 1926–35.

_____. *The Papers of Andrew Jackson.* Edited by Sam B. Smth and Harriet Chappell Owsley. 13 vols. Knoxville: University of Tennessee Press, 1980–2009.

James, Marquis. *The Life of Andrew Jackson.* Indianapolis: Bobbs-Merrill Company, 1933.

_____. "Napoleon, Junior." *American Legion Monthly,* vol. 3, no. 4 (October 1927), pp. 14–17.

James, William. *A Full and Correct Account of the Military Occurrences of the Late War Between Great Britain and the United States of America.* Vol. 2. London, 1818.

Kanon, Tom. *Tennesseans at War, 1812–1815*. Tuscaloosa: University of Alabama Press, 2014.

Kouwenhoven, John Atlee, and Lawton M. Patten. "New Light on 'The Star Spangled Banner.'" *Musical Quarterly*, vol. 23, no. 2 (April 1937), pp. 198–300.

Lafitte, Jean. *The Journal of Jean Lafitte*. New York: Vantage Press, 1958.

Landry, Stuart Omer. *Side Lights on the Battle of New Orleans*. New Orleans: Pelican, 1965.

Langguth, A. J. *Union 1812: The American Who Fought the Second War of Independence*. New York: Simon & Schuster, 2006.

Latimer, Jon. *1812: War with America*. Cambridge, MA: Belknap Press of Harvard University Press, 2007.

Latour, Arsène Lacarrière. *Historical Memoir of the War in West Florida and Louisiana in 1814–15: With an Atlas*. 1816. Reprint edited by Gene A. Smith. Gainesville: University Press of Florida, 1999.

———. *Historical Memoir of the War in West Florida and Louisiana in 1814–15: With an Atlas*. 1816. Reprint, with an introduction by Jane Lucas de Grummond. Gainesville: University Press of Florida, 1964.

Lossing, Benson J. *Pictorial Field-Book of the War of 1812*. New York: Harper & Brothers, 1868.

McClellan, Edwin N. "The Navy at the Battle of New Orleans." *Proceedings of the United States Naval Institute*, vol. 50 (December 1924), pp. 2041–60.

Mahon, John K. "British Command Decisions Relative to the Battle of New Orleans." *Louisiana History: The Journal of the Louisiana Historical Association*, vol. 6, no. 1 (winter 1965), pp. 53–76.

———. *The War of 1812*. Gainesville: University of Florida Press, 1972.

Martin, François-Xavier. *The History of Louisiana from the Earliest Period.* 2 vols. New Orleans: Lyman & Beardslee, 1827–29.

Morazan, Ronald R. *Biographical Sketches of the Veterans of the Battalion of Orleans, 1814–1815.* Baton Rouge, LA: Legacy Publishing Company, 1979.

Morriss, Roger. *Cockburn and the British Navy in Transition: Admiral Sir George Cockburn, 1772–1853.* Exeter, UK: University of Exeter Press, 1997.

Nolte, Vincent. *Fifty Years in Both Hemispheres; or, Reminiscences of the Life of a Former Merchant.* New York: Redfield, 1854.

Owsley, Frank Lawrence, Jr. "Jackson's Capture of Pensacola." *Alabama Review,* vol. 19, July 1966, pp. 175–85.

———. "The Role of the South in the British Grand Strategy in the War of 1812." *Tennessee Historical Quarterly,* vol. 31, no. 1 (spring 1972), pp. 22–38.

———. *Struggle for the Gulf Borderland: The Creek War and the Battle of New Orleans, 1812–1815.* Gainesville: University Press of Florida, 1981.

Pack, James. *The Man Who Burned the White House: Admiral Sir George Cockburn, 1772–1853.* Annapolis, MD: Naval Institute Press, 1987.

Parton, James. *Life of Andrew Jackson.* 3 vols. New York: Mason Brothers, 1861.

Patterson, Benton Rain. *The Generals: Andrew Jackson, Sir Edward Pakenham, and the Road to the Battle of New Orleans.* New York: New York University Press, 2005.

Pickett, Albert James. *History of Alabama, and Incidentally of Georgia and Mississippi, from the Earliest Period.* 2 vols. Charleston, SC: Walker and James, 1851.

Powell, Lawrence N. *The Accidental City: Improvising New Orleans.* Cambridge, MA: Harvard University Press, 2012.

Prentice, George D. *The Biography of Henry Clay.* New York: J. J. Philips, 1831.

Reid, John, and John Henry Eaton. *The Life of Andrew Jackson, Major-General in the Service of the United States.* Philadelphia: M. Carey and Son, 1817.

Reilly, Robin. *The British at the Gates.* New York: G. P. Putnam's Sons, 1974.

Remini, Robert V. *Andrew Jackson and His Indian Wars.* New York: Viking, 2001.

_____. *Andrew Jackson and the Course of American Democracy, 1833–1845.* New York: Harper & Row, 1984.

_____. *Andrew Jackson and the Course of American Empire, 1767–1821.* New York: Harper & Row, 1977.

_____. *The Battle of New Orleans.* New York: Viking, 1999.

Roosevelt, Theodore. *The Naval War of 1812.* G. P. Putnam's Sons, 1889.

Royall, Anne. *Letters from Alabama on Various Subjects.* Washington, 1830.

Smith, Gene A. "Arsène Lacarrière Latour: Immigrant, Patiot-Historian, and Foreign Agent." In *The Human Tradition in Antebellum America,* edited by Michael A. Morrison. Wilmington, DE: Scholarly Resources, 2000.

Smith, Harry. *The Autobiography of Lieutenant-General Sir Harry Smith.* Vol 1. London: John Murray, 1902.

Smith, Z. F. *The Battle of New Orleans.* Louisville, KY: K. P. Morton, 1904.

Stagg, J. C. A. *Mr. Madison's War.* Princeton, NJ: Princeton University Press, 1983.

Surtees, William. *Twenty-Five Years in the Rifle Brigade.* Edinburgh: William Blackwood, 1833.

Tatum, Howell. "Major H. Tatum's Journal While Acting Topographical Engineer (1814) to General Jackson, Commanding 7th Military District." In *Smith College Studies in History,* vol. 7, edited by John Spencer Bassett and Sidney Bradshaw Fay. Northampton, MA: Department of History of Smith College, 1922.

Thomson, John Lewis. *Historical Sketches of the Late War, Between the United States and Great Britain*. 4th ed. Philadelphia: Thomas Desilver, 1817.

Updyke, Frank A. *The Diplomacy of the War of 1812*. Baltimore: Johns Hopkins Press, 1915.

Vogel, Steve. *Through the Perilous Fight: Six Weeks That Saved the Nation*. New York: Random House, 2013.

Walker, Alexander. *Jackson and New Orleans*. New York: J. C. Derby, 1856.

Wellington, Field Marshal Arthur Wellesley, Duke of. *Supplementary Despatches, Correspondence, and Memoranda*. Vol. 10. London: John Murray, 1863.

Windship, John Cravath May. "Letters from Louisiana, 1813–1814." Edited by Everett S. Brown. *Mississippi Valley Historical Review*, vol. 11, no. 4 (March 1925), pp. 570–79.

Woodward, Thomas S. *Woodward's Reminiscences of the Creek, or Muscogee Indians*. 1859. Reprint, Tuscaloosa: Alabama Book Store, 1939.

INDEX

Brian Kilmeade and **Don Yeager** are the coauthors of *George Washington's Secret Six* and *Thomas Jefferson and the Tripoli Pirates*, both *New York Times* bestsellers. Kilmeade cohosts Fox News Channel's morning show *Fox & Friends* and hosts *The Brian Kilmeade Show* on Fox News Radio. He lives on Long Island. Yeager has written or co-written twenty-six books and lives in Florida.

It's easy to get regular updates and
highlights from *The Brian Kilmeade Show*,
plus occasional special offers. Just visit
www.BrianKilmeade.com
and put your e-mail address in the box on the
right. Or, if you prefer, send an e-mail to
subscribe@briankilmeade.com.

You can also stay in touch with
Brian on social media:
- Facebook (facebook.com/kilmeade)
- Twitter (@kilmeade)
- Instagram (@kilmeade)

To invite Brian to speak to your
group or organization, please e-mail
speak@briankilmeade.com.
For media requests, please e-mail
media@briankilmeade.com.

Also available from Brian Kilmeade

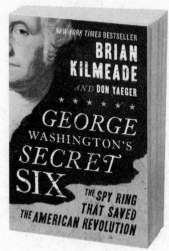

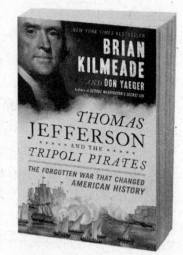

SENTINEL